I M A G E S
of America

POUGHKEEPSIE

HALFWAY UP THE HUDSON

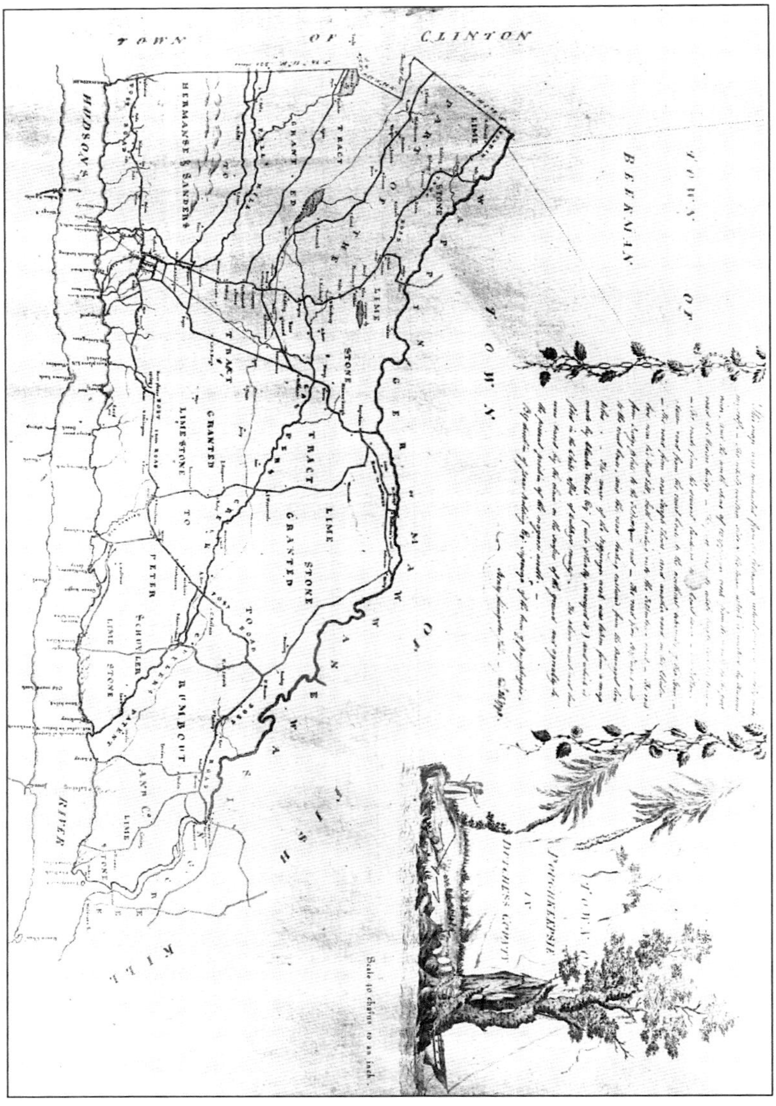

The Poughkeepsie Town and Village 1798 Patent Map. (Dutchess County Historical Society [DCHS]; photograph by Peter Klose [PK].) This map created by Henry Livingston Jr. in 1798 shows land divisions and residences within the present city and town of Poughkeepsie a decade after Poughkeepsie became a town. It was included in historian Helen Wilkinson Reynold's definitive 1924 monograph, *Poughkeepsie, the Origin and Meaning of the Word* as a guide to early settlement and ownership patterns. It may be noted that the original outlines of the town have remained stable through the centuries.

IMAGES
of America

POUGHKEEPSIE
HALFWAY UP THE HUDSON

Joyce C. Ghee and Joan Spence

ARCADIA
PUBLISHING

Copyright © 1997 by Joyce C. Ghee and Joan Spence
ISBN 978-0-7385-6203-2

Published by Arcadia Publishing
Charleston, South Carolina

Printed in the United States of America

Library of Congress Catalog Card Number: 2008935176

For all general information contact Arcadia Publishing at:
Telephone 843-853-2070
Fax 843-853-0044
E-mail sales@arcadiapublishing.com
For customer service and orders:
Toll-Free 1-888-313-2665

Visit us on the Internet at www.arcadiapublishing.com

Contents

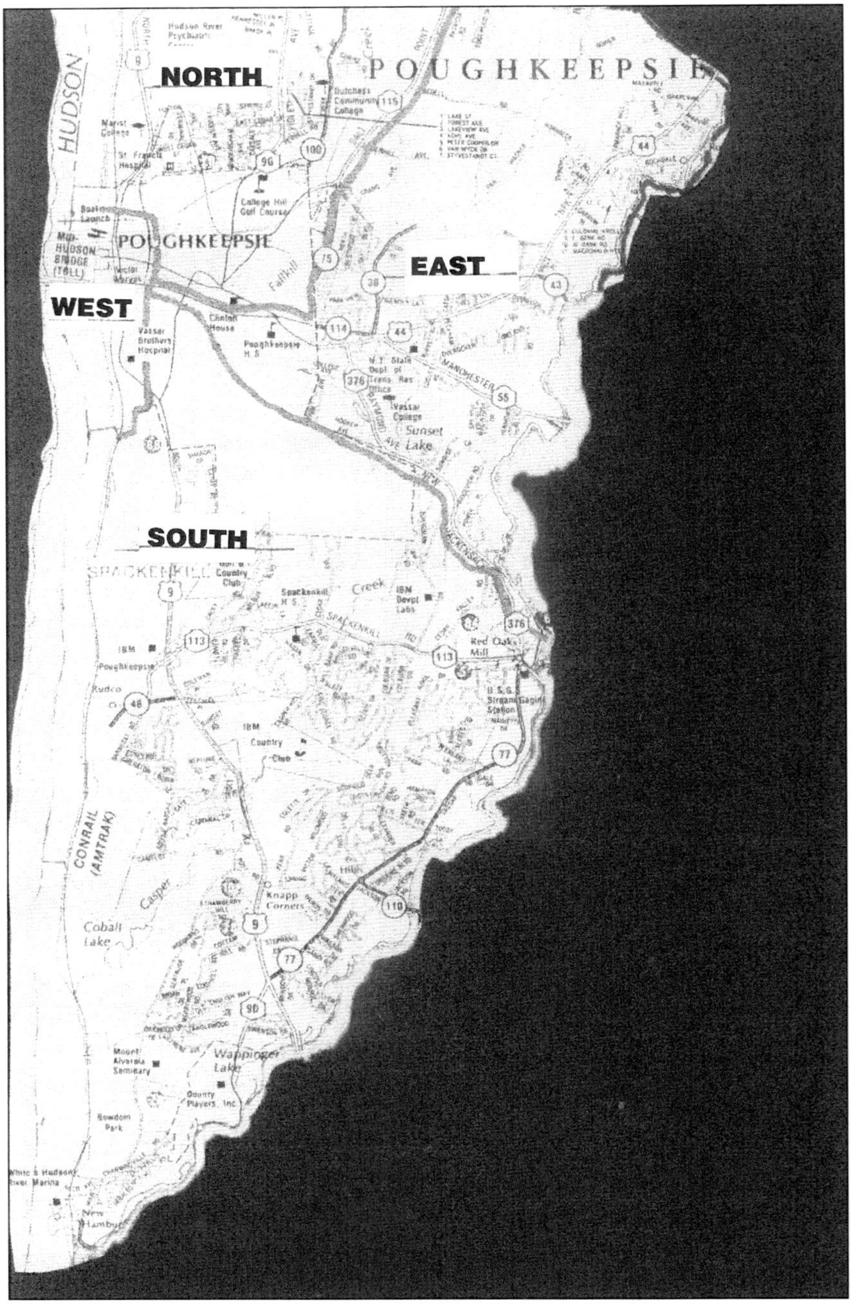

A Computer Generated Map, 1997. (DCHS.) Jon Hayden's map created for the Dutchess County Historical Society addresses the geographic divisions outlined in the first four chapters. "West" covers the original settlement area of the city on the river between Upper and Lower Landings, inland to the Market Street corridor. "East" follows Main Street, fanning out southeast and northeast to the Wappingers Creek. "North" extends to the Hyde Park line from the city's north side and east to the Salt Point Turnpike. "South" extends from the city's south side to the Wappinger Creek and the river.

Introduction

"Uppuqui-ip-ising," as the place was identified by early Wappinger Indian residents, or Poughkeepsie, as we call it, is hard to spell, hard to say, but easy to find. The city and town share the name and lands delineated in several seventeenth-century adjoining crown patents. The area was first settled near the Casparkill by Pieter Lassingh *c.* 1688, and near the Fallkill in 1687 by Sanders/Harmense patent tenants, Baltus Van Kleeck and Hendrick Jan Ostrom. The city and town have been inextricably bound throughout history—physically, demographically, and politically.

The geographic location of Poughkeepsie—mid-way on the Hudson River between New York harbor and Albany—has been key to its success. The estuarine tides and deep channels of the Hudson encouraged water traffic long before Europeans arrived in numbers starting in the seventeenth century. Bluffs lining the riverbanks were broken at coves here, providing easy access inland. Waterpower from creeks (kills) supported different types of development and encouraged industry. Native American trails became roads traveled on horseback and in carriages. The coming of the railroad made Poughkeepsie a vital center for business and commerce. And with the advent of the automobile, Poughkeepsie continued to be at the forefront of progress.

The central location of Poughkeepsie has also made it a regional stage for pivotal action: it has served as an early state capital, the site of New York's Ratification Convention of the United States Constitution in 1788, the nineteenth-century center of rail connections from the south and east, the twentieth-century location of a key bridge and road system, and the staging area for IBM's expanding global empire.

From its earliest days, Poughkeepsie has also been a barometer of national immigration patterns. Neighborhoods continue to change as each wave of immigrants arrives.

No format is better suited to show such change over time than this type of book, which is more an exhibit or index than a formal history. The images selected from local archival and personal collections convey the evolution of Poughkeepsie from Native American territory to European settlement to American village, city, and town. The pictures reinforce the importance and sense of place.

The captions include historical information to support the authors' two theses: a) the location of Poughkeepsie makes it a likely stage for important events and b) the community's development reflects national demographic and historical trends.

The evolution of the city and town, treated as one entity, is followed chronologically within neighborhoods in each of four quadrants. The first chapter focuses on the riverfront area and bluff between the two original landings. Here fundamental decisions were made which defined a nation and continue to define the political, business, social, and cultural life of Poughkeepsie and of the county. The second chapter details the growth of Poughkeepsie along Main Street east to Vassar College and to areas known as Bull's Head (Arlington), Manchester, Rochdale, and Red Oaks Mills. The third chapter deals with the northern area where river estates, farms, and industries all flourished. The fourth chapter chronicles the history of areas known as Channingville, Camelot, and New Hamburgh, as well as the Livingston, Morse, Vassar, and Kenyon estates, and includes the development of the south side of Poughkeepsie and the coming of IBM. A map at the beginning of each chapter will help the reader to relate past environments and place names to what exists today. The final chapter summarizes the geographic, social, and political connections that have bound the different areas into a whole. The physical environment, transportation links, and economic, political, cultural, and social institutions have all played a role.

Authors' Note: When a source of images is credited for the first time, it is identified by the full name of the institution and/or individuals who provided pictures. Thereafter, the source is identified by its initials. Acknowledgments and a brief reading list are also included.

One

From the Riverbank to the Top of the Hill

The earliest settlers here must have congratulated themselves on snagging a great piece of real estate. It had everything: accessible mid-river landings, water power, a trail, and friendly Native Americans. Business opportunities from river travel were sure to come. And they did. But to insure the community's success, Jacobus Van den Bogert made one important move. He gave two pieces of land to the settlement, one for a church and another for a courthouse, with the provision that if the land were not used for its designated purposes the family could reclaim it. His 1714 decision marked Poughkeepsie as a permanent center for government and commerce, and provided the setting for great historical events played out at the intersection of the Post Road and the path to Union Landing (Main and Market). From the days of Hamilton, Clinton, and Jay to the era of Ham Fish Sr. and FDR, the fortunes, lives, and visions of people great and small have been recorded by courts and meeting rooms in five courthouses on the same site since 1717. The courthouse attracted development: homes, offices, hotels, and stores appeared nearby. Between Upper and Lower Landings along the river, business and industry flourished, changing with the times, the talents of new populations, technology, and transportation. This smallest of Poughkeepsie's divisions has always been the place to be in order to keep abreast of current events.

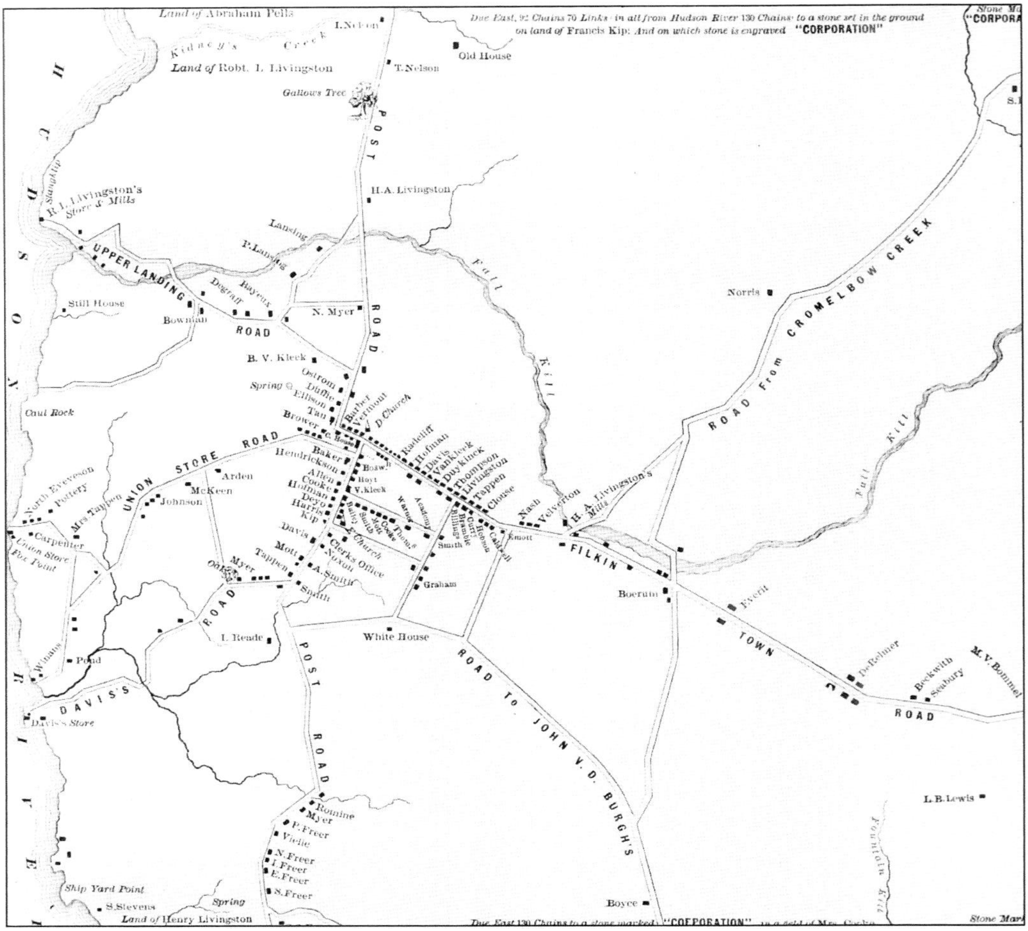

Poughkeepsie Village, from a 1799 Livingston Map. (*Poughkeepsie Journal* [PJ].) Henry Livingston Jr.'s survey maps are excellent sources of historical information. "Uppuqui-ip-ising" is probably the "spring" identified between Post Road and Henry Livingston's land along the river to the south. Following changes in the course of the road and land exchanges, the spring now lies opposite the Poughkeepsie Rural Cemetery, through which its overflow meanders.

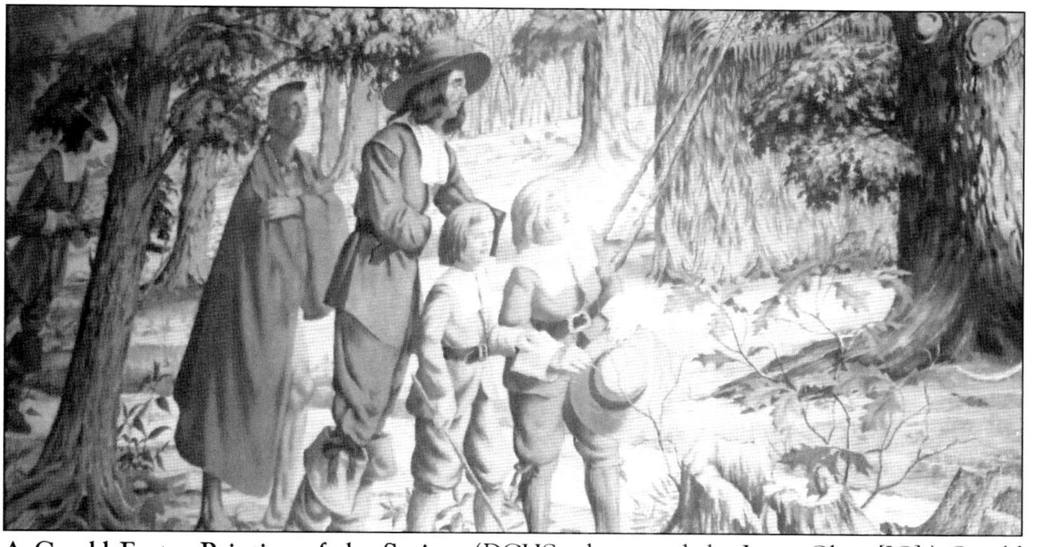

A Gerald Foster Painting of the Spring. (DCHS; photograph by Joyce Ghee [JG].) Gerald Foster's 1939 mural shows young Myndert Van Den Bogert and Johannes Van Kleeck c. 1692 discovering the long-ago obscured Native American trail rest stop that gave Poughkeepsie its name. FDR's contention that public places should reinforce local history was supported by historian Helen Wilkinson Reynolds, who provided the inspiration for Foster's artistic vision by identifying the site of the spring near the Poughkeepsie Rural Cemetery.

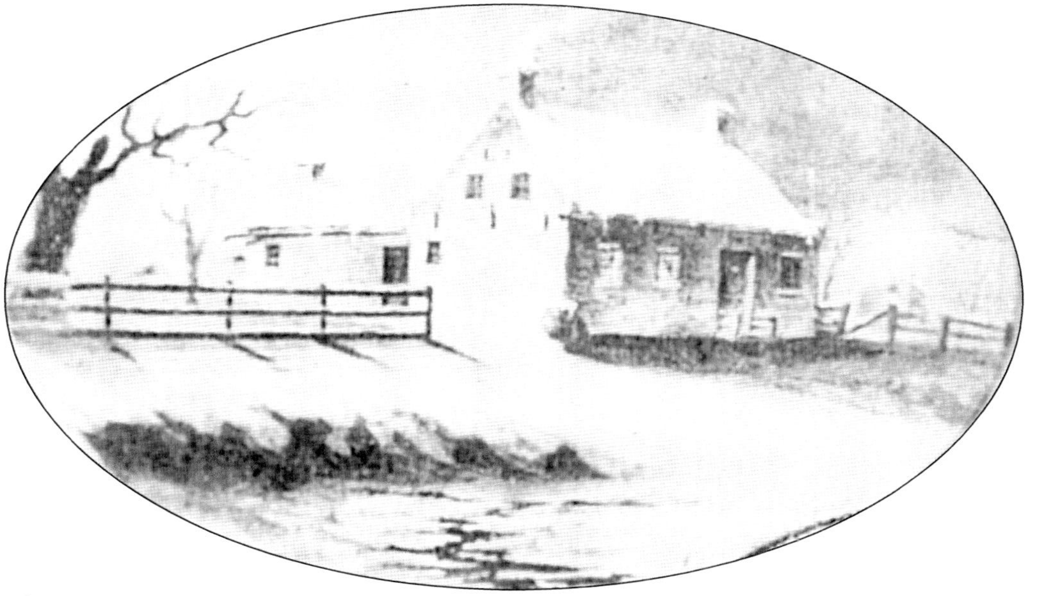

The Van Kleeck House, 1702. (DCHS.) Historian Benson Lossing's drawing shows Baltus Barents Van Kleeck's 1702 stone house, completed two decades after local Native Americans and Patentees Sanders and Harmense reached an accord on a land exchange at the river mid-point. Tenant agreements from 1687 show required improvements and common land, indicating a commitment to settlement. Dutchman Van Kleeck and his English brother-in-law Sanders expressed the diversity that still marks the city. The house at 222 Mill Street near the Fallkill Upper Landing survived into the nineteenth century.

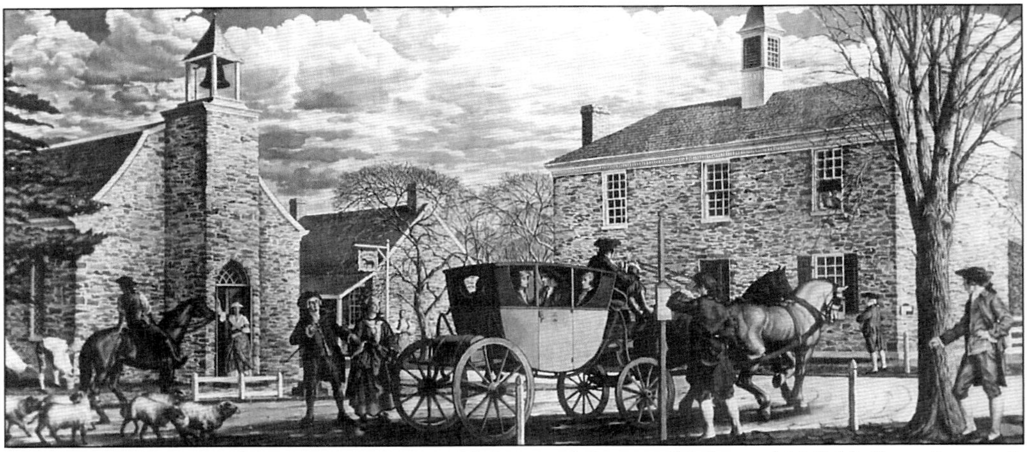

The Hamlet of Poughkeepsie, c. 1740. (Adriance Memorial Library [AML].) Foster's mural, *Main and Market c. 1740*, pictures the colonial hamlet recently named as the center of county government. The Dutch church is in the middle of the Main/New Market intersection, northeast of the courthouse. Five courthouses have stood here since the Colonial Assembly decided in 1715 that Dutchess was sufficiently populated to support self-government. Construction of the first courthouse is implied by building supply bills dating from *c.* 1717. When the 1714 Van Den Bogert deed of gift was filed in 1747, a second courthouse was already in place.

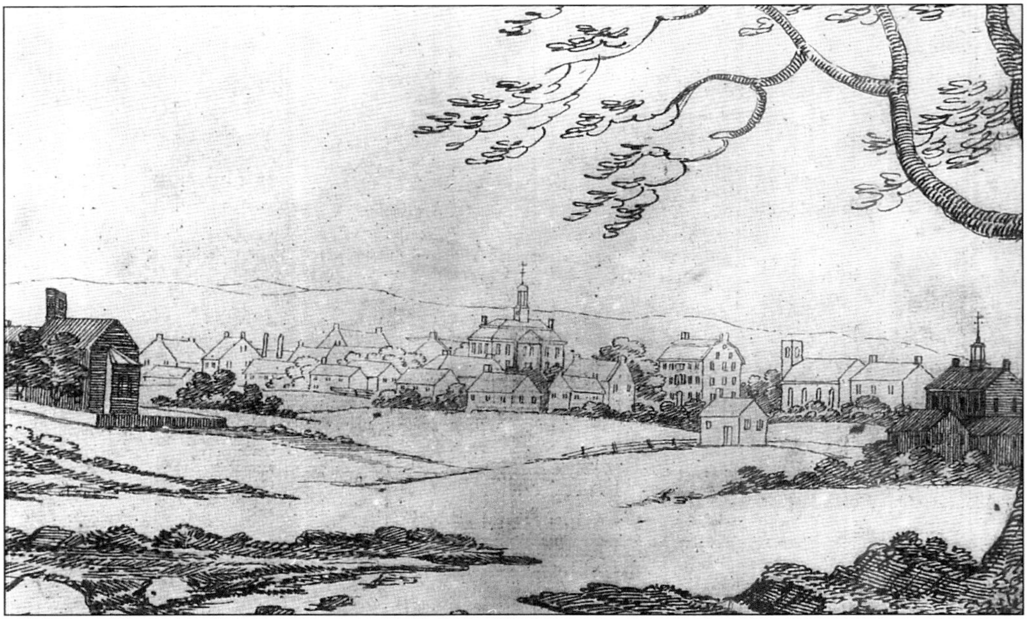

The Courthouse, September 1792. (New-York Historical Society.) In April 1785, fire destroyed the second courthouse, which was replaced in time for the 1788 New York State Ratification Convention. The inns and homes of Poughkeepsie, the default state capital after Kingston was burned in 1777, overflowed with delegates and visitors. Archibald Robertson's drawing is the only image of the hamlet in which New York State ratified the United States Constitution by three votes. Federalist/Anti-federalist debate that threatened to destroy the infant nation ended with Melancthon Smith's proviso for a Bill of Rights.

Clinton and Hamilton Agree on Ratification. (DCHS; photograph by JG.) Foster's dramatic 1939 Poughkeepsie Post Office painting captures the historic moment in 1788 when Anti-federalist George Clinton and Federalist Alexander Hamilton agreed to compromise on a Bill of Rights. Helen W. Reynolds' historical architectural research made the artist's vision of the original interior scene possible. A surprise witness to the event is a tiny full-time resident of the building. The courthouse mouse, pictured just beneath the men's handshake, continues to charm those who study the painting closely.

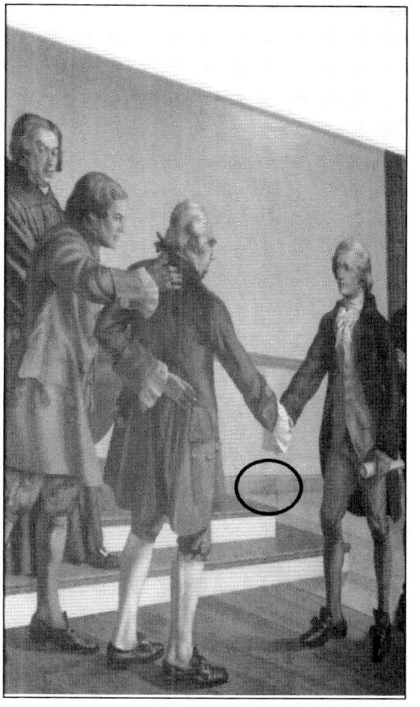

FDR Dedicating the Post Office, 1937. (AML.) The president, surrounded by a multitude of area, state, and national leaders, dedicated the post office in 1937 as a model for public buildings. The architect, Eric Kebbon, used the 1788 Dutchess County Courthouse as his prototype, according to President Roosevelt's wish. Nationwide, Works Progress Administration (WPA) construction of schools, post offices, and municipal halls repeated the concept, using regional architectural styles as inspiration and putting artists and historians to work recreating scenes of past local history.

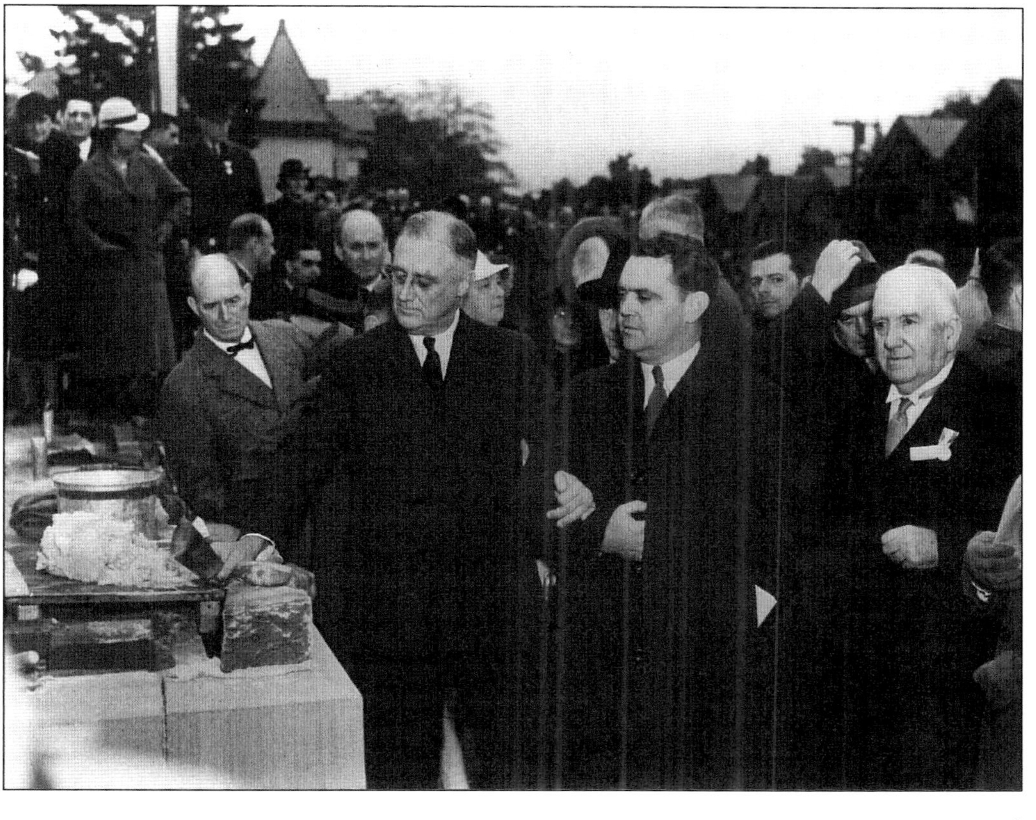

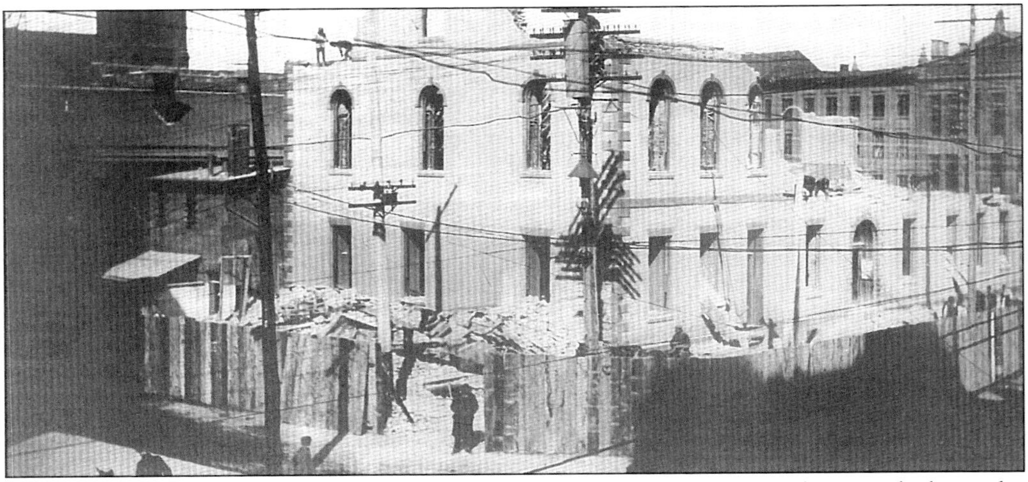

Demolition of the 1809 Courthouse. (AML.) This turn-of-the-century photograph shows the demolition of the third courthouse. Completed in 1809, it replaced the short-lived structure destroyed by fire in 1806 in which the Constitution was ratified. Every courthouse since the first has maintained a "gaol" cell as required by the deed of gift from the Van Den Bogert family, but this one also supported Matthew Vassar's Oyster Bar, a barber, and other commercial services required by those who did business here. Space limitations mandated its replacement.

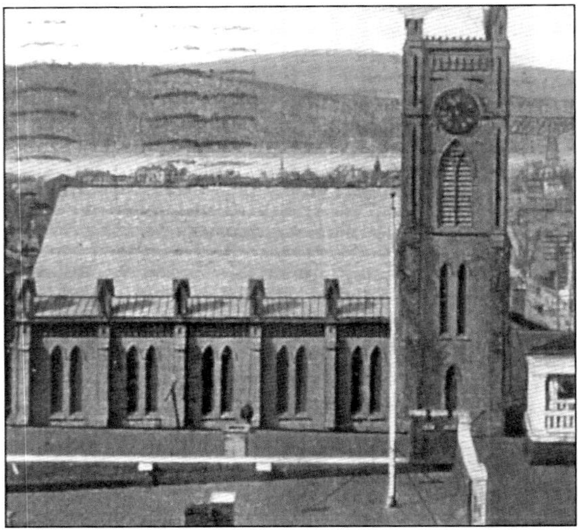

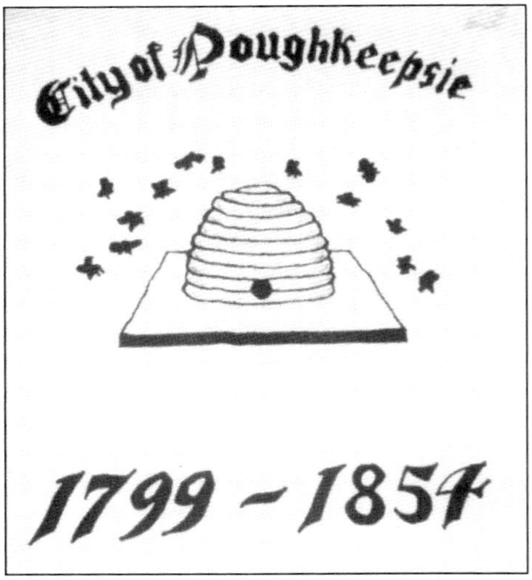

The Reformed Dutch Church. (DCHS.) The steeple of the Reformed Dutch Church with its highly visible clock, viewed from the courthouse roof in this turn-of-the-century postcard, was a beloved landmark of Poughkeepsians. The congregation, established *c.* 1716 by Van Kleeck family members, built their church on Van Den Bogert land near the courthouse. Several subsequent sanctuaries, all particularly prone to fire damage, were built in the same vicinity over a two-hundred-year period. This one was built in the mid-nineteenth century.

The Poughkeepsie City Seal. (DCHS, JG.) An orange, blue, and white city flag shows the municipal seal, the beehive, selected as a symbol of industry and energy when the village, created in 1799, became the "Queen City" in 1854. The city's colors hark back to its Dutch roots. The decision to become a city came before the Civil War, when entrepreneurs full of ideas for civic improvement felt limited by village status and overlapping authorities. Village Hall and Market, built in 1831, became the city hall.

Smith Brothers Restaurant. (AML/DCHS.) Smith Brothers Restaurant, seen in turn-of-the-century commercial booklets, was one of the most popular mid-town dining/meeting places. The confectionery/soda fountain featured candy—including those famous cough drops—ice-cream delights, and by the 1920s, luncheon fare. The large formal dining room in the rear, noted for its fine food, décor, and quiet revolving ceiling fans, was a favorite spot for business luncheons and before-theater dinners.

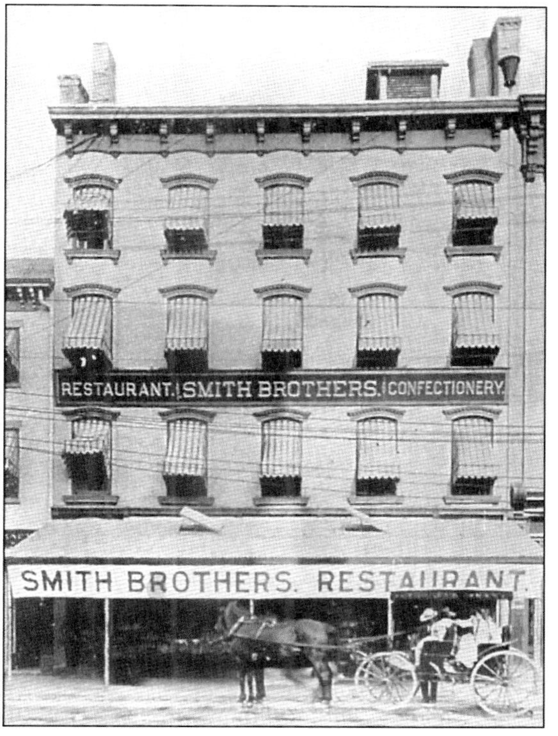

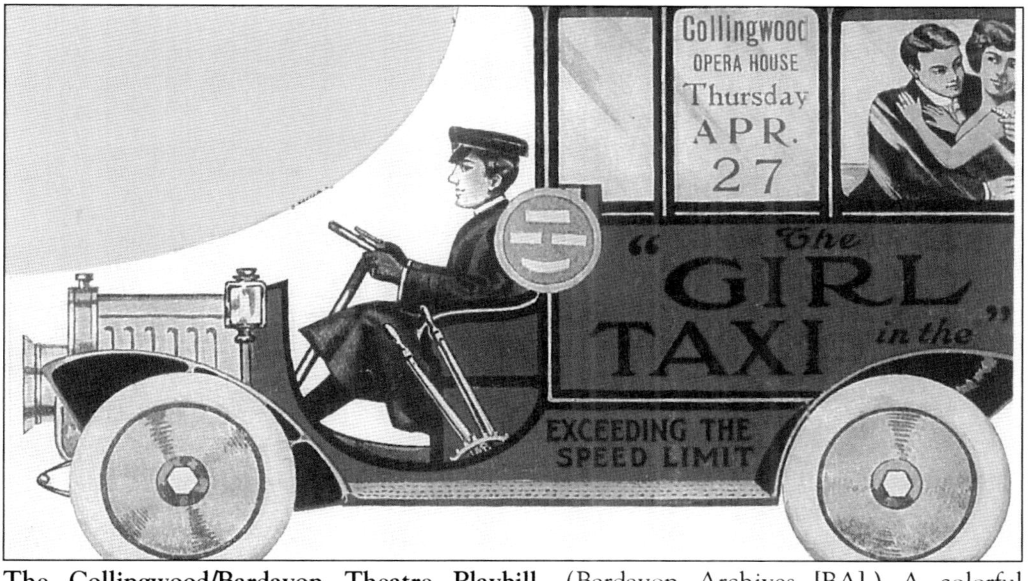

The Collingwood/Bardavon Theatre Playbill. (Bardavon Archives [BA].) A colorful playbill from the Bardavon 1869 Opera House Archives gives a glimpse of the Bardavon's rich theatrical fare. Concerts, plays, dance groups, and acts of all kinds featuring some of the finest performers known are sketched in Elizabeth Oakley's slide set on the history of this National Register performing arts center and successful arts business. J.A. Wood, prominent city architect, designed the first structure in 1868 for owner James Collingwood, who also ran a coal business.

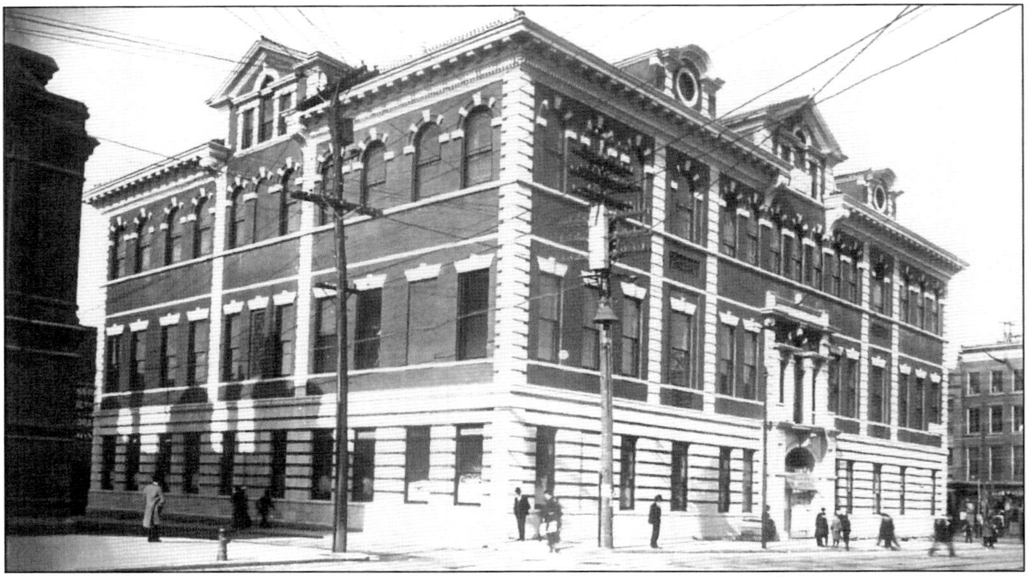

The 1902 Courthouse. (Catherine Bala [CB].) This photograph made from a glass negative can be dated by a sign advertising "Campbell and Sons General Contractors," the "new" courthouse construction company. Begun in 1902 and completed in 1904, the Italianate-influenced design by architect William Beardsley was a departure from former buildings using early American motifs. Like all those that preceded, this courthouse has undergone numerous internal and external additions and changes pitting aesthetics against practicality. The monumental building still survives, heading for a longevity record.

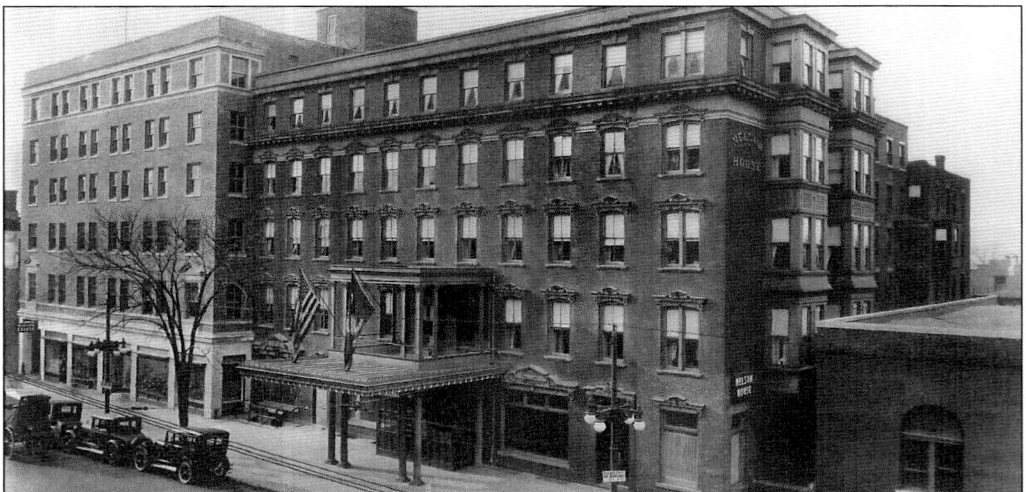

The Nelson House, 1920s. (AML.) The elegant Nelson House, close to the courthouse and the Bardavon, traced its roots to Van Den Bogert's early farm that took in travelers. Stephen Hendriksen built the first inn in 1777, seeking courthouse business. Guests included Clinton, Jay, Hamilton, and Thomas Jefferson (who stopped on a trip through New York, noting in his diary Hendriksen's excellent service). New owners brought name changes: the Forbus Hotel and finally, the Nelson House. FDR delivered many a speech there while the dining room and bar buzzed with politicians politicking.

Theater Ads, 1923. (BA.) A Bardavon archives ad shows the theater as the premiere city "combination house," later part of the Paramount chain, featuring first-run movies and vaudeville. Renovations after World War I by architect William Beardsley kept abreast of changes in audience entertainment preferences and made the seating area, originally designed to seat two thousand, smaller. Fine acoustics, enhanced by the center dome, made stage productions, lectures, concerts, and films equally enjoyable experiences for patrons and presenters alike.

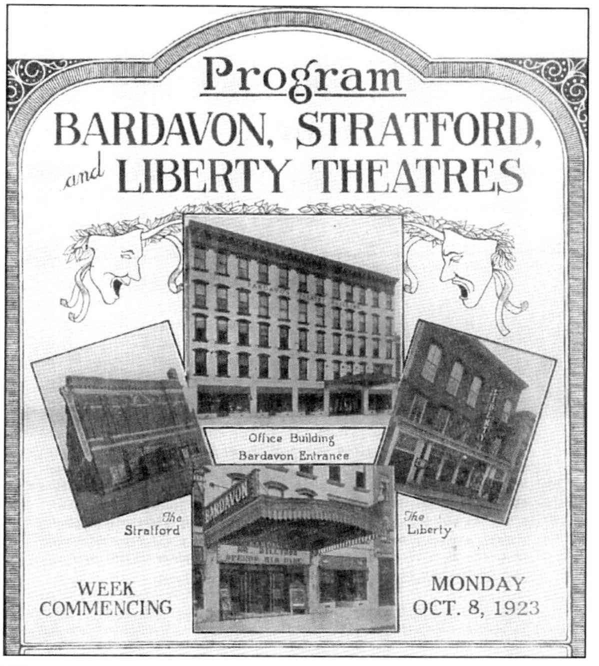

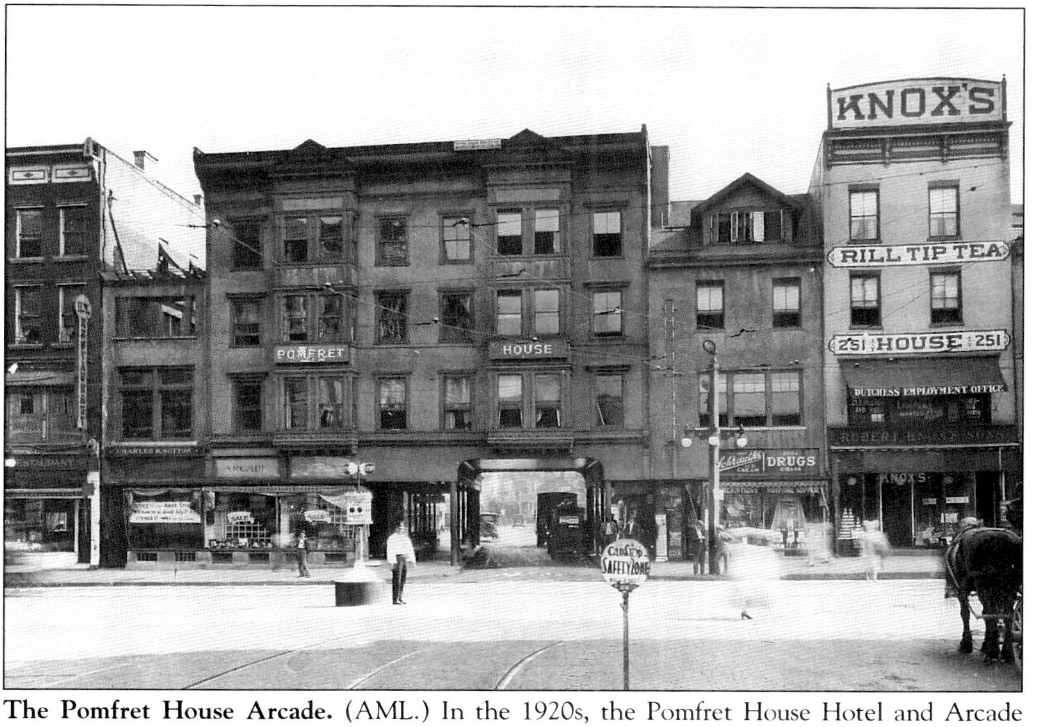

The Pomfret House Arcade. (AML.) In the 1920s, the Pomfret House Hotel and Arcade occupied the center of the street at the intersection of Main and Market. When the decision to construct New Market Street was made (to ease Albany Post Road traffic congestion), the hotel, facing Main Street, was not torn down, but simply turned into a first-floor tunnel and arcade for several years until surrounding demolition and reconstruction were complete.

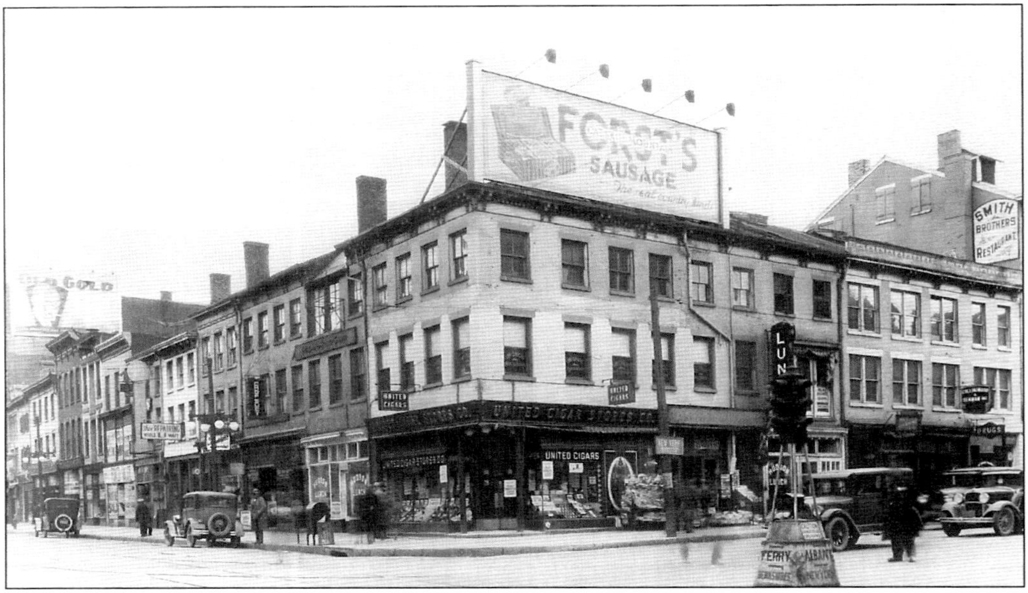

Church Building Corner. (AML.) This *c.* 1930 photograph shows the southeast corner of Main and Market before the buildings were replaced by a single Art Deco structure. Called "the Church Corner" for two centuries, this was the site of the cemetery of the original Dutch church. During the nineteenth century, the property was developed commercially and became occupied by a row of small stores leased to private businessmen.

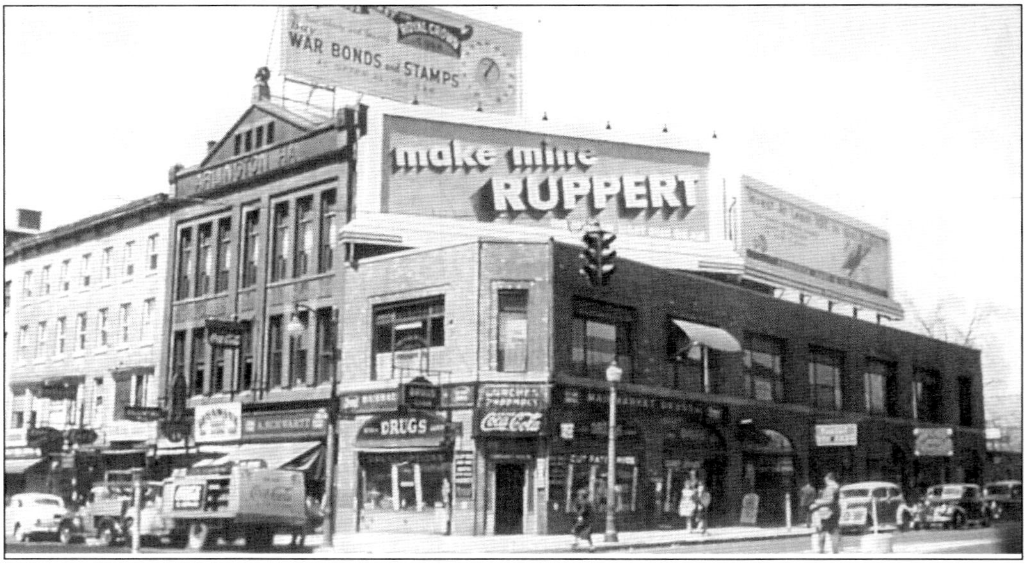

The Northwest Corner of Main and New Market Streets. (DCHS, William H. Hubbard [WH].) William Hubbard's photograph of the northwest corner of Main and Market is dated as early 1940s by the rooftop sign selling War Bonds and Stamps. This corner was rebuilt in the 1930s when New Market Street was constructed. The Rexall Drug Store had a popular soda fountain and sandwich counter. Two doors down on Main Street, a Chinese family operated an upstairs restaurant serving local patrons more exotic dishes at reasonable prices.

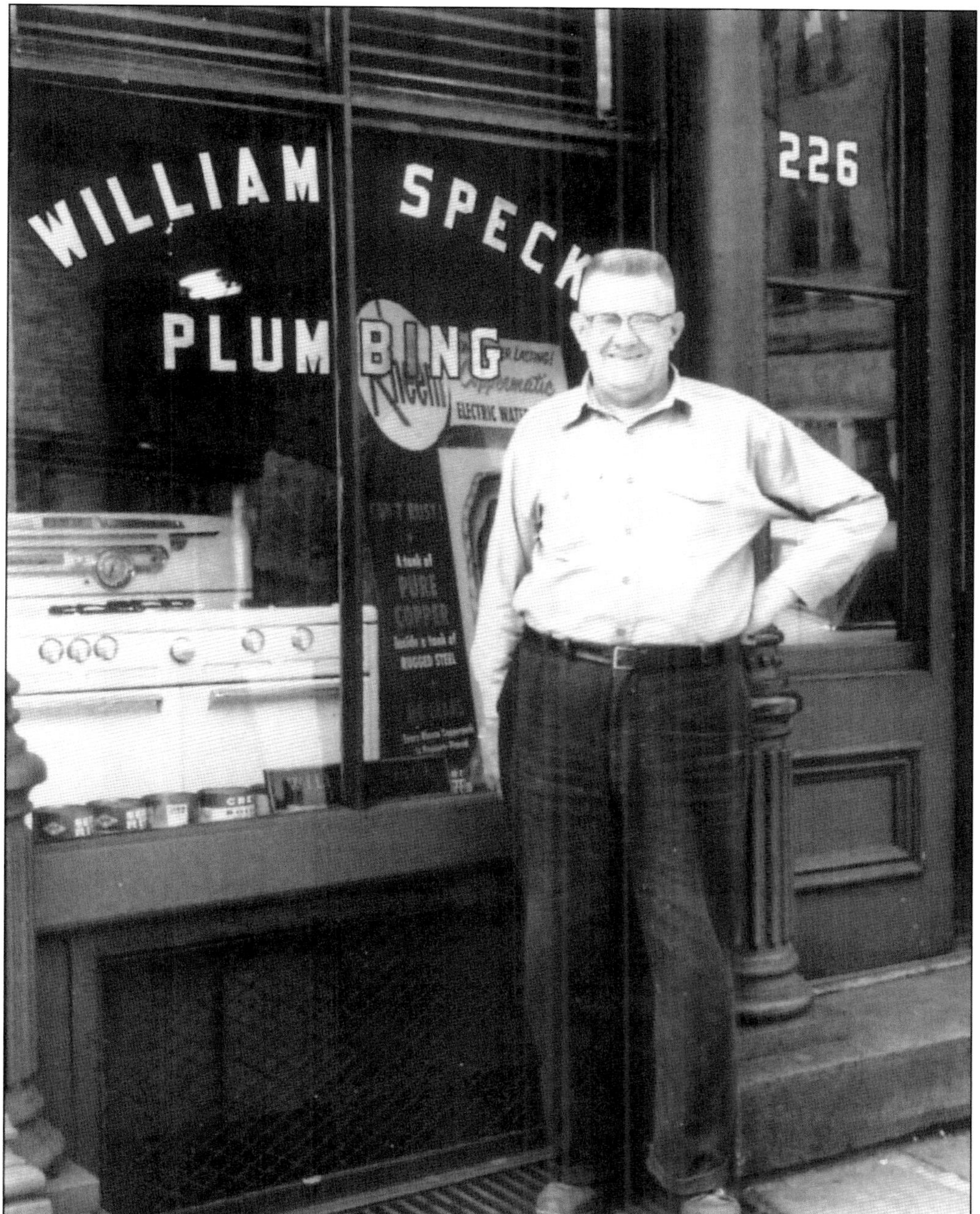

William Speck, Plumbing. (Christine Jacoby [CJ].) William Speck's successful mid-twentieth-century plumbing, heating, and metal work firm specialized in beer and soda fountain work. However, Speck's business at 226 Union Street at the intersection with Little Washington Street was conveniently near county and city offices and the old city jail, where inmates frequently took out their anger on plumbing fixtures. In the 1890s, the building, known as "the Hackett Law Building," housed lawyers' offices upstairs and the James Reynolds' Elevator Company retail store on the first floor.

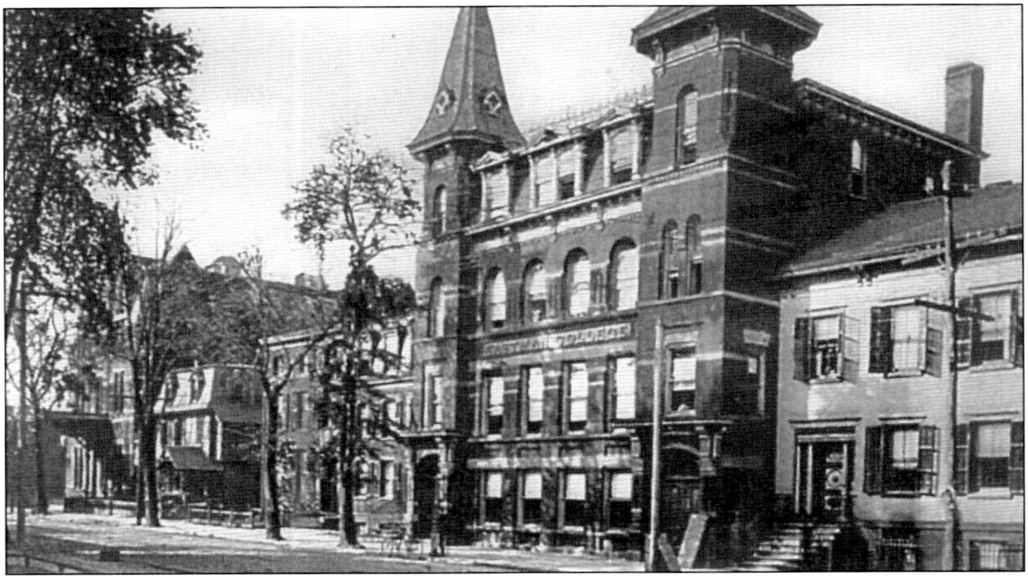

Eastman Business College. (DCHS.) Around the corner on Washington Street was the main building of the Eastman Business College, the brainchild of Harvey Eastman, a creative entrepreneur likened to "The Music Man." He descended like a tornado in 1859 and vigorously advertised his nascent business school, whose campus was scattered all over downtown Poughkeepsie in rented rooms, hotels, and storefronts. Despite the ephemeral infrastructure, his inventive teaching style was sound, producing skilled businessmen for generations.

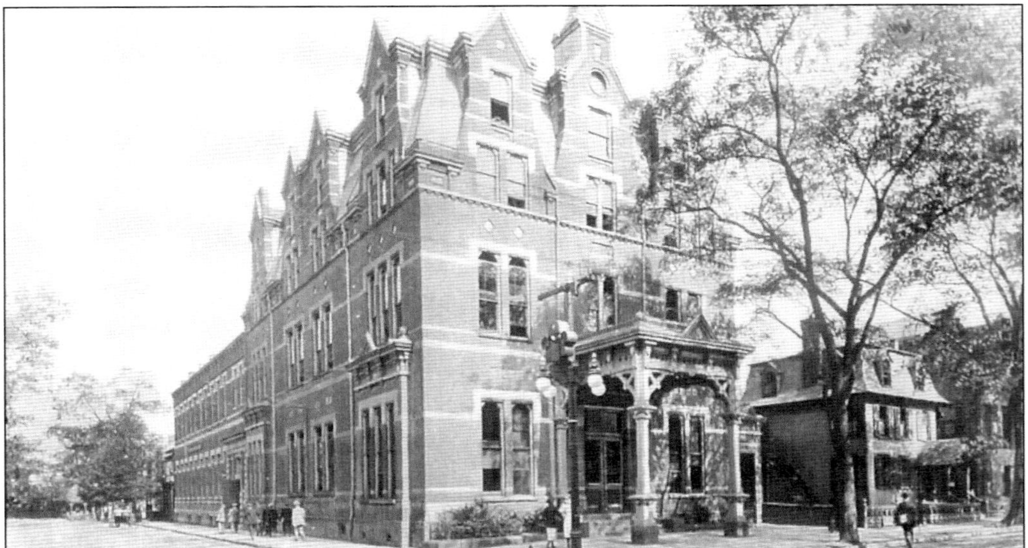

Old Poughkeepsie High School. (DCHS.) An old postcard shows the Poughkeepsie High School/Library on Washington Street, erected *c.* 1871. This institution was the nineteenth-century equivalent of community college in the days when a grammar school education was considered adequate by most young people. It served not only the city's post-elementary school students, but accepted students who came on a tuition basis by train and trolley from all over the county. A new building was needed by the turn of the century.

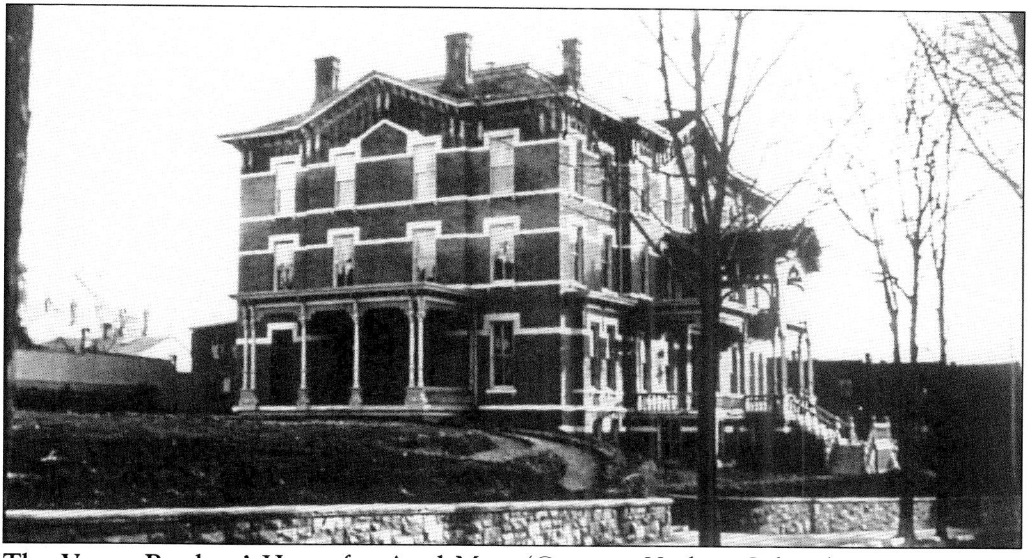

The Vassar Brothers' Home for Aged Men. (Cunneen-Hackett Cultural Center, Virginia Hancock [CH, VH].) A block west on Vassar Street, the Vassar Brothers' Home for Aged Men was built on the site of Matthew Vassar's home near his successful brewery. It was incorporated in 1880 by John Guy and Matthew Vassar Jr., nephews of the founder of Vassar Female College, who were community philanthropists in the family tradition. The home that for many years cared for elderly Protestant gentlemen is now occupied by the Cunneen-Hackett Cultural Center.

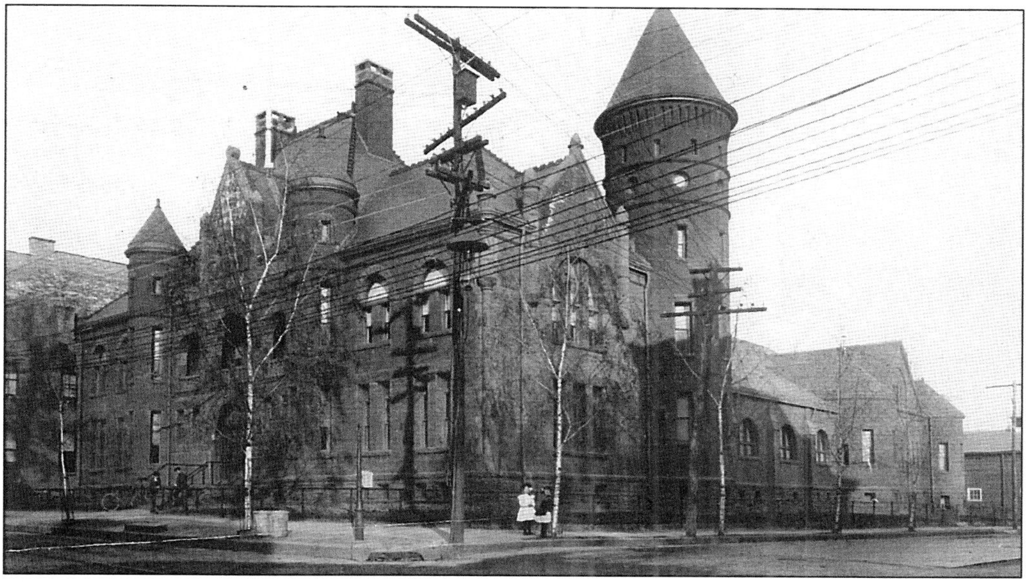

The Armory. (AML.) The Armory was erected in 1891 at the corner of Market and Church Streets on the site of the first Episcopal church, which was built before the Revolution and for which the street was named. Although the "English" church was closed in protest during that war, Episcopalians returned in numbers thereafter. Christ Church moved to its present Academy Street location in 1888, making way for the Armory. Two chattering little girls seem indifferent to the nearby mighty fortress housing local militia units.

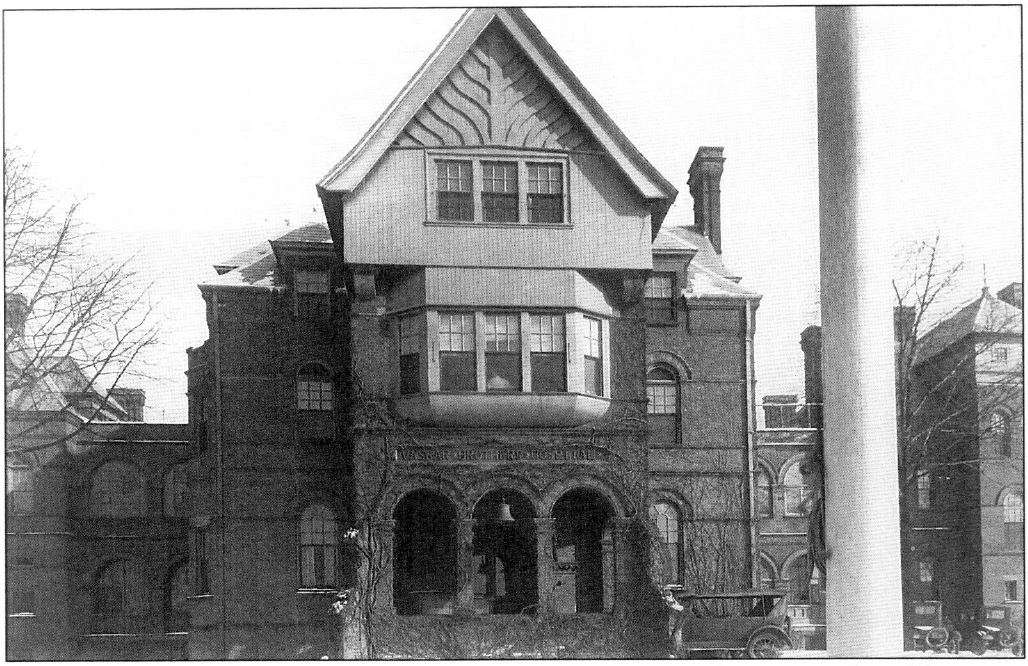

Vassar Brothers' Hospital. (DCHS.) This *c.* 1890 photograph of Vassar Brothers' Hospital is another reflection of the Vassar family community largesse. Matthew Vassar Jr.'s initial bequest in 1882 built the main building on Reade Place in 1884 and John Guy Vassar's endowment in his will gave the institution the capability to grow in accordance with community needs. Along with the money came a cherished bell from the Vassar Brewery. With an early capacity of 225 beds, Vassar Brothers' became the largest, most well-equipped hospital between New York City and Albany.

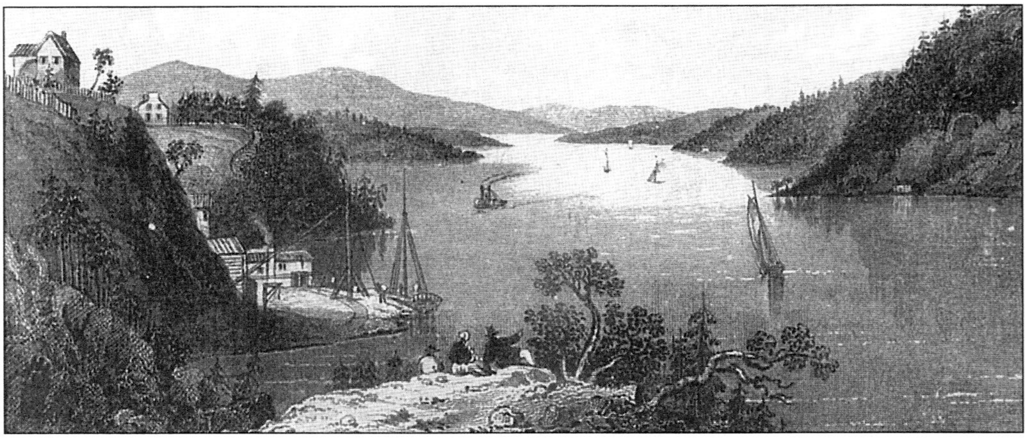

The Lower Landing Area in the Nineteenth Century. (DCHS.) Fanciful nineteenth-century river engravings abound, such as this *View (south) of the Hudson from Poughkeepsie*. The mixture of land forms and structures in pleasing, aesthetic arrangements in these engravings cannot always be trusted to provide accurate historical information. Here, however, the configuration of inlet, heights, and ship-building activity is strikingly consistent with information found in eighteenth-century maps of the riverfront between the present Poughkeepsie Rural Cemetery and the Livingston/Morse property.

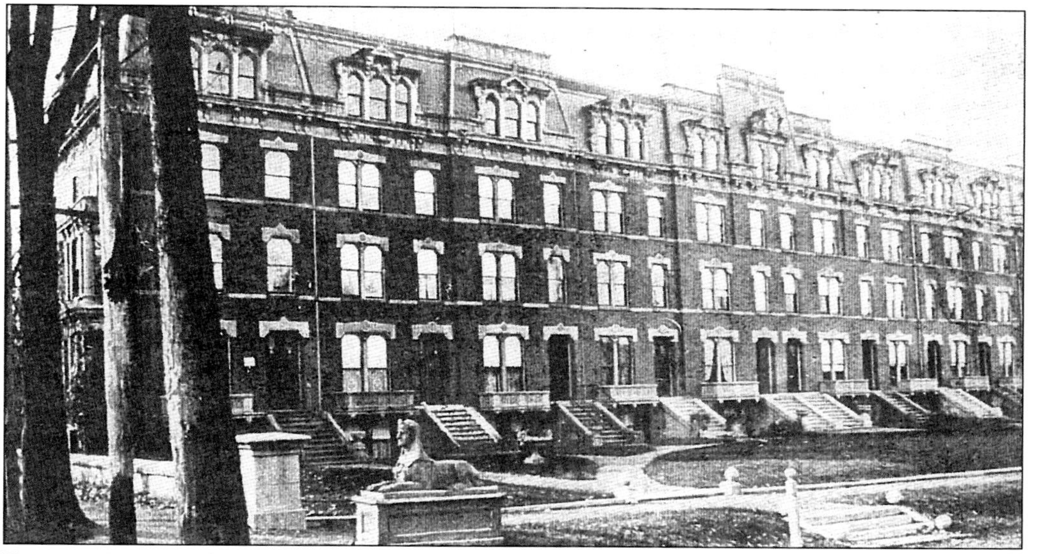

Eastman Terrace. (DCHS.) A vintage postcard shows Eastman Terrace, a handsome Victorian townhouse development project that was the linchpin of Harvey Eastman's plan for ongoing south-side development. A brochure from 1873 shows his vision of elegant brick homes overlooking a carefully landscaped park setting that was to include walkways, a deer park, a fountain, and the Eastman residence. The message was aimed at well-to-do city dwellers who might also need to commute. Sadly, sales were disappointing and the plan never was completed.

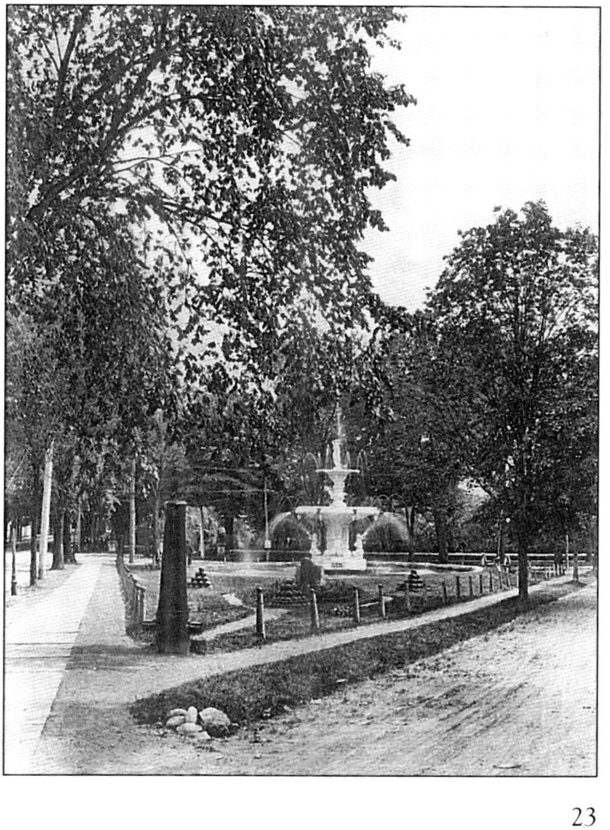

Soldiers' Fountain. (DCHS.) This old postcard shows one of the city's most cherished landmarks, the Soldiers' Fountain near Eastman Park. With $70,000 from Harvey Eastman, much fanfare, and a balloon ascension, this flower-filled triangle honoring Civil War soldiers was dedicated on July 4, 1870. The annual ritual of lighting the fountain signals that spring is here. One of a handful of fountains molded in the same design, it has a "sister" monument in Savannah, Georgia.

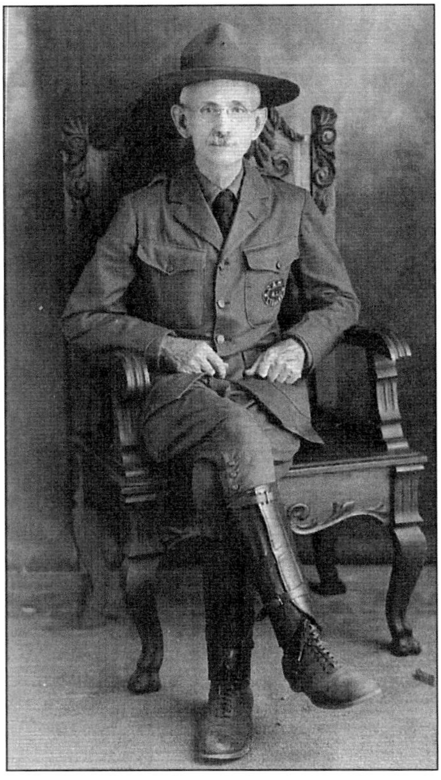

John C. Sickley. (AML.) John C. Sickley, city library director from 1882 to 1920, poses in his World War I army uniform. Sickley put his considerable talents as a librarian to work for the war effort in 1918 at Camp Wadsworth in Spartanburg, North Carolina. Mr. Sickley also oversaw every detail of the construction of the new public library building, the Adriance Memorial Library, assuring its position as one of the finest in the state.

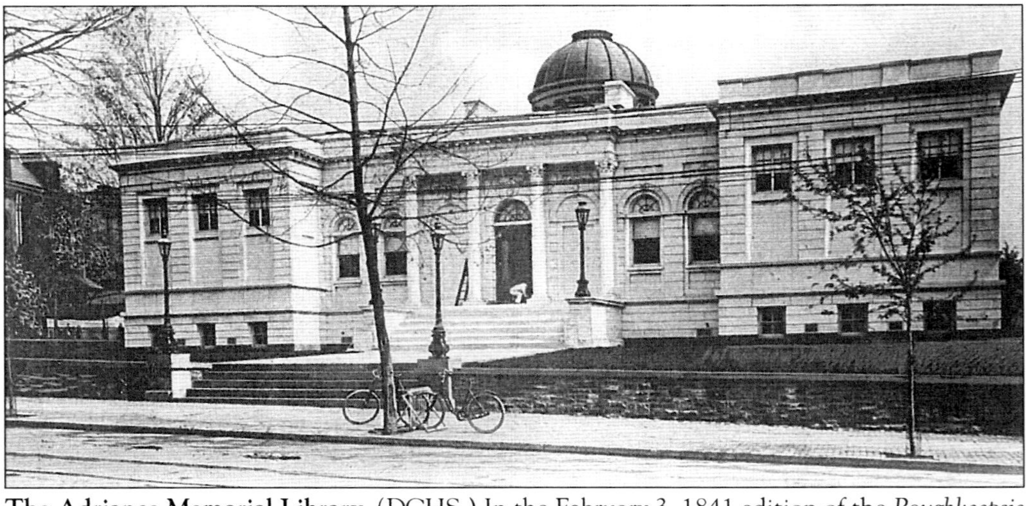

The Adriance Memorial Library. (DCHS.) In the February 3, 1841 edition of the *Poughkeepsie Telegraph*, Lancaster School Trustees announced the opening of a public reading room. Adriance, as its direct legal descendant, is the oldest tax-supported municipal library in the state. Until construction was finished on Market Street in 1898, materials had been housed in several locations, including the courthouse and the high school on Washington Street. The extensive local history collection at Adriance is a valued regional research resource. The marble French Renaissance-influenced structure honors John P. Adriance, a local industrialist, and his wife, Mary; the construction was financed by the couple's children.

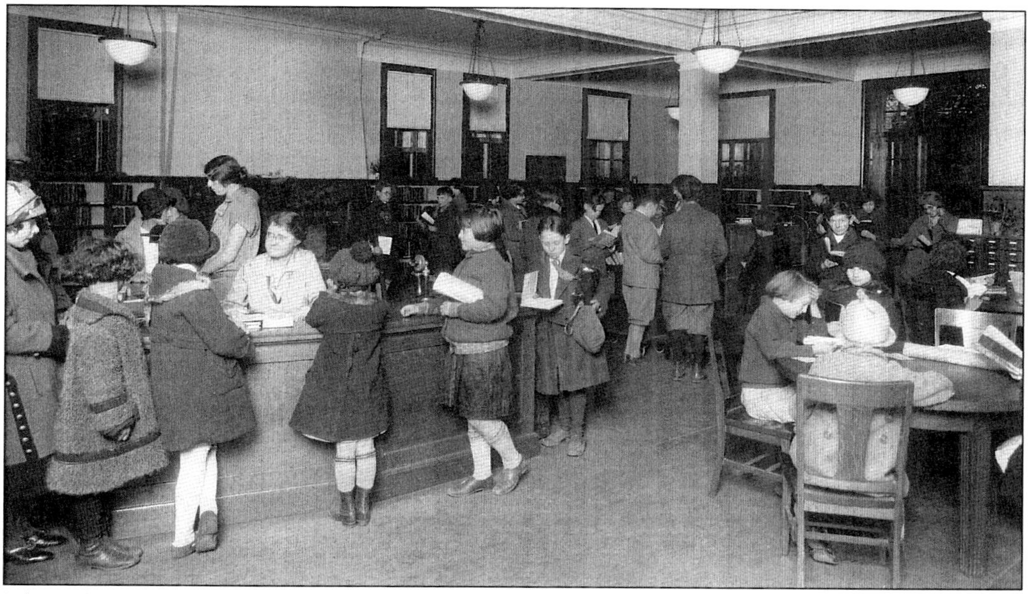

The Adriance Children's Room. (AML.) The welcome addition at Adriance in 1923 of a new children's room brought hundreds of new young patrons to attend its opening. The refined high-style structure, designed with the interests of a literate adult population in mind, saw additions to the collection and physical changes as well. Small chairs, low tables and a wide selection of children's literature—plus child-friendly librarians—have made this room one of the most popular spots at the library.

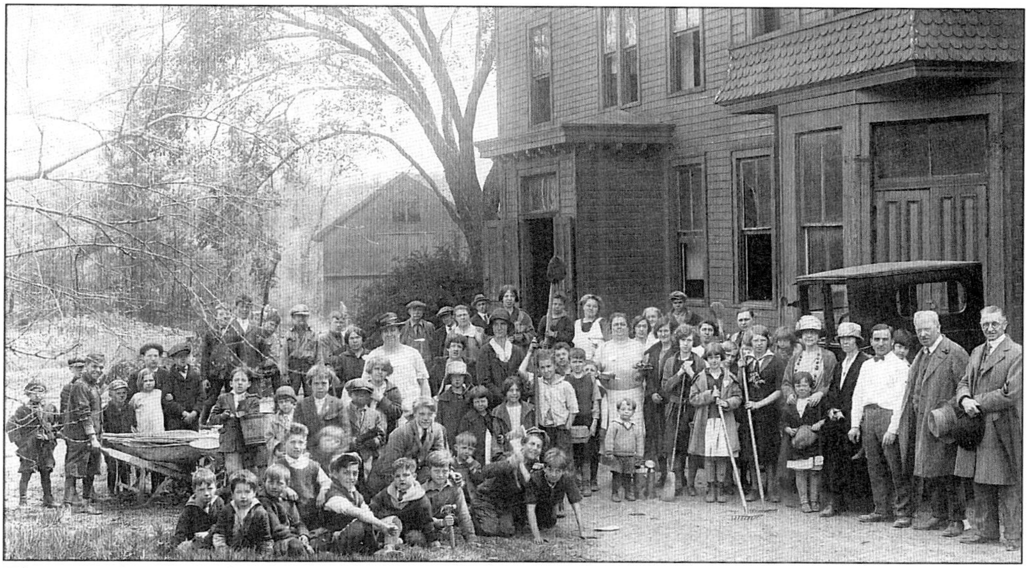

The Lincoln Center/Riverview Academy Site, c. 1926. (AML.) The 1920s saw rapid changes near Vassar Brothers' Hospital at the site of Riverview Military Academy. When the school closed, the building was taken over by Lincoln Center, which provided neighborhood services and programs for all ages. Riverview Military Academy had offered a classical curriculum within a highly disciplined regimen to young men of the upper classes. Lincoln Center expressed new learning concepts emphasizing the social implications of education.

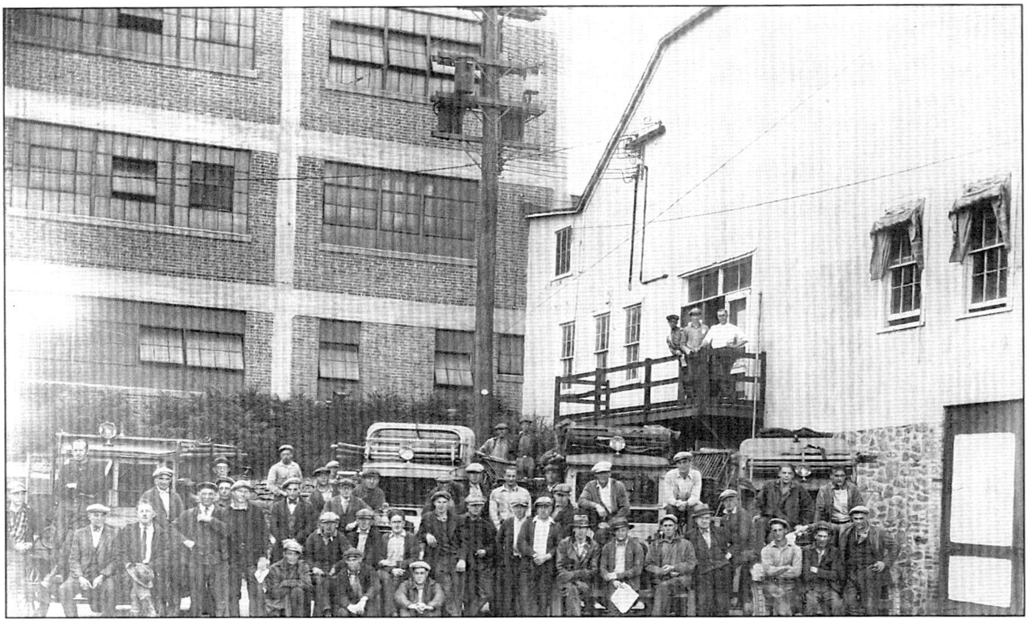

The Central Hudson Crew. (Mary Lou Sotanski [MLS].) The Sotanski family album shows a 1930s group portrait of Central Hudson Gas and Electric Corporation workers at the main plant near the Poughkeepsie Rural Cemetery. Grandfather John, on the far left in the first row, lived nearby on Grand Street. Public utilities got an early start here in 1884 when Dorsey Neville erected a dynamo at Bullard's Foundry on Main Street. The Poughkeepsie Electric Light and Power Company bought his rights and incorporated in 1886.

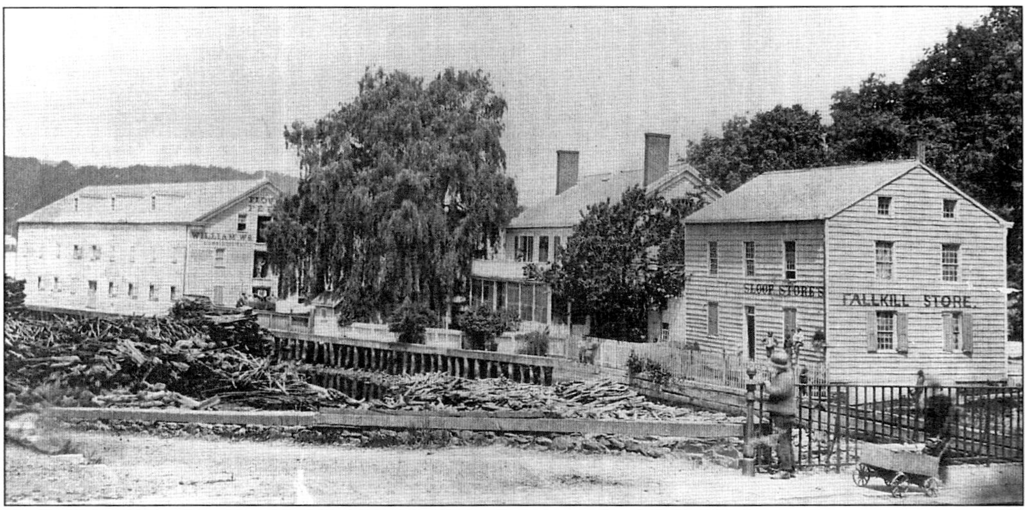

The Upper Landing/Fallkill Store. (AML.) Mills and stores had been located at Upper Landing from the start of settlement when James Reynolds came in 1800 to begin a weekly freight and passenger sloop business between Poughkeepsie and New York City. In 1818 he and Aaron Innis bought the Hoffmann Mill and expanded services to include a store and milling and grain transport. The opening of the Erie Canal and the Civil War increased trade. A growing company was passed to family members who learned the wholesale business from the bottom up.

St. Peter's Catholic Church and Rectory. (DCHS.) From a bluff overlooking the river, St. Peter's white steeple and gold cross have been landmarks welcoming Roman Catholics from all European cultures since 1837. Although Catholics were few in number until the Great Potato Famine of the 1840s brought waves of Irish immigrants to the area, they established a small congregation *c.* 1833 with support from the Improvement Party's John Delafield. Twentieth-century Italian immigrants were given use of St. Peter's basement for services until the community built Mt. Carmel Church a block away at Cataract Square.

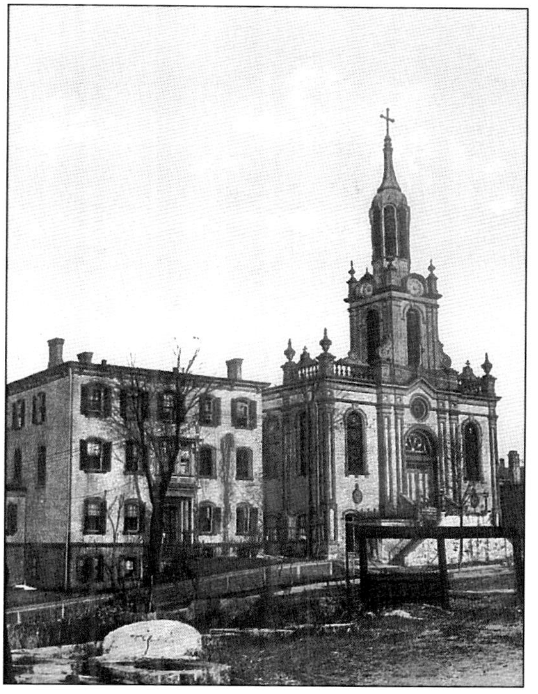

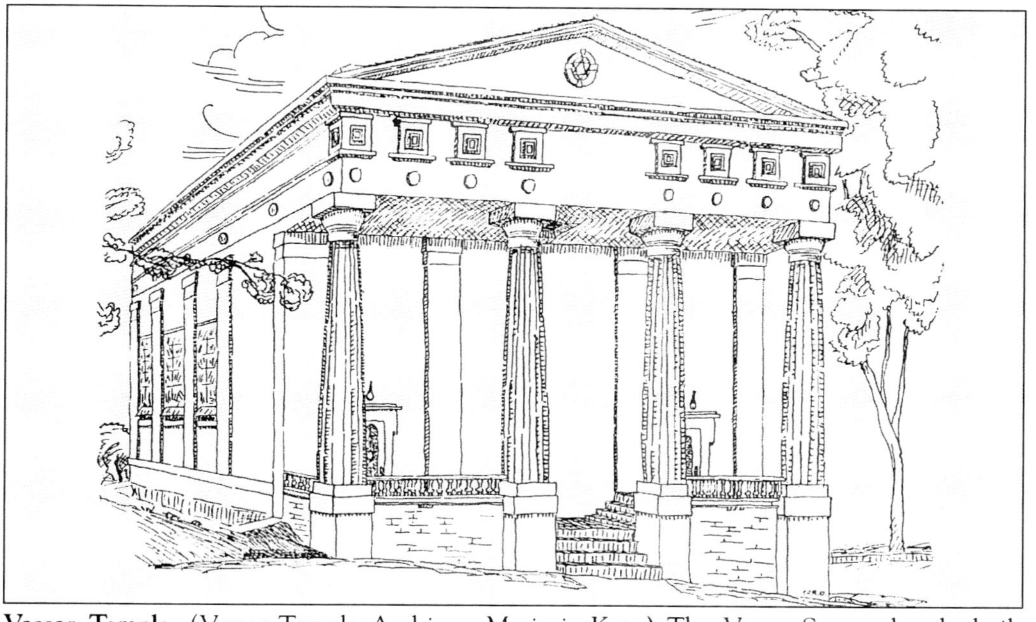

Vassar Temple. (Vassar Temple Archives, Marjorie Katz.) The Vassar Street church, built *c.* 1835 by dissenting Presbyterians, has sheltered several religious communities. By 1845, Jews escaping Europe's pogroms moved to riverside neighborhoods, where a group of five Germans formed the Congregation Children of Israel. Three years later, a Certificate of Incorporation changed the name to Congregation Brethren of Israel, and this became the only synagogue between Albany and New York City. In 1860 the congregation remodeled this Greek Revival structure with a mortgage secured by Matthew Vassar Jr., who lived nearby on Mill Street.

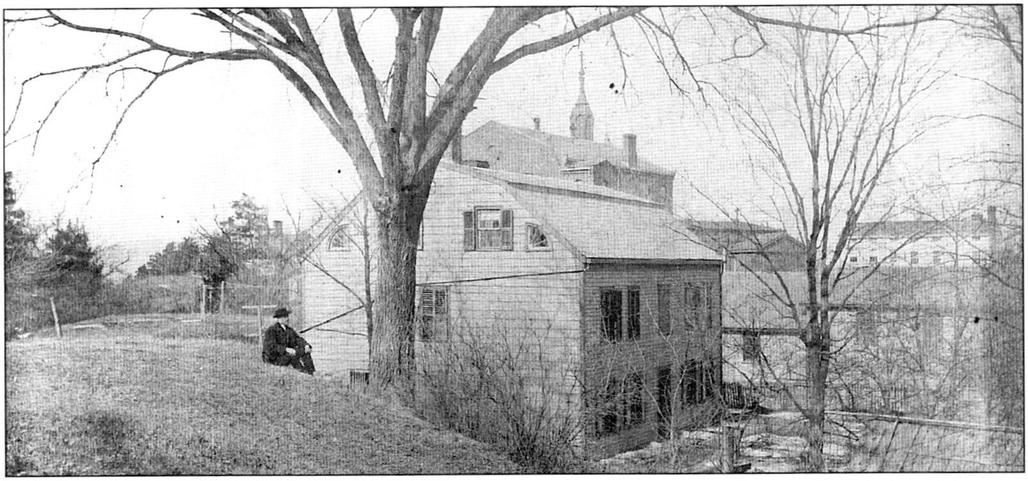

The George Booth Residence, c. 1870. (AML.) Factory owner George Booth lived by the river near St. Peter's Church. Booth, who came from England, introduced the first wool carding machine used in the United States. His woolen factories on the Fallkill and Wappinger Creeks experienced a boost during the War of 1812's embargo on foreign goods. Members of the Booth family were prominent in civic affairs, establishing schools and fire control systems. The O.H. Booth Hose Company honors son Oliver; daughter Lydia's Cottage Hill Seminary was Matthew Vassar's model for his college.

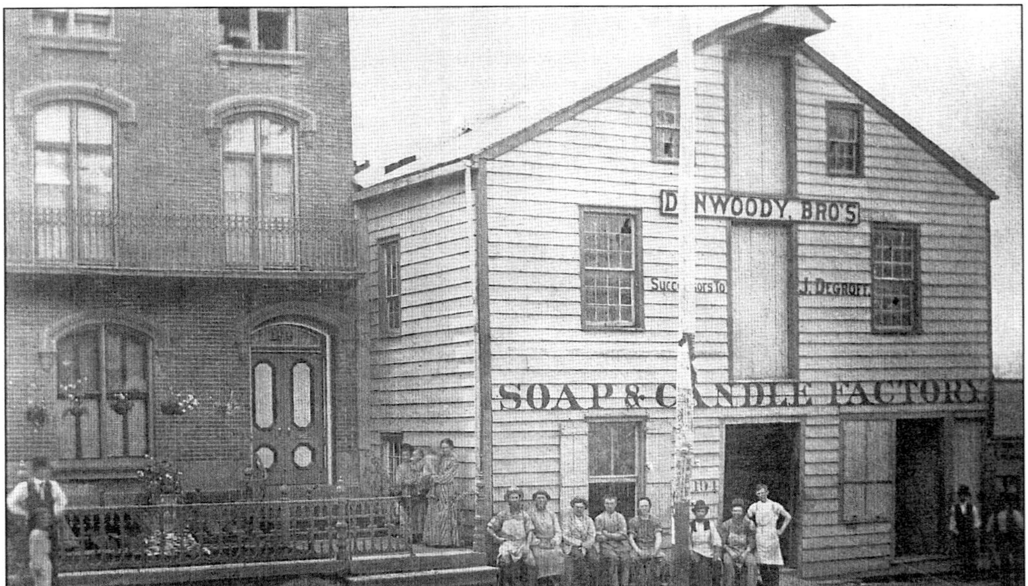

The Dunwoody Bros. Soap Factory. (AML.) The Dunwoody Brothers Soap Factory, successor to J. DeGroff, soap and candlemakers at 194 Main Street since 1795, was one of three soap factories in the city, producing 18,000 pounds of soap every three weeks. The company's building, originally a schoolhouse, was converted to industrial use and expanded. In neighborhoods near the waterfront where laborers in local factories and new immigrant populations lived, mixed uses of buildings, however incompatible, were common and considered a convenience by residents who needed to walk to work.

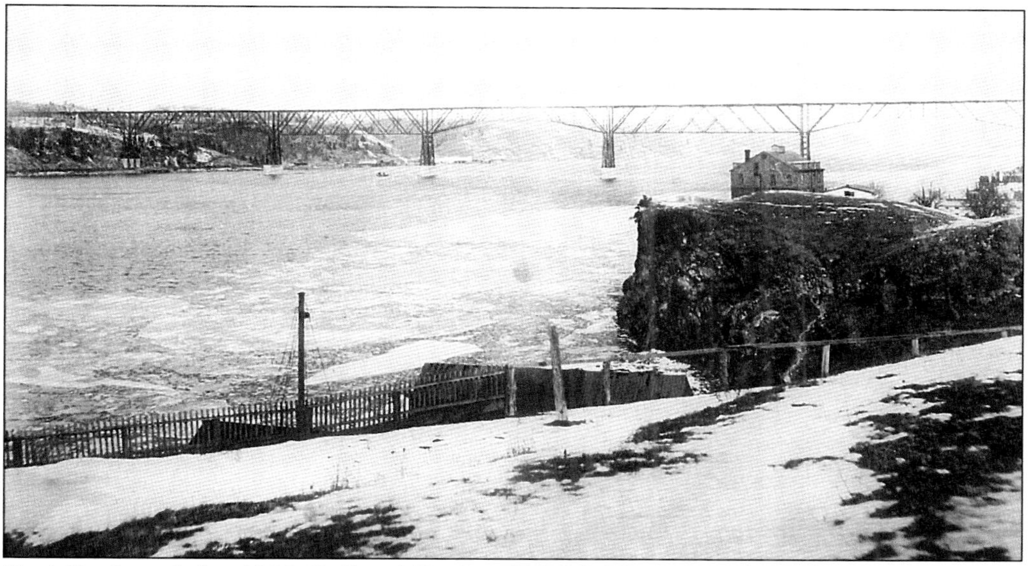

Caul Rock and the 1888 Railroad Bridge. (AML.) This view of Caul/Kaal Rock (Dutch for Bald Rock) and the 1888 railroad bridge reveals the importance of both landmarks to Poughkeepsie. Caul Rock's visibility made it easily spotted by schooners and sloops heading for nearby landings in the years when the river was the main road. One look at the ice makes Harvey Eastman's insistence on the need for a railroad bridge obvious. While it did not have the immediate impact on Poughkeepsie that he envisioned, the bridge kept supplies and products moving by rail year-round.

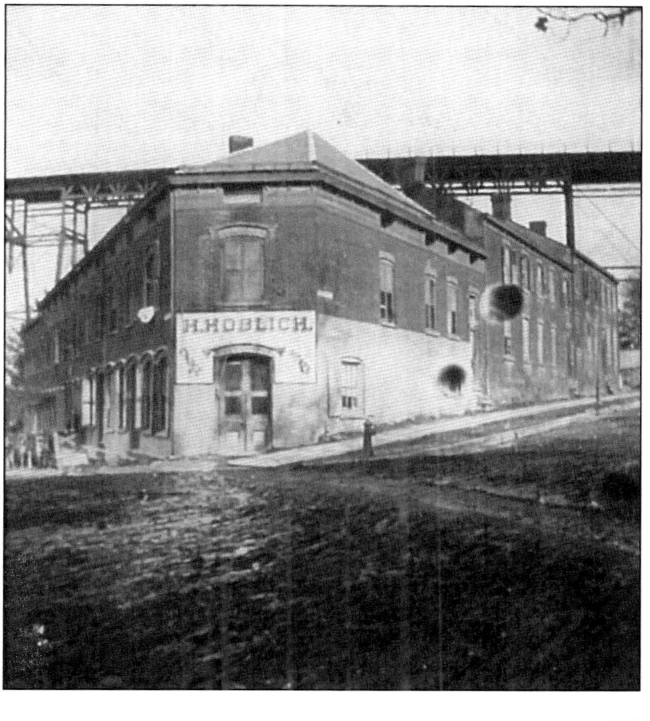

Hoblich's Butcher Shop. (AML.) "H. Hoblich, Choice Meats," a German butcher shop, stood on the corner of Dutchess Avenue and Delafield Street at the turn of the century with the new railroad bridge looming overhead. Customers came from around Cataract Square, now called Mount Carmel. German immigration early in the nineteenth century contributed to the growth of organizations like the Germania Singing Society, established in 1850, whose concerts enriched area cultural resources. German Catholics faithfully supported the Nativity Church they built on Union Street in 1853 and the school added later.

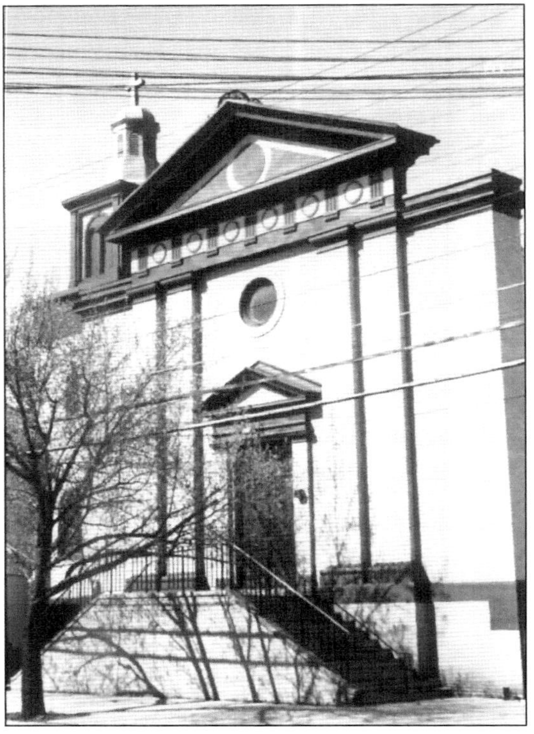

Mt. Carmel Church. (DCHS, JG.) Mt. Carmel Church, the heart of the Italian community here since 1903, informally rebaptized the "Cataract" area "Mount Carmel." Italians began coming in 1888 when men from the same Italian town found work on the Central New England Railroad. Following the Leos, Tesones, and Amatos came others: the Peluses, Barones, Finns, and Cards who, despite the respelling of their names, retained Italian linguistic and cultural links still evident in neighborhood architecture, landscapes, shops, restaurants, celebrations, and community life.

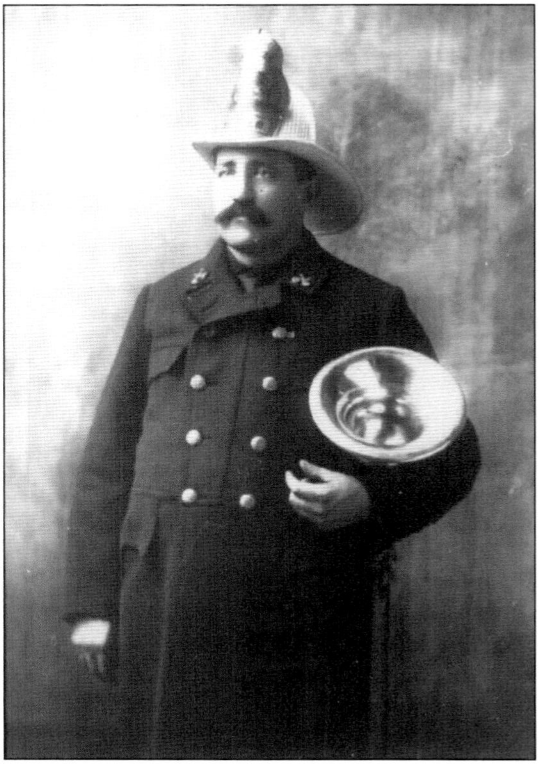

William E. Slater, Fireman. (Lucy Edgcomb [LE].) This glass-plate negative print shows William E. Slater, respected first assistant chief engineer of the Lady Washington Hose Co. #1, who retired after twenty-six years of service in 1906. Related negatives uncovered by Lucy Edgcomb and Catherine Bala, supported by Bardavon historian Annon Adams' research, provide glimpses of life c. 1900 in the riverfront area. Listed by city directories as a carpenter, Mr. Slater worked at part-time jobs, including being a ticket taker for the Collingwood Theater, for which he earned $4 for the season and was paid by a Fallkill Bank check).

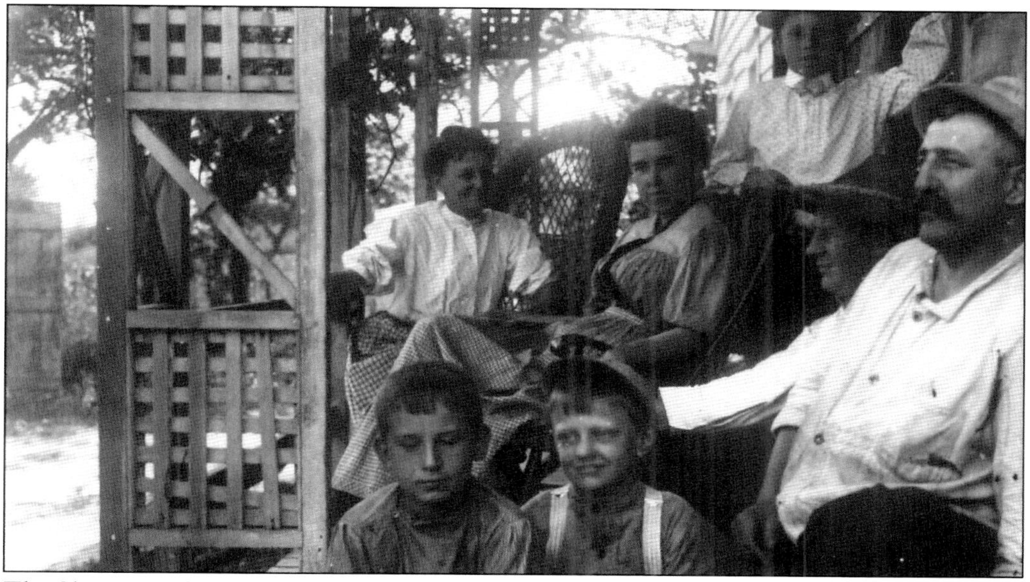

The Slater Family, c. 1900. (BA/LE/CB/Annon Adams.) The William E. Slaters were typical of neighborhood residents. Hard-working and civic-minded, both parents were children of German immigrants who had lived in Poughkeepsie almost all their lives. Pauline, a housewife, bore three children and saw two boys live to maturity. The small backyards of the rented houses on South Bridge and Union Streets and later Southeast Avenue show carefully tended kitchen gardens where neighbors and extended family gathered in the evening to gossip, smoke a pipe, or occasionally help each other with difficult chores.

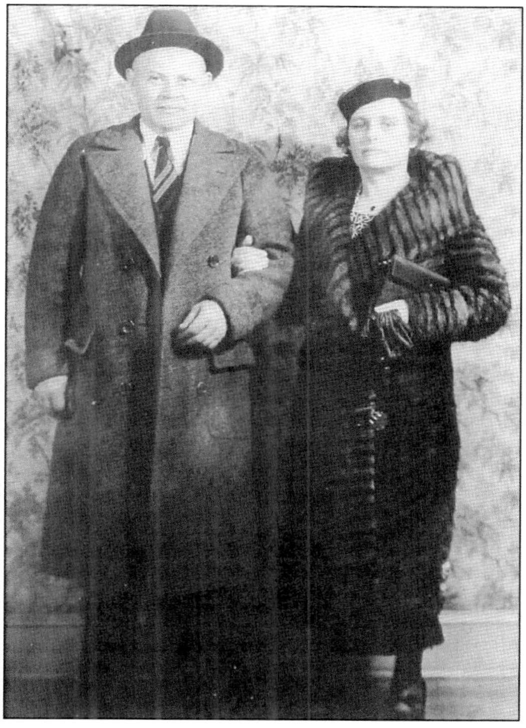

Mary and Thomas Potocki. (Leonard Babiarz Sr. [LB].) The Potockis, Len Babiarz' grandparents, emigrated to the United States from Poland at the turn of the century. Just before World War I, Mrs. Potocki returned to Poland with her small daughter to visit her mother. Caught by the war, she was forced to remain there much longer than she had planned and was relieved to return finally to Poughkeepsie. The family lived first on Gate Street and later on Charles Street. Mr. Potocki worked at the Fairview Foundry.

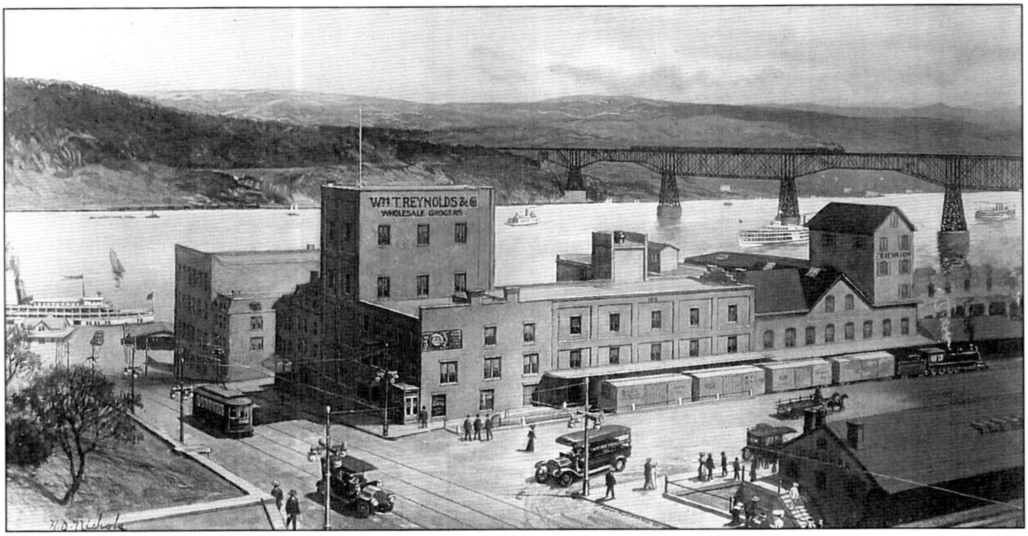

Wm. T. Reynolds' Business, 1910. (AML.) H.D. Nichols' architectural drawing of Wm.T. Reynolds & Company's planned development shows burgeoning industry and commerce along the riverfront at the Main Street dock before World War I. Reynolds' family-owned river properties and their wholesale businesses at the transportation hub had grown proportionately with the local economy, providing work for the neighboring community. In the foreground on the right is the old New York Central and Hudson River Railroad passenger terminal.

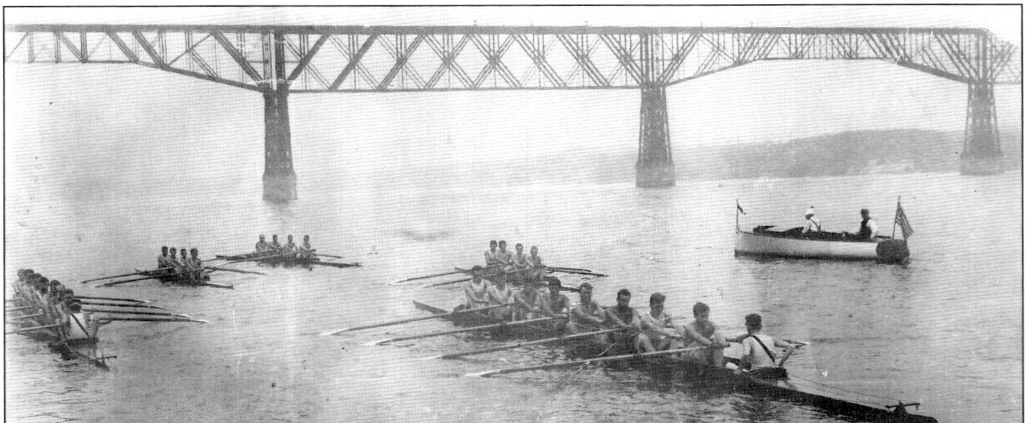

The Poughkeepsie Intercollegiate Regatta. (Jonah Sherman [JS].) The intercollegiate regatta was first held in Poughkeepsie in 1895 and was won by Columbia. Most of the leading young men of the area belonged to the amateur rowing association, which was instrumental in bringing the regatta to Poughkeepsie. The crews raced on part of the "Lange Racke," a long straight reach between Hyde Park and New Hamburgh. The regatta attracted thousands to cheer on their favorite college crews; there was even an observation train for spectators. The last year of the regatta was 1947; California won.

Dongan Statue. (DCHS, JG.) The only statue to recognize Irishman Thomas Dongan's contributions as the colonial governor who established New York's original counties was dedicated by Governor Franklin D. Roosevelt in June of 1930 at the newly created Dongan Square in Poughkeepsie at the intersection of Delafield and Mill Streets. Monsignor Joseph Sheahan, pastor of St. Peter's Church, was a principal proponent of the memorial designed to call attention to Irish contributions to New York history.

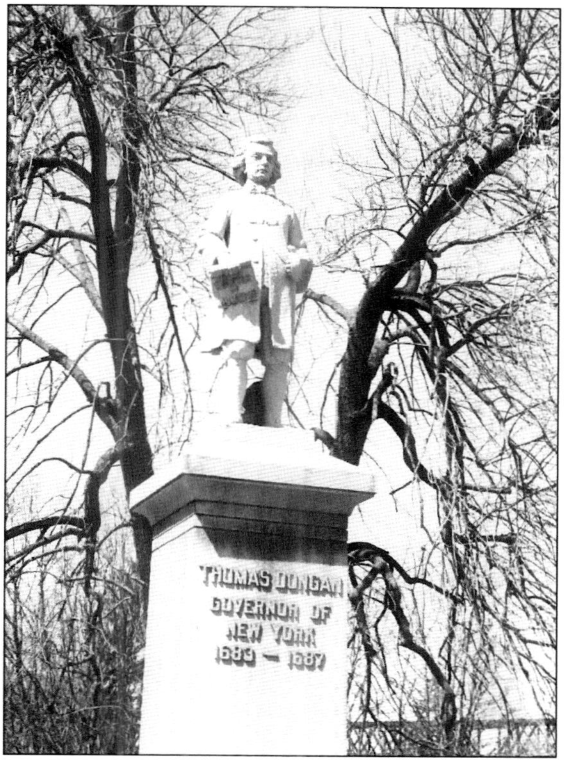

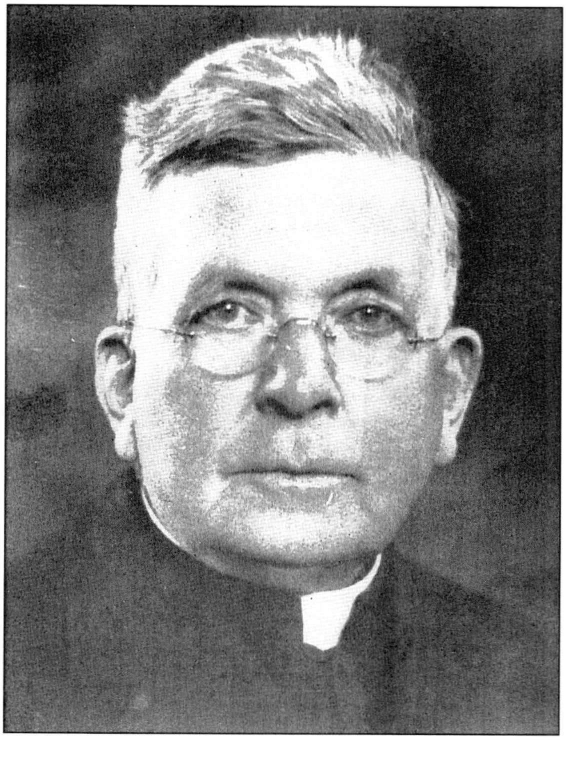

Monsignor Sheahan. (William D. Ghee [WDG].) This was a parish priest who made the community his pulpit and community action the subject of his homilies. His tireless advocacy of the Mid-Hudson Bridge, his work to develop St. Francis Hospital, and his success in bringing respect for Irish contributions to local history through the Dongan Memorial were only the most visible parts of the work that he pursued diligently throughout his years of service at St. Peter's.

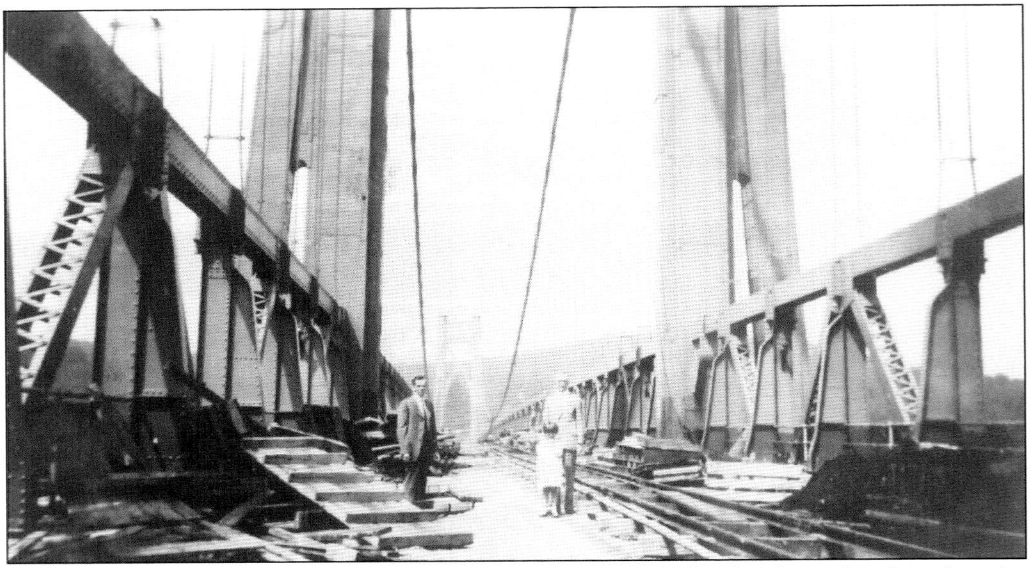

Mayor Lovelace Checking Construction. (Dave Krzeminski.) Like the railroad bridge, the Mid-Hudson vehicular bridge was in the talking stages for years, advocated by leaders like Monsignor Joseph F. Sheahan of St. Peter's. In this family album shot from Dave Krzeminski, Mayor Frank Lovelace and his young granddaughter Vivian get an insiders' tour of the bridge during construction c. 1928–29. The five-and-a-half-year construction period offered an opportunity for local "sidewalk superintendents" to take photographs and comment on the six-million-dollar project.

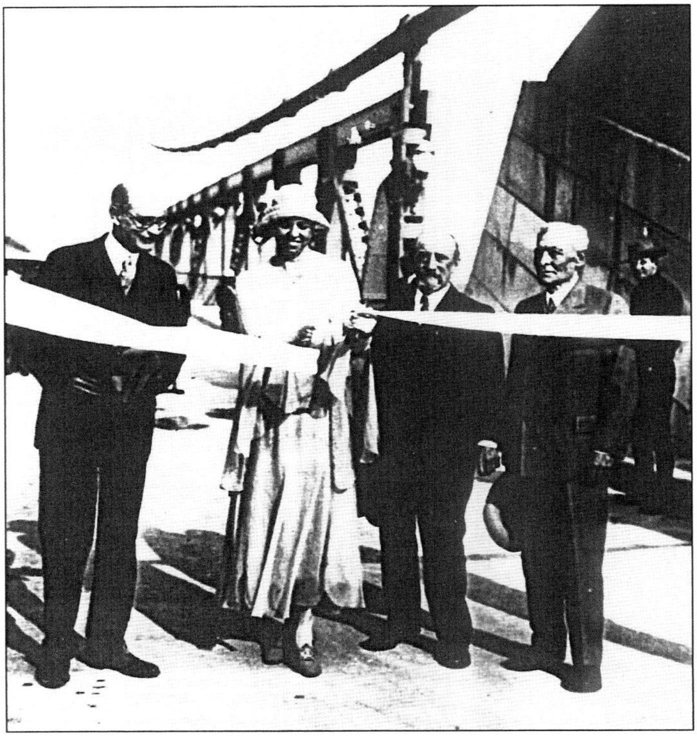

The Mid-Hudson Bridge Opening, 1930. (FDR Library.) On August 25, 1930, New York State First Lady Eleanor Roosevelt opened the Mid-Hudson Bridge. Ralph Modjeski and Daniel E. Moran designed one of the nation's most beautiful suspension bridges at the mid-point of the river between New York City and Albany. It was a key link in the East Coast highway system. The 80¢ fare was almost double the ferry fee, but cut crossing time by the better part of an hour.

Kay Kondor Gets the Prize. (DCHS, JG.) A tintype of Catherine (née Walsh) Kondor and her father, Thomas J. Walsh, an electrician of Irish descent from Poughkeepsie's riverside neighborhoods, marks a special memory. *The Poughkeepsie Eagle* sponsored a contest in 1926 for selling subscriptions, and a "singing doll" was given as a prize to this five-year-old student at Benjamin Franklin School. The excitement was shared with her mother, who worked on "The Whip" at Woodcliff, and was relived in her Girl-Scouting years, as she retold the story to Vassar student counselors at Lincoln Center.

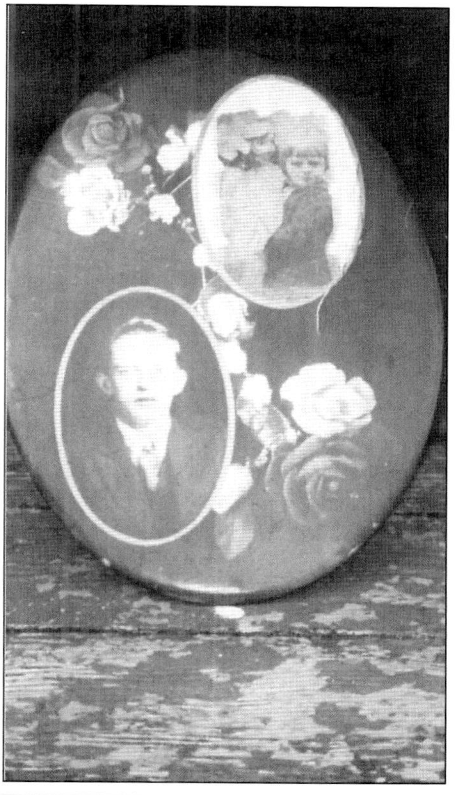

St. Joseph's Graduation. (LB.) It was a proud moment for Leonard Babiarz (in the second row on the left), the students of St. Joseph's Parochial School, and Father Kaminski, a beloved Polish community leader, at graduation in 1946. Father Kaminski was a favorite also in boating circles: the Pirate Canoe Club, the Poughkeepsie Yacht Club, and the Cataract Steamer Company counted him as a member. A growing Polish presence in the twentieth century contributed to establishment of St. Joseph's Church on Lafayette Place in 1903 and the Polish-American Citizens' Hall, erected in 1932 at 19 North Bridge Street.

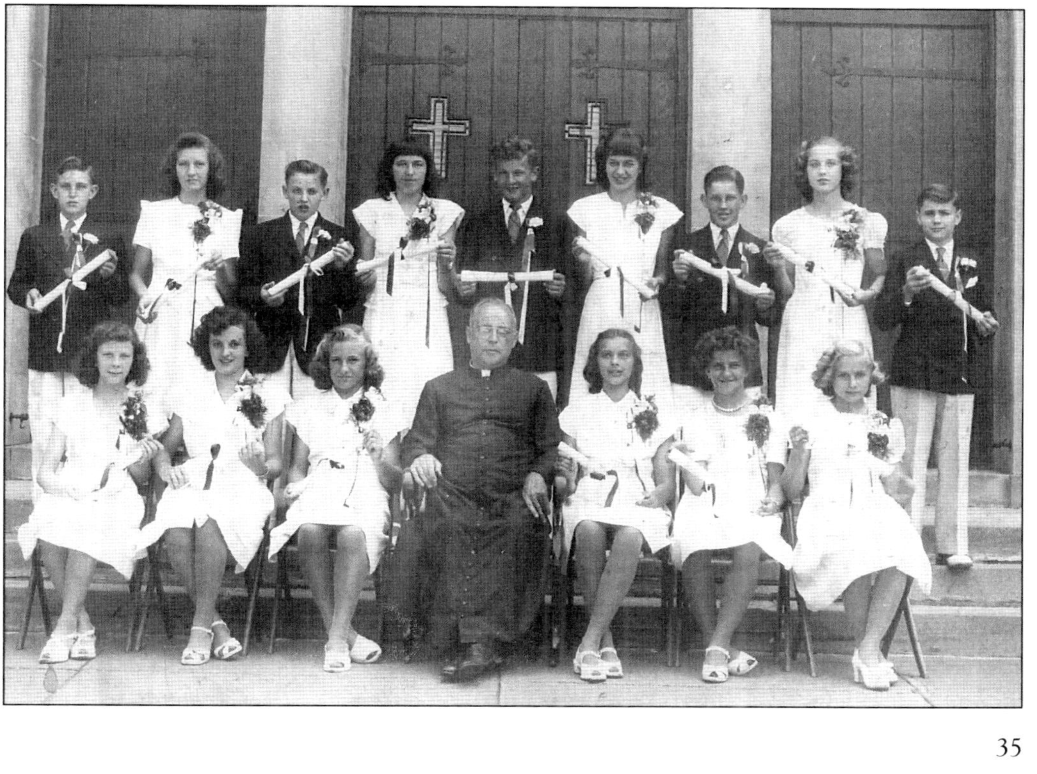

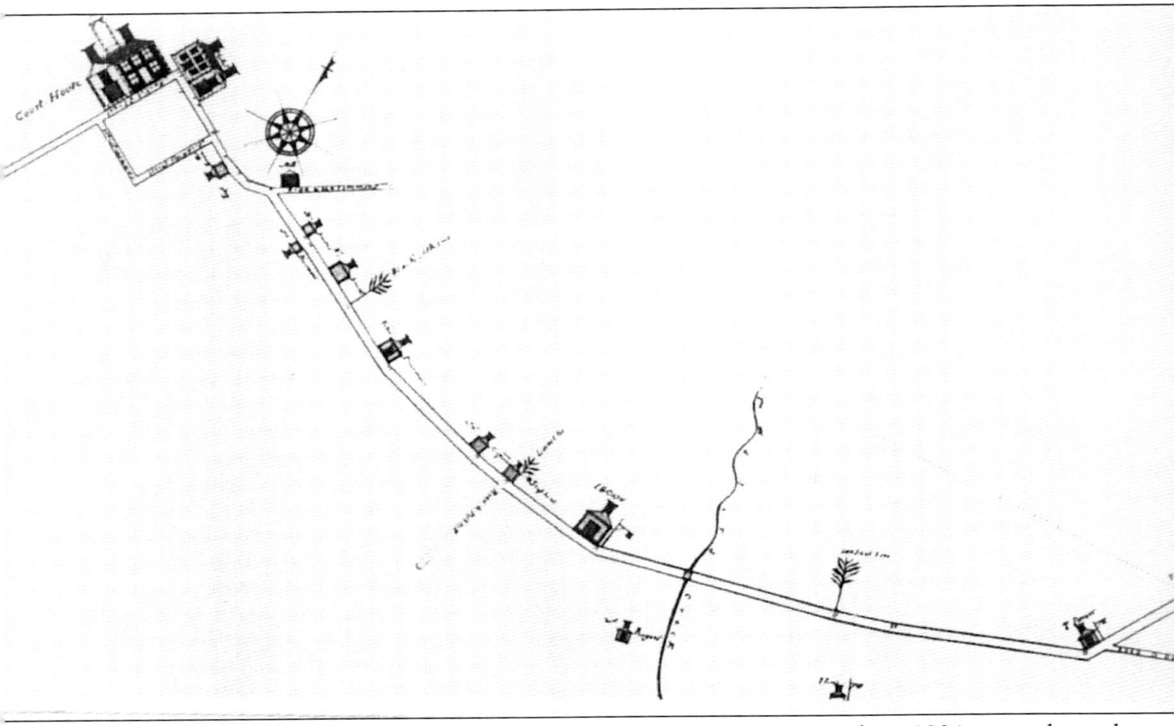

Courthouse Map, 1804. (JG.) A 60-foot-long county survey map made in 1804 traces the path of unpaved Filkintown Road east from the brand-new third courthouse to the Connecticut border. The start of the map features a charming drawing of the courthouse and identifies property owners and arboreal landmarks along the route with equally delightful renderings. Beyond the Bull's Head area the original paths soon became log toll roads, today's state east-west highways.

Two

Paths Eastward to New England

By the late eighteenth century, a path called Filkintown Road had been beaten east from the courthouse to the border with Connecticut by farmers and patent holders in that sector wishing to trade and get their stock and products to market. This road, named for storeowner Henry Filkin, eventually became Main Street, connecting the Hudson via the Pleasant Valley (Route 44) and Manchester (Route 55) Roads to New England. As the "Landings" area became crowded, demands to expand eastward increased.

The original settlement, which described itself first as a village in 1799 and as a city in 1854, soon surpassed the town in population. Beyond the city's unfolding boundaries, open fields and farmland retreated from encroaching urban growth until there were few fields by the mid-twentieth century. Closeness to the road seemed advantageous for both residents and businesses, so growth was linear. Successive maps of Poughkeepsie show development filling all gaps along these routes from Post Road beyond town borders. At Bull's Head (later called Arlington) a drovers' station was located beyond the village/city limits, at the intersection of the way to New Hackensack. Along the Wappinger Creek at fording places and around mills fed by the creek, self-sufficient hamlets grew: Rochdale, Manchester, and Red Oaks Mill.

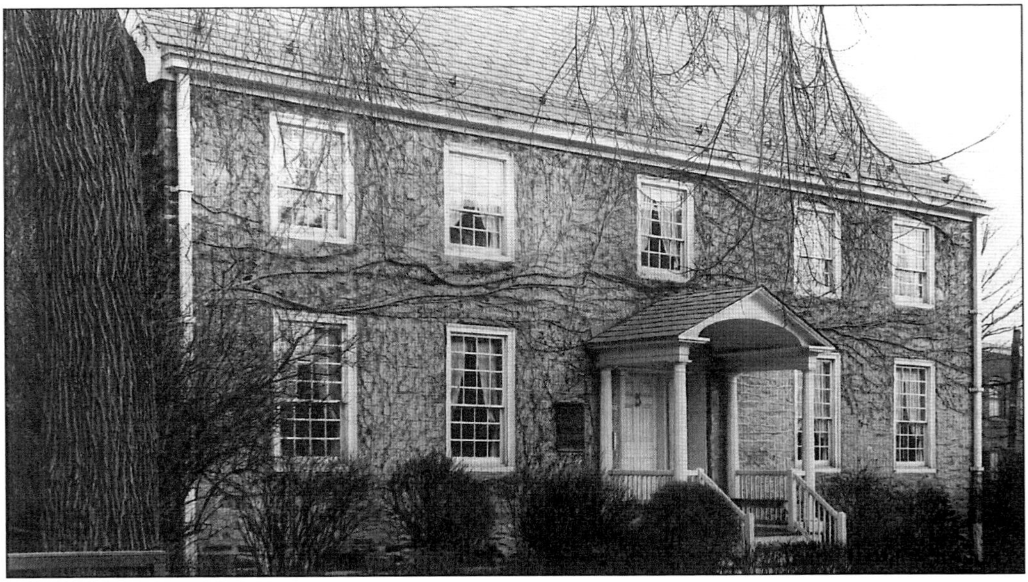

The Dutchess County Historical Society/Governor Clinton House. (DCHS.) "Governor Clinton House" may be a misnomer, as the house was built before Clinton's residency in Poughkeepsie during the American Revolution, when it became New York's capital. Owned by Clear Everitt and farther down Filkintown Road or East Lane from Clinton's modest rented home, it may have been used as the governor's office. This status prompted the Mahweniwasigh DAR to ask Governor Theodore Roosevelt to declare the building a historic site *c.* 1900. It is now the headquarters of the Dutchess County Historical Society.

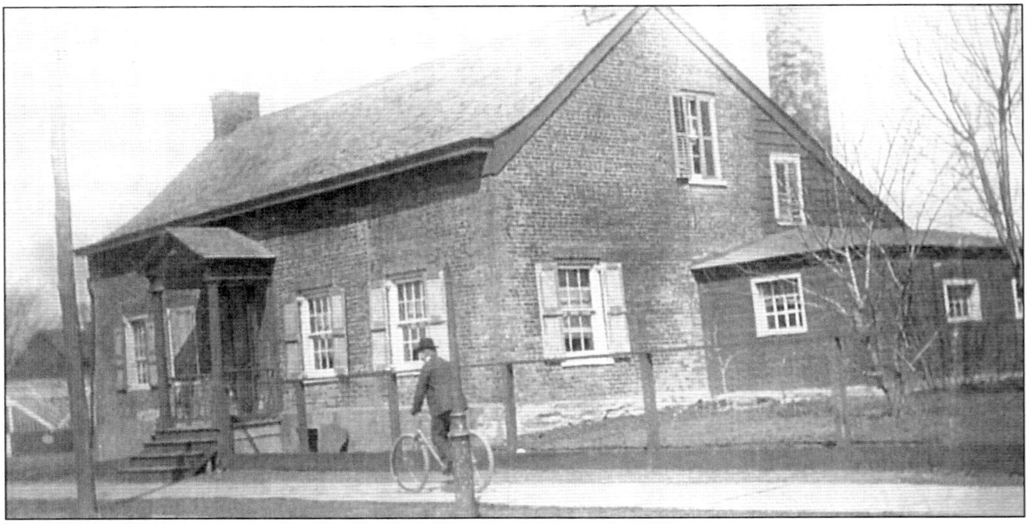

The Glebe House. (DCHS.) In 1767 the Reverend John Beardsley, newly appointed Episcopal minister of Christ Church, purchased 87 acres for a "Glebe" or rectory/farm on Filkintown Road in the countryside east of the Poughkeepsie hamlet and built a modest brick house. As a family with divided Loyalist and Patriot sympathies, the Beardsleys suffered banishment during the Revolution and the loss of their home. Nevertheless, the structure, shown here in an early photo, still stands as a city house museum administered by the Dutchess County Historical Society with support from the Junior League.

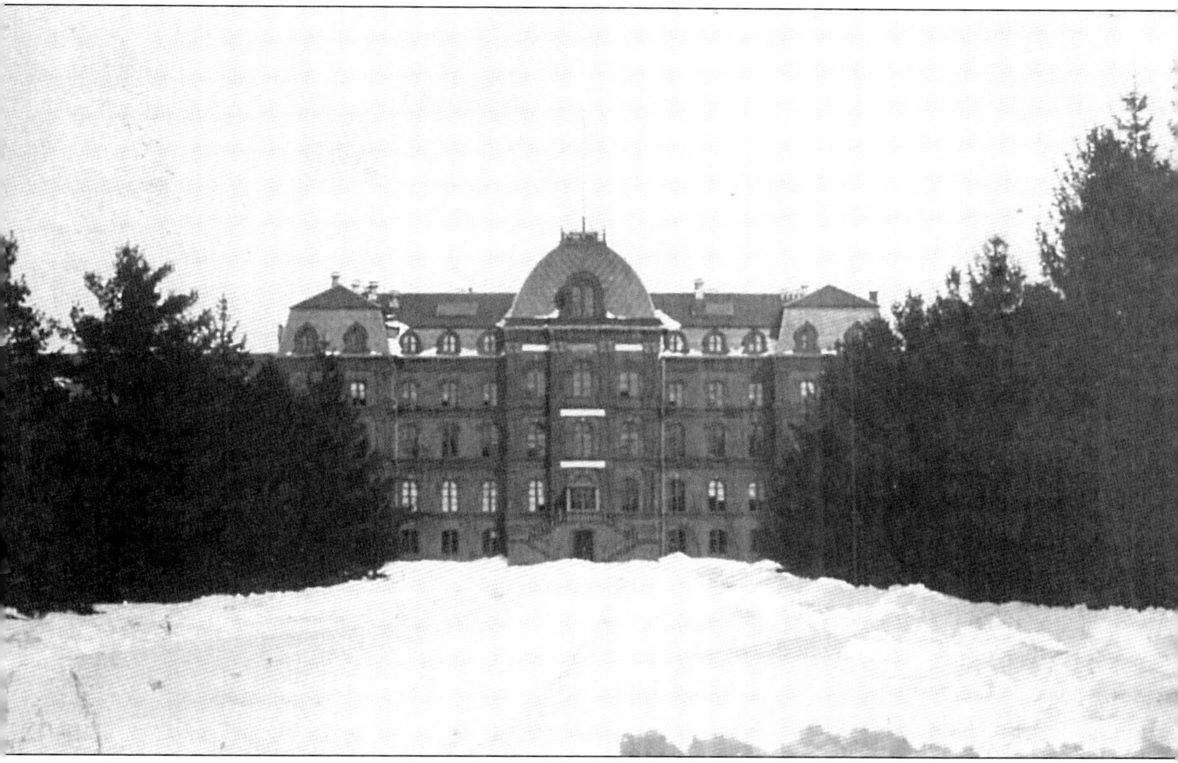

The Vassar College Main Building. (DCHS.) Vassar Female College, founded in 1861 by Matthew Vassar, was established on land he owned east of Poughkeepsie. "Main," designed by James Renwick Jr.in the Second Empire style, is said to have been inspired by the Tuileries Palace in France. Vassar's interest in women's education had grown, nurtured by his step-niece, Lydia Booth, a talented teacher. His plans for an institution for women's higher education to rival Yale and Harvard included a superb art gallery and collection and an observatory under the direction of Maria Mitchell, noted astronomer.

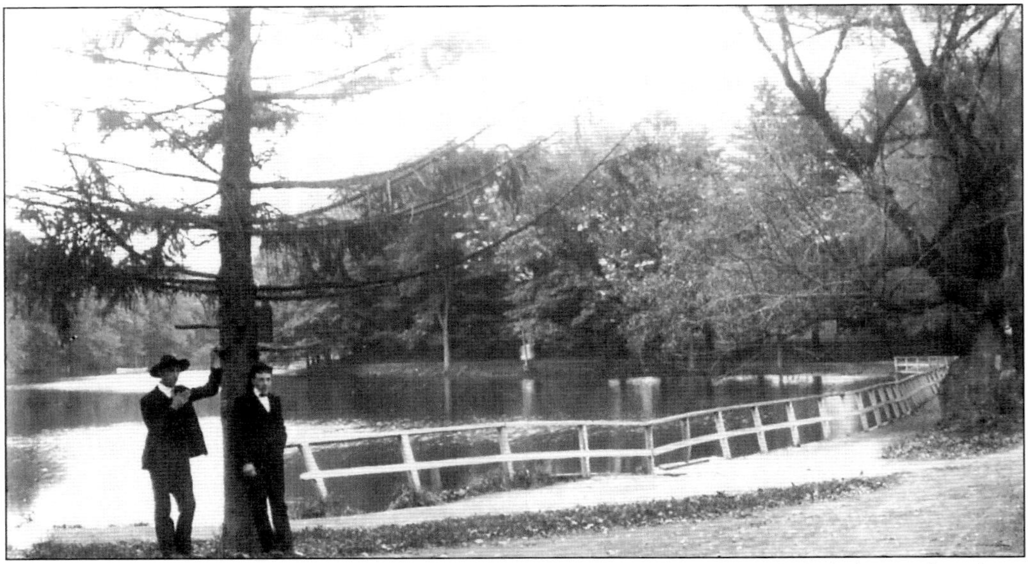

Vassar Lake. (CB.) The glass plates recovered by Catherine Bala included shots of a Slater outing to man-made Vassar Lake (near Vassar College), which was created by damming part of the Casparkill. The shady pathway around its banks beckoned strollers. Stonewalls that bordered country fields along the road to New Hackensack only a generation earlier lined the gardens of a skillfully landscaped campus by 1900. College development meant increased interest in neighborhood development.

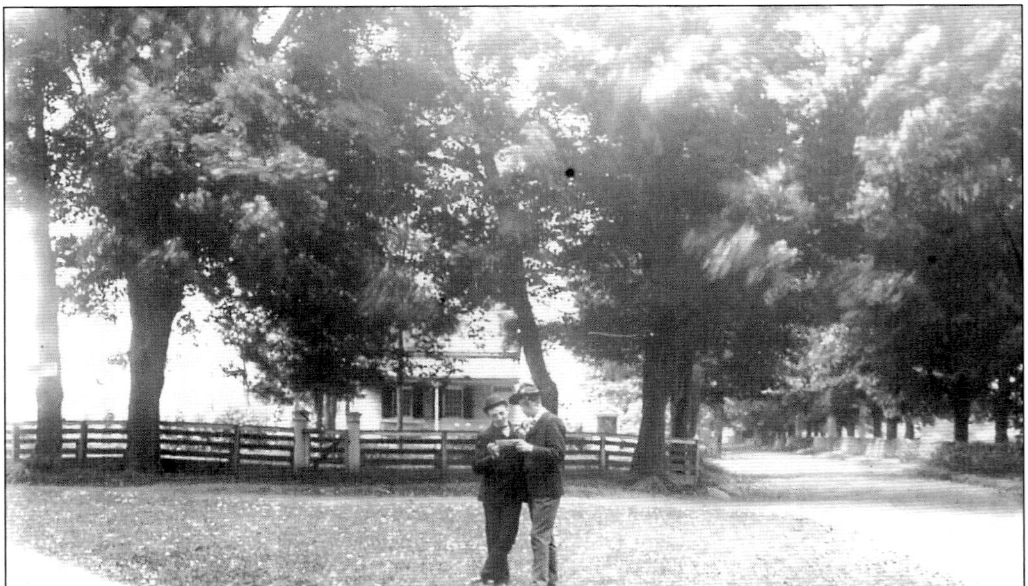

Vassar Farm. (CB.) The path of the Slaters' outing along the road to New Hackensack and around Vassar Lake curved back into the city at the intersection with Hooker. Here on a triangular piece of property sat the cottage of a Vassar College farmer. The college raised much of its own food supply on an extensive farm that stretched south and west toward Red Oaks Mill and the Driving Park. The Slaters probably followed the road sign back to the riverside.

The Vassar Warner Old Ladies Home. (Vassar-Warner Home [VWH], Marjorie Thompson [MT].) With eastward growth, South Hamilton Street became residential. Dutchess Academy was purchased by Jonathan Warner for the Old Ladies Home and incorporated by a group of Protestant churches in 1870 to care for elderly Protestant ladies. "Poughkeepsie, celebrated for her beauty of situation, her schools of learning, her Children's Home, yet lacked a home like this," said the Honorable J. Thompson, president of the trustees board at its 1871 opening. Warner and gifts from Matthew Vassar Jr. made it possible.

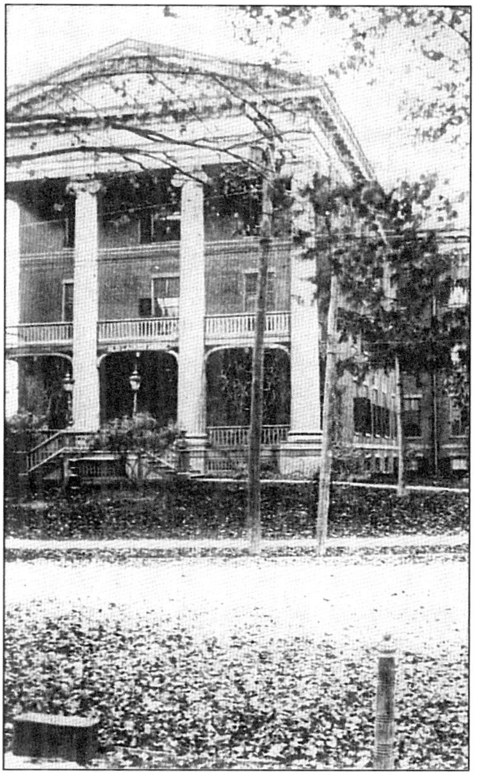

The Vassar Warner Board of Lady Managers, 1936. (VWH, MT.) Renamed Vassar-Warner Home to honor the original donors, the home initially established an unique governance system. While male trustees handled the pocketbook, a board of lady managers handled decisions directly affecting the residents. The 1936 board officers included (seated) Mrs. Edmund Young (center, president), Mrs. Samuel Scott (second from left, vice president), and Miss May L. Reynolds (second from right, treasurer).

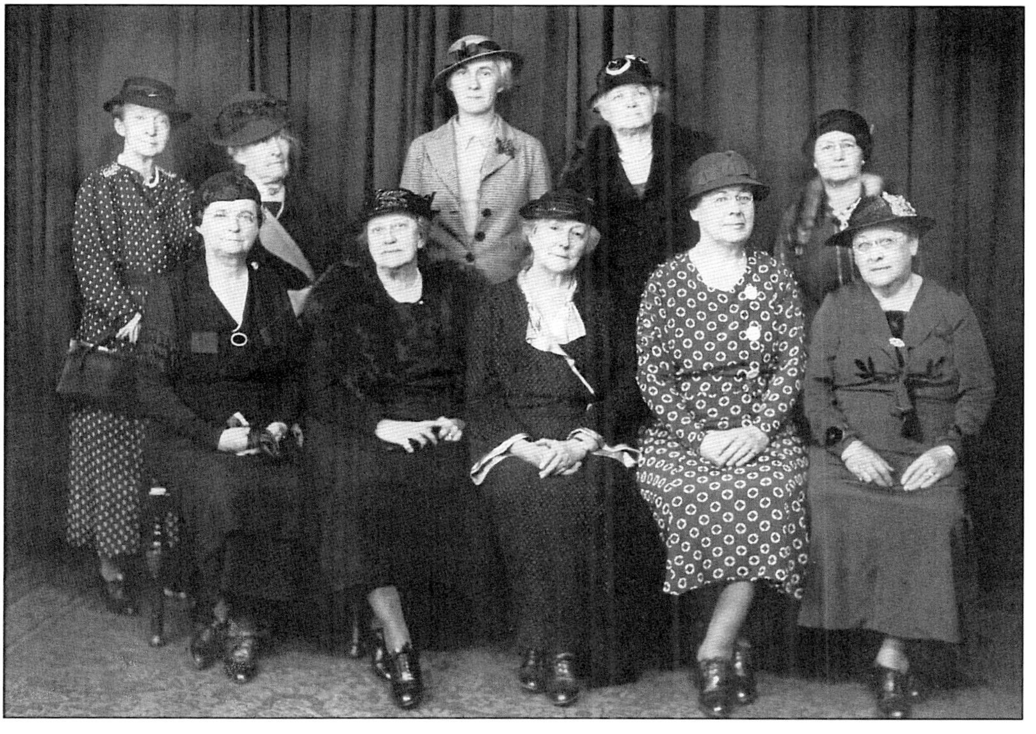

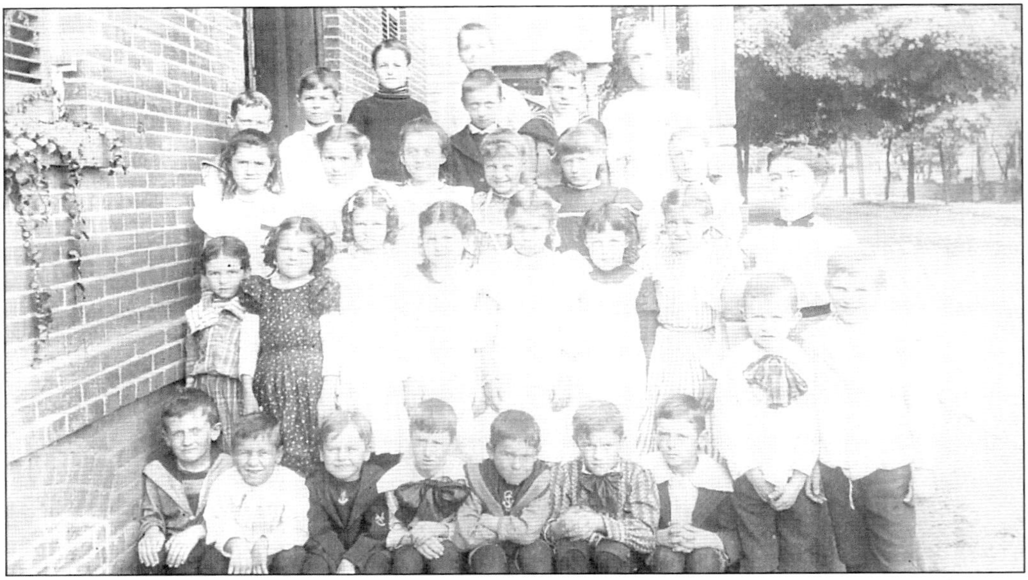

A Cannon Street Class. (AML.) Public education was encouraged by Governor Clinton's administration in 1795, but there were no free public schools until a March 1841 survey found that a quarter of the children here between the ages of five and sixteen received no education at all. In the "City of Schools," private academies and Lancaster School largesse overlooked many. An independent board of education began by renting rooms for primary classes. Ward schoolhouses, like the Cannon Street School #8 where young normal school graduate teachers held sway, were constructed later.

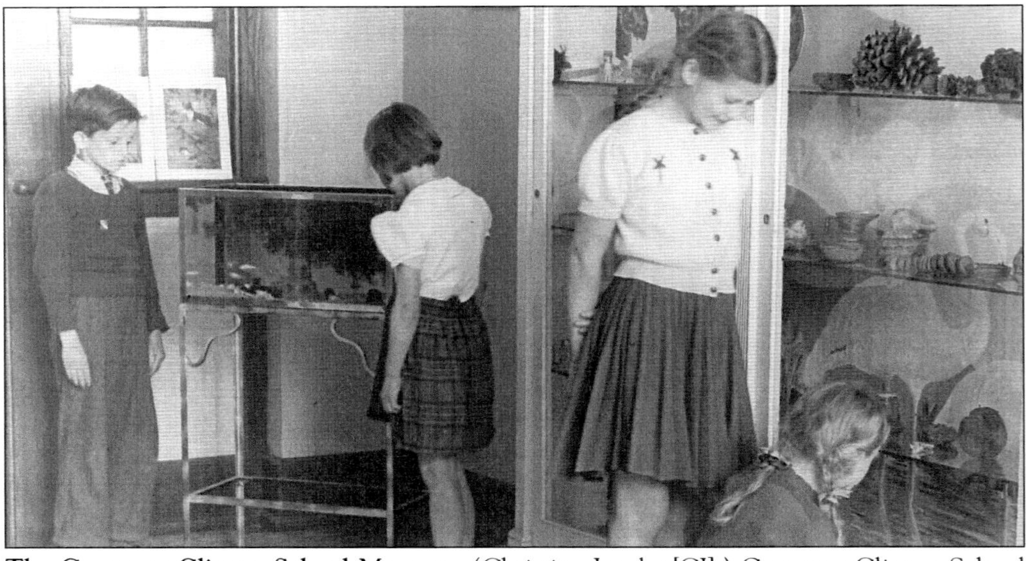

The Governor Clinton School Museum. (Christine Jacoby [CJ].) Governor Clinton School on Montgomery Street got a new building in the 1920s. By the 1940s when this shot of children examining materials in the school library's "museum" was taken, it was the pride of the system. Before the creation of central school districts in the late 1930s, the better-funded city schools with more modern buildings, libraries, cafeterias, auditoriums, and professional staff were models for small independent districts just beginning to organize.

Slee Bros./Luckey's Forerunner. (AML.) The forerunner of what would become the leading store of the Mid-Hudson Valley was a small dry goods store started late in the 1840s by Isaac Dribble, whose partner, Robert Slee, who also had a photography business, engaged Charles P. Luckey as "boy in the store." In 1869 the store became Luckey and Platt, and it became Luckey, Platt and Company in 1872 when William DeGarmo Smith became a partner.

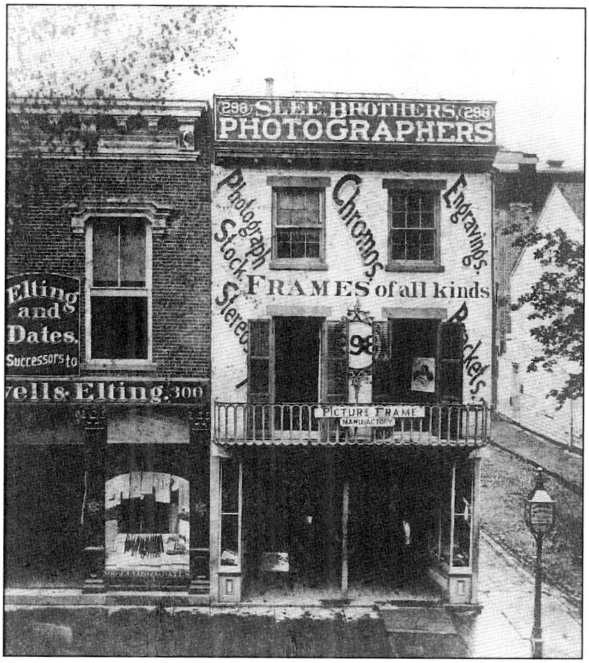

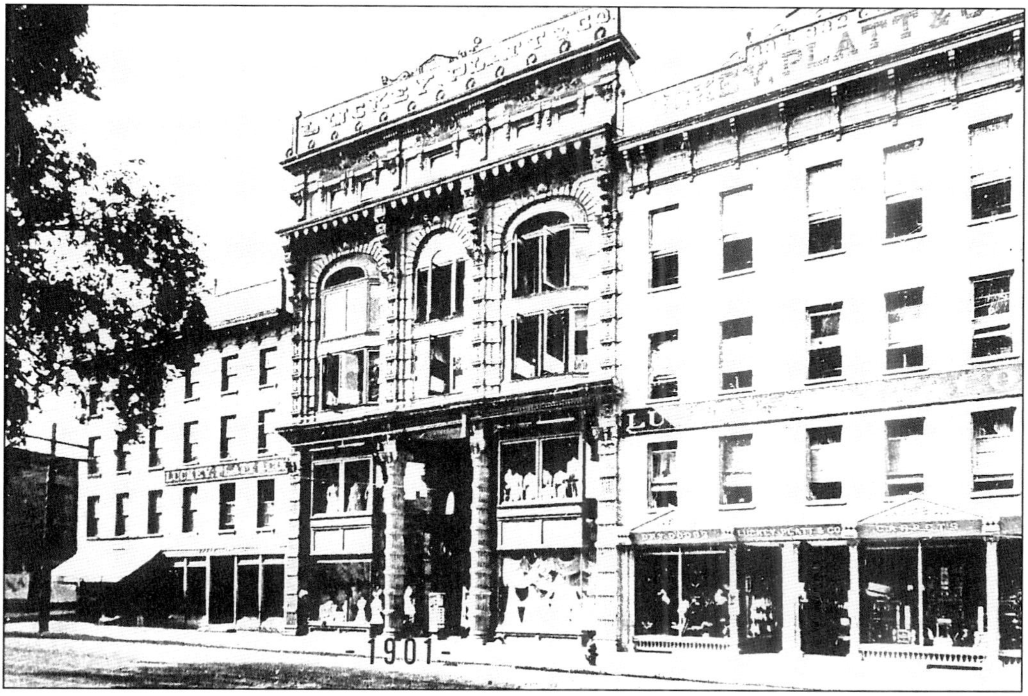

Luckey and Platt Expands. (DCHS, Landmarks.) From its beginnings, Luckey and Platt earned a reputation for introducing enterprising initiatives: a "set price" policy, telephone service for home delivery, and the first passenger elevator in the city. During the rest of the 1800s it progressively expanded, until by 1904 it was a five-story structure. In 1920 the old building was torn down and in 1924 a new store was opened to much fanfare.

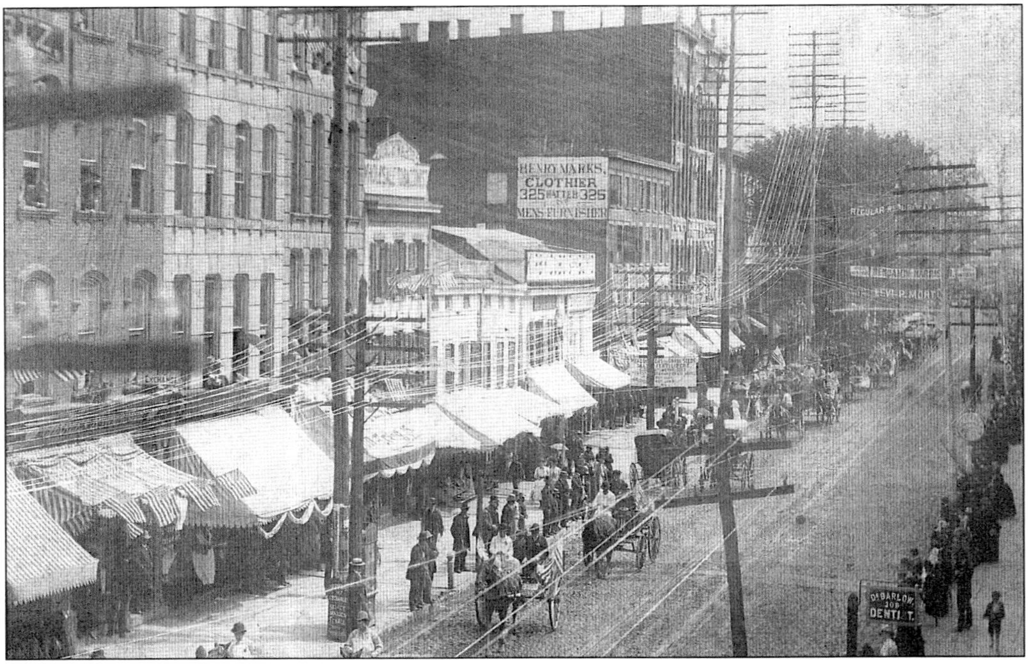

Main Street, 1892. (AML.) What appears to be horse-drawn traffic is a parade along the city's Main Street. Flags and bunting suggest a patriotic theme, which may be the Fourth of July . . . or could be election enthusiasm. A banner over the street, extolling the virtues of Benjamin Harrison for president and Levi P. Morton of Rhinebeck for vice president (the team ran successfully for office in 1888), suggests the latter.

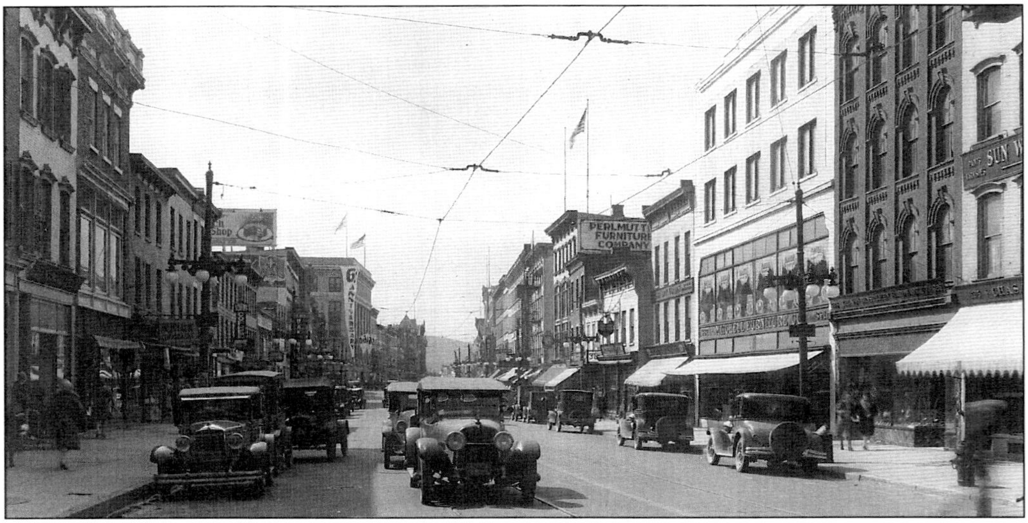

Main Street, 1929. (DCHS.) A Central Hudson street lighting survey in 1929 just before the stock market crash depicts a town with trolley tracks still in place, heavy auto traffic, and few parking places. Luckey's, celebrating its 60th anniversary in its almost-brand-new store, was having a big sale as advertised by a four-story banner hung from the roof. Although commercial businesses stretched the length of Main Street from the river to Cherry Street, Academy and Main defined the center of retail.

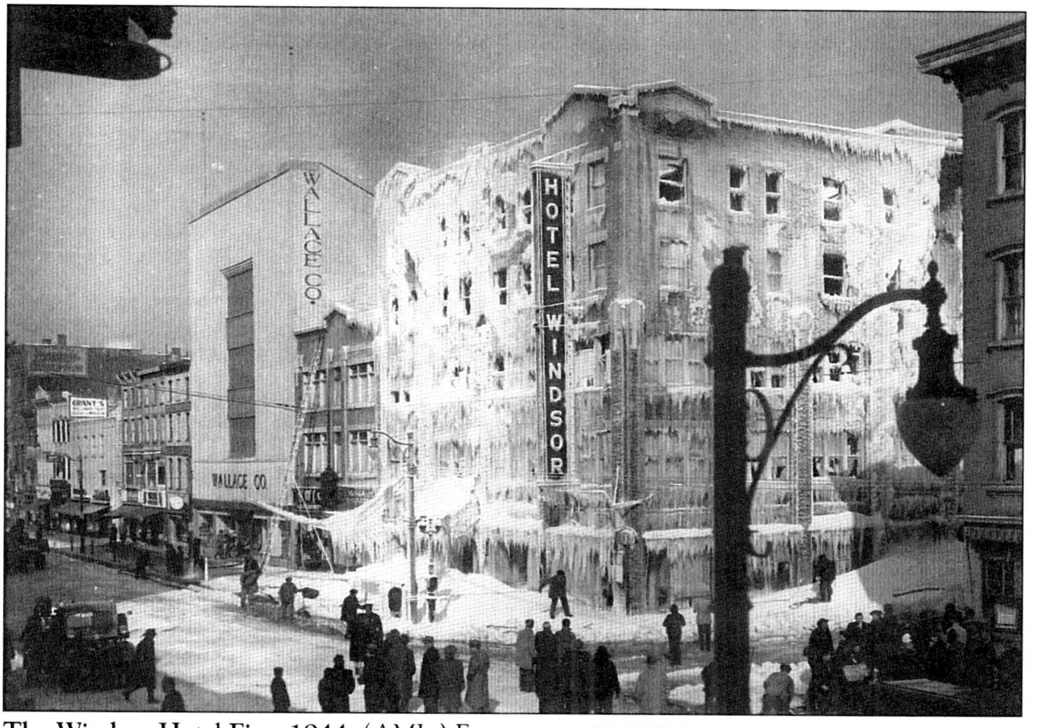

The Windsor Hotel Fire, 1944. (AML.) For a century, Main and Catharine Street was the corner for fine hotels that unfortunately burned. In 1853, Eastern House, established in 1831, burned. Gregory House, its replacement, was purchased in 1865 by George Morgan, who changed the name, but not the building's luck. It, too, burned and was eventually replaced by the Windsor Hotel. Despite the Windsor's proximity to firehouses, it had the granddaddy of all fires in the winter of 1944 when enormous icicles coated the destruction, luring gawkers. Fortunately, nearby Wallace's was untouched.

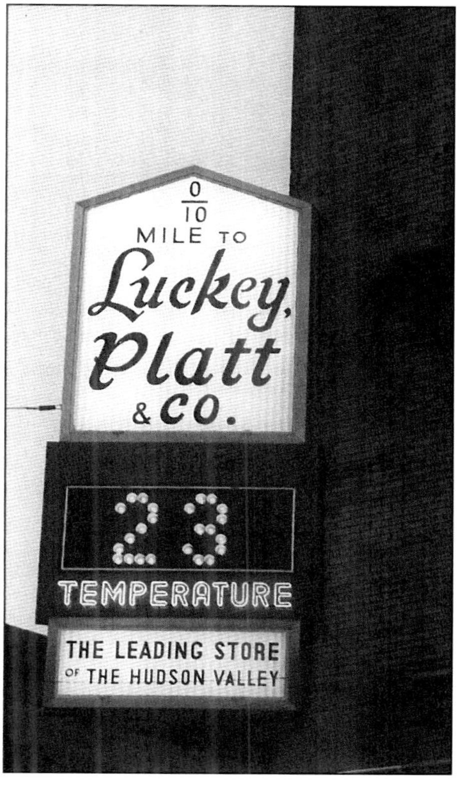

Luckey's Milepost. (JS.) This photograph highlights one of Luckey's most successful marketing ploys, the "Milepost." In the late 1940s, a huge electronic clock and thermometer were hung at the Main Street corner and replicated all over the area with wooden Mileposts giving directions and mileage to Luckey's. Donald and Elizabeth Budd also recall it as the name and logo for the employees' newsletter. There soon were very few people in the region who didn't know how to find Luckey's in Poughkeepsie.

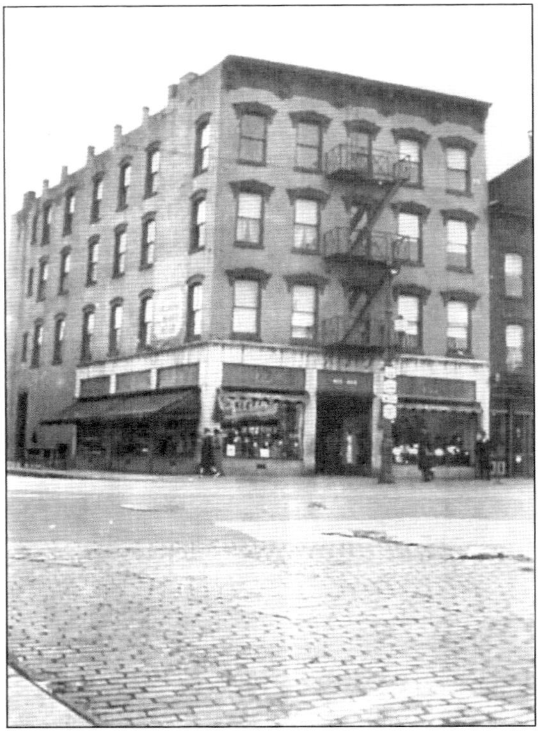

Effron's Clothing Store. (DCHS, William Hubbard [WH].) When this pre-World War II photograph was taken, many Jewish families had improved their fortunes, putting skills honed through centuries of enforced wandering to work in local enterprises. Morris Effron's horse and cart in 1895 provided the foundation for his successful children's clothing business at Clinton Square. The wagon gave way to a Main Street general store, which expanded into larger quarters, eventually into Effron's own building. The store became a specialty shop featuring infants', children's, and teens' clothing.

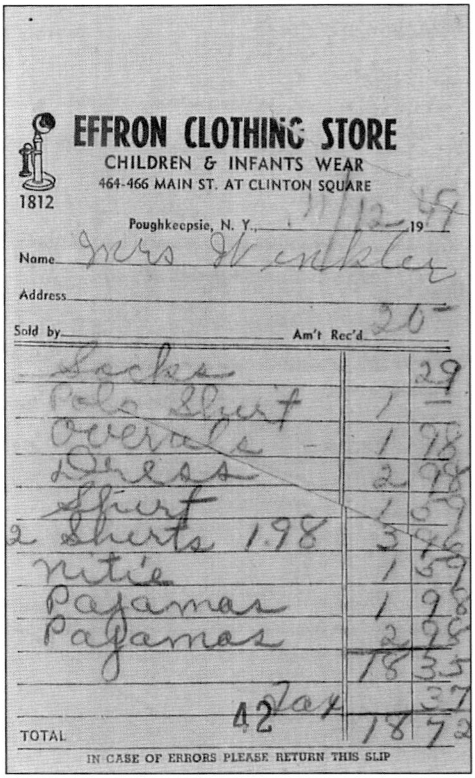

EFFRON CLOTHING STORE
CHILDREN & INFANTS WEAR
464-466 MAIN ST. AT CLINTON SQUARE
1812

Poughkeepsie, N. Y., 11/12 1949

Name Mrs W Winkler

Address

Sold by Am't Rec'd 20

Socks		29
Polo Shirt	1	—
Overalls	1	98
Dress	2	98
Shirt	1	59
2 Shirts 1.98	3	96
Nitie	1	59
Pajamas	1	98
Pajamas	2	98
	18	35
42 Tax		37
TOTAL	18	72

IN CASE OF ERRORS PLEASE RETURN THIS SLIP

Mrs. Winkler's Bill, 1949. (Marshall and Jesse Effron [M/JE].) Their children's clothing store was not only a blessing to the Effron family, but represented one-stop, modestly priced wardrobe shopping for families all over town who returned seasonally to restock the closets of growing children. Mrs. Winkler's bill in 1949 gives mute testimony to why customers returned.

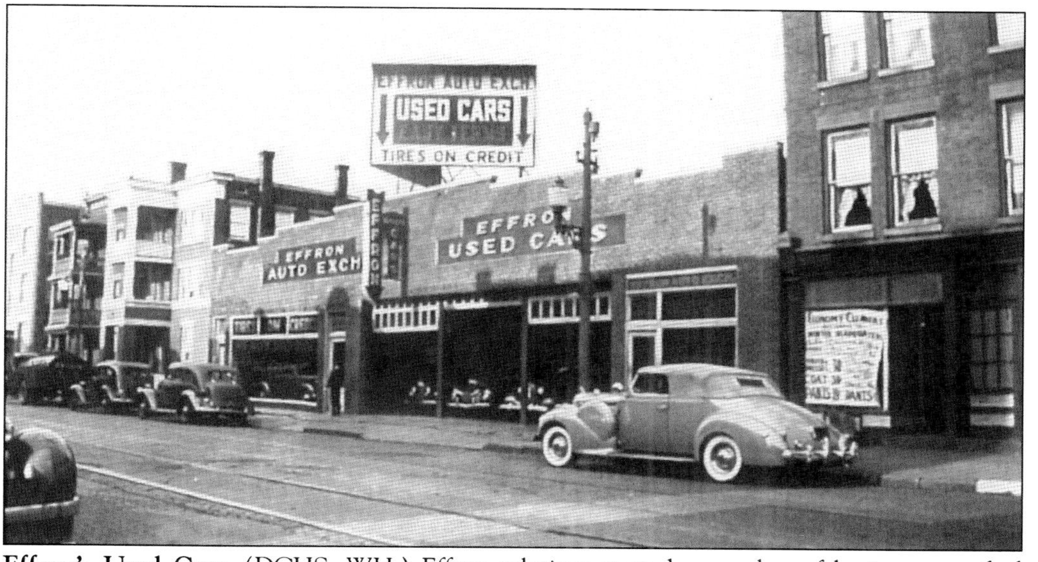

Effron's Used Cars. (DCHS, WH.) Effron relatives started a number of businesses: a fuel company, a wholesale flour distributorship, a dry goods stores, a bookstore, and a car dealership. After cars had been around awhile, there was a market for used cars. Joseph Effron at 569–71 Main, near the Keyes Ford-Mercury dealership, advertised Effron Auto Exchange as "Dutchess County's largest and oldest used car dealer." Nearby were Arben Chrysler-Plymouth dealers and S.J. Reynolds auto body works. Those needing anything automotive found it on Main Street near the Governor Clinton House.

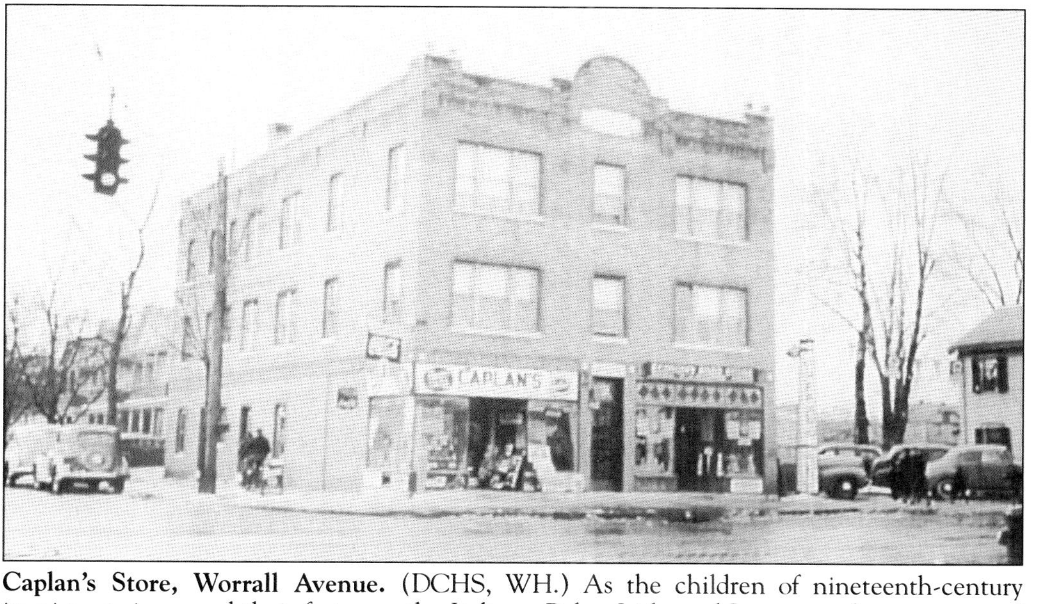

Caplan's Store, Worrall Avenue. (DCHS, WH.) As the children of nineteenth-century immigrants improved their fortunes, the Italians, Poles, Irish, and Jews moved to eastern and southside suburbs. Their businesses followed, with modest commercial buildings and apartments filling empty lots between Arlington and the city limits. Milton and Martin Caplan opened a neighborhood variety store and confectionery seen in the 1930s at 706 Main on the corner of Worrall Avenue, an area that developed rapidly after World War I.

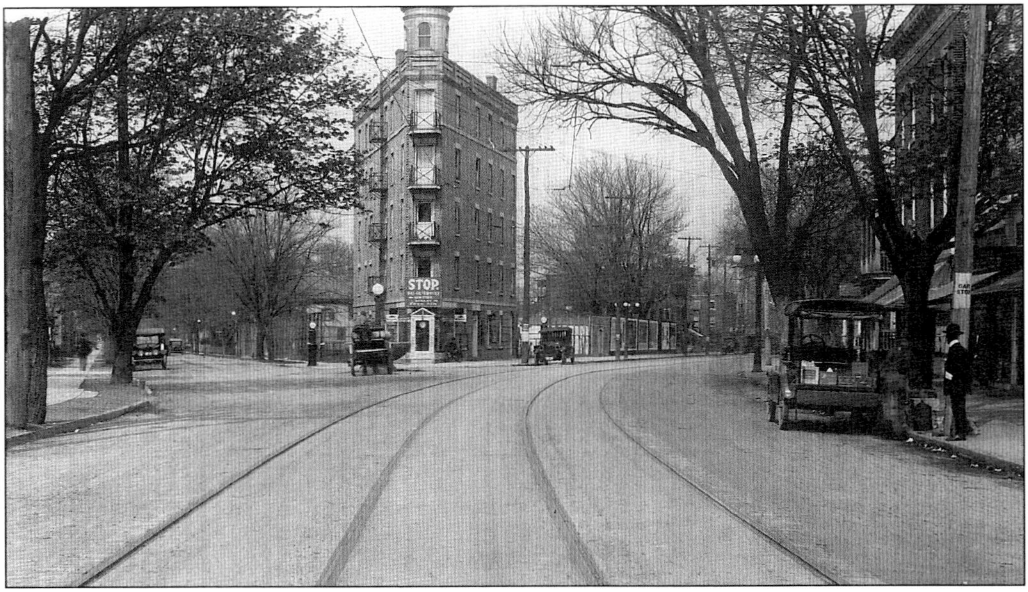

A Flatiron Building. (AML.) After the turn of the century, virtually every sizeable community boasted a "Flatiron" building, which typified a style popularized by city skyscrapers whose steel frames overcame the limitations of traditional wooden "balloon" construction. Triangular lots could be completely filled up. Poughkeepsie's, at the intersection of two of the town's oldest paths—Church and Main near Beardsley's Flemish brick Glebe House—came down before World War II and was replaced by a filling station.

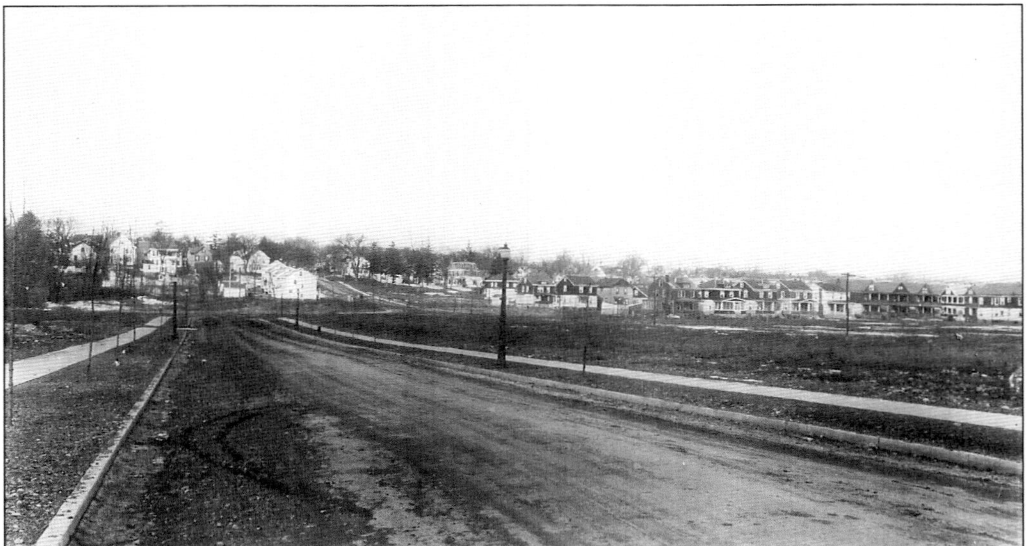

Harding Heights/Forbus Street Development. (DCHS.) The pressure to expand into the suburbs began between 1912 and the 1920s. Middle-class housing development, including Harding Heights, featuring single- and double-family houses, covered an immense triangular area between Main, Hooker, and Grand Avenues. Forbus Street and a host of other side streets were created as this photograph of construction shows, contributing to the growth of the Eighth Ward and extending city boundaries into the town.

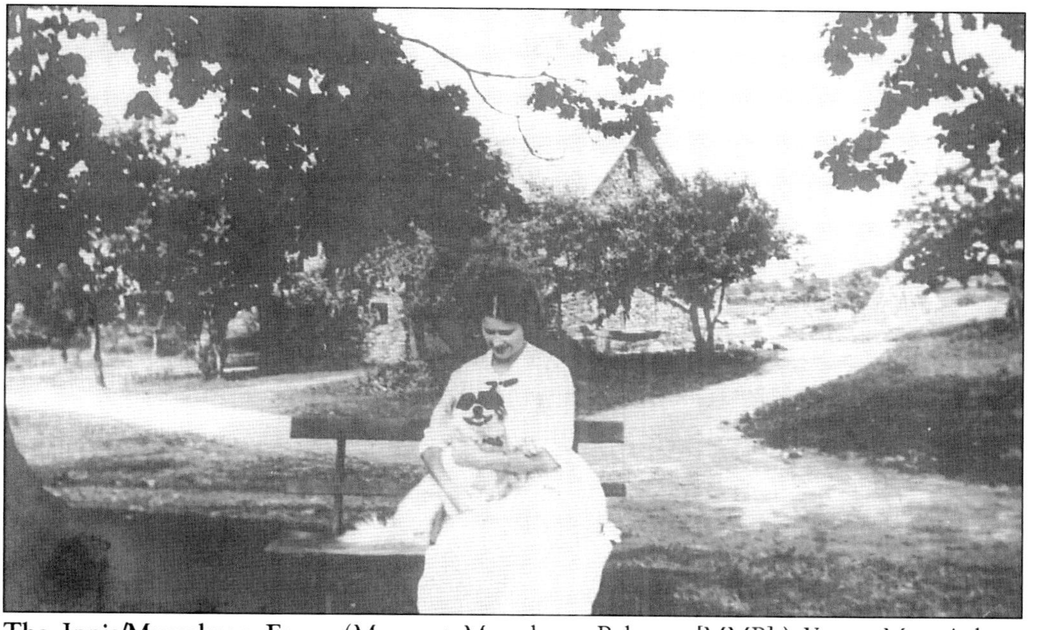

The Innis/Musselman Farm. (Margaret Musselman Behrens [MMB].) Young Mrs. Aylmer Musselman is captured in this engaging family album photograph taken by her husband, a talented cornetist and photographer, on the lawn of their farmhouse on Innis Avenue hill at the turn of the century. The couple redesigned the landscape of their property, "the Knolls" (carved out of the extensive Innis farm), with the distinctive turreted stone house and outbuildings that still mark the crest of the hill.

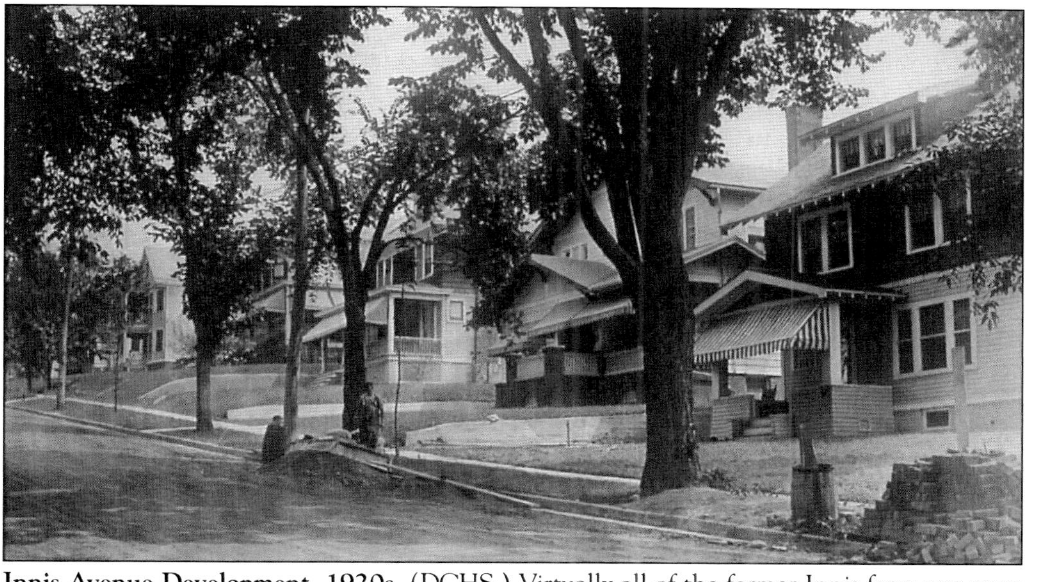

Innis Avenue Development, 1920s. (DCHS.) Virtually all of the former Innis farm was open fields until the Musselman property was developed in the early 1900s. These handsome, brand-new single- and double-family homes, sensitively planned to nestle into the hill and designed with occasional stone touches echoing the Musselman house, became part of the movement into the suburbs that expanded the city borders and population.

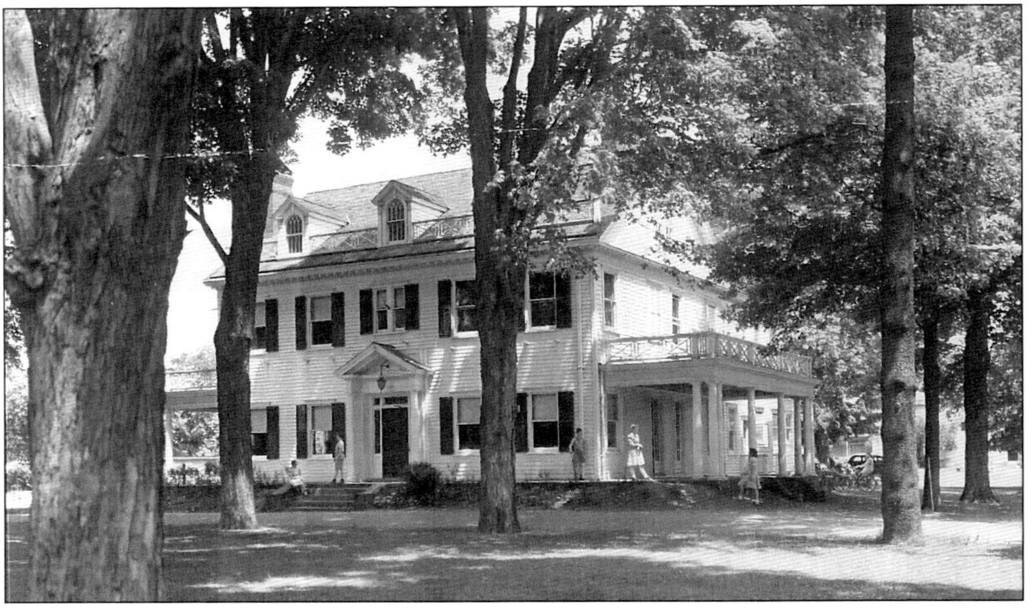

Poughkeepsie Day School. (Poughkeepsie Day School.) Poughkeepsie Day School was founded in 1934 by a group of parents who believed that the early years of a child's life are the most formative. The building site selected by a committee headed by S. Kaplan was the Spaulding property at Hooker and Grand Avenues. A Vassar College faculty advisory committee was established early on to make recommendations on the curriculum and to see that the close relationship with Vassar College continued.

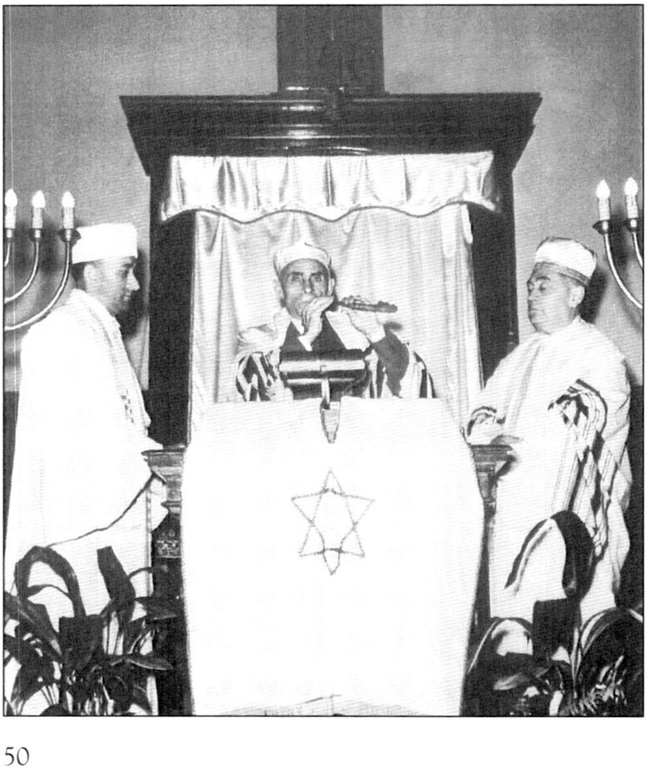

Temple Beth-El/Rabbi Zimet. (M/JE.) Poughkeepsie has become home to three main branches of Judaism: Orthodox (Schomre Israel), Reformed (Vassar Temple), and Conservative (Temple Beth-El). In 1927, individuals from already existing Orthodox and Reformed congregations incorporated as Temple Beth-El, and purchased the former Friends Meeting House on Montgomery Street. Rabbi Irwin Zimet (left), a beloved member of the community, was called to lead the new congregation in 1946.

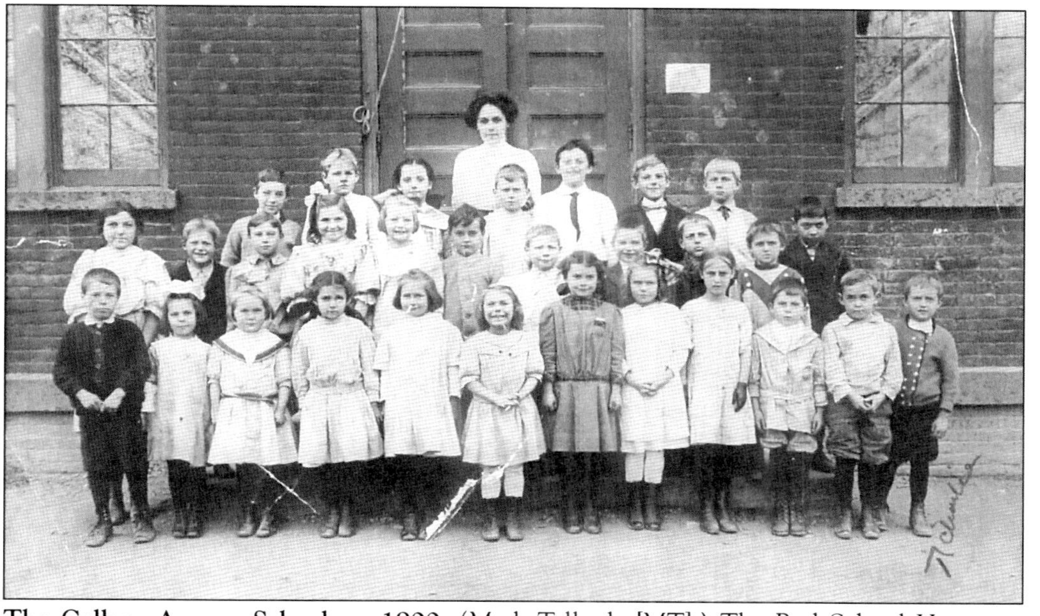

The College Avenue School, c. 1900. (Mark Tallardy [MT].) The Red School House on College Avenue was still a country school when this picture of second graders was taken at the turn of the century. Residential development of College Avenue was on the rise and small local schools were becoming overcrowded. In the days before centralization and busing, these little persons sometimes walked miles every day from Arlington neighborhoods to classes.

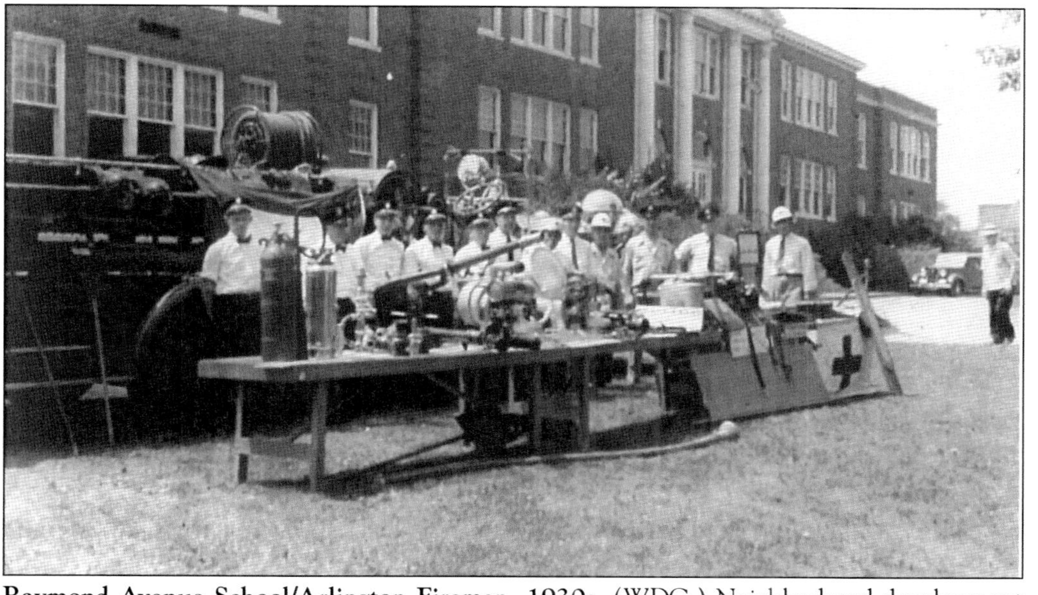

Raymond Avenue School/Arlington Firemen, 1930s. (WDG.) Neighborhood development around Vassar College at the beginning of the twentieth century called for new community institutions: schools and a fire department. In a hamlet with no government of its own, these institutions became the heart of the community. The Raymond Avenue School, built as a high school originally, is seen in the 1930s when it had become an elementary school undergoing a rigorous fire drill with help of Arlington Fire Department volunteers.

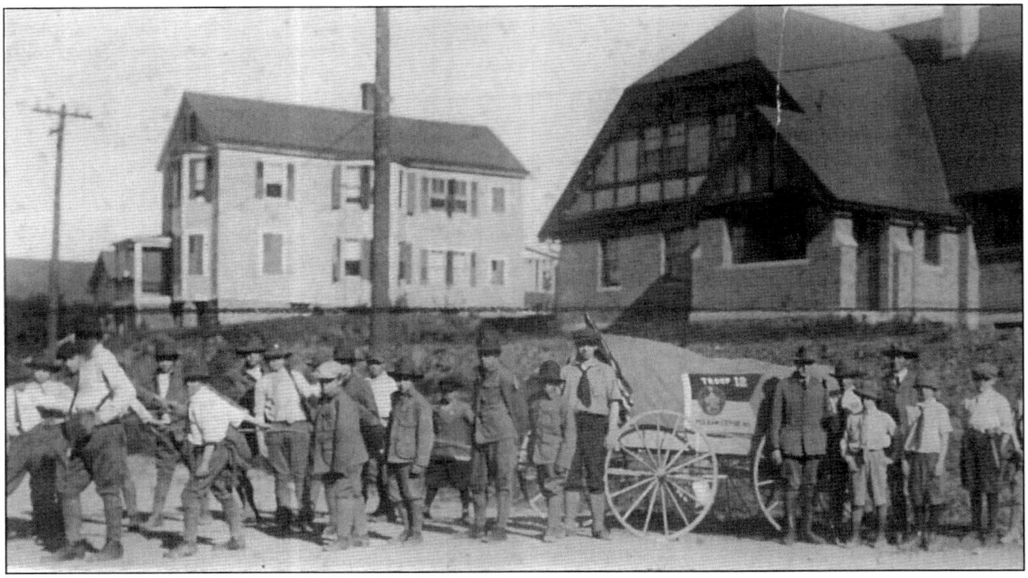

Reformed Dutch Church Boy Scouts. (MT.) The early 1900s brought three new churches to the renamed and renewed hamlet of Bull's Head. St. Andrew's Episcopal Church, Holy Trinity Catholic Church, and the Arlington Dutch Reformed Church were constructed within a block of each other near the Raymond Avenue High School and the Arlington Fire Department. All were centers of community activity. Here a scout troop is engaged in a service project in front of the new reformed church.

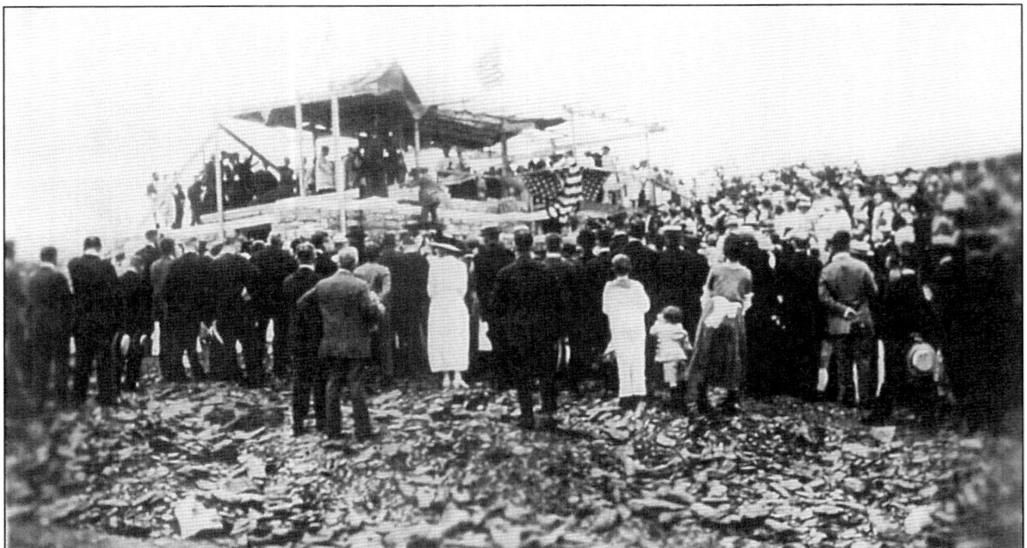

The Holy Trinity Cornerstone Laying. (WDG.) Growth of the Catholic population in the Arlington area in 1920 moved the New York Archdiocese to decide to build a new church, which was incorporated in 1921. Under the watchful eye of Father Peter Conaty and a huge crowd, the cornerstone for Holy Trinity was laid on June 11, 1922. The church, placed on a knoll overlooking Main Street, was completed in 1923 and the rectory shortly thereafter. In 1952, the school was added.

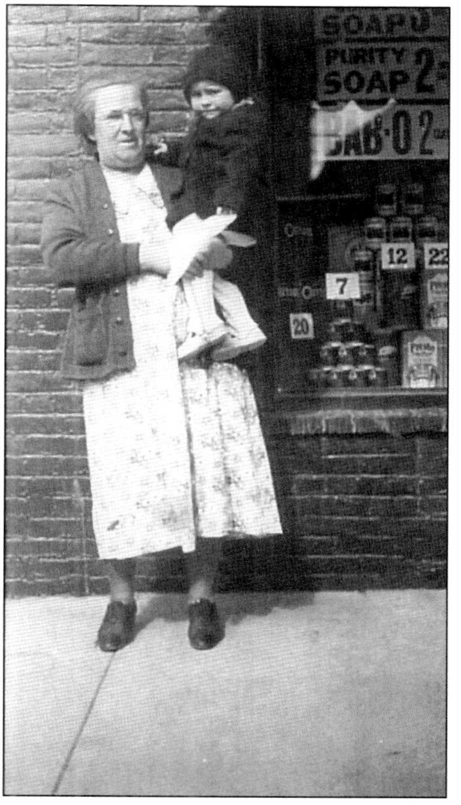

Aunt Susie, 901 Main Street, 1933. (JG.) Boyd's Grocery at Main Street and Van Wagner Road was typical of early-twentieth-century "Mom and Pop" neighborhood stores. Susie Tompkins Boyd from Verbank and her husband Boye, a Norwegian, purchased the property after the turn of the century, living over the business they ran twenty-four hours a day for over fifty years. A customer's "chit" (signature) for purchases was his bond, settled up periodically. "Aunt Susie," beloved by grandnieces Joyce and Nancy Connelly, was both fair and generous.

Mrs. Tallardy. (MT.) The energetic lady pushing a wheelbarrow was Mark Tallardy's grandmother, for whom Tallardy Place is named. She was a developer, in the days when the field was dominated by men, who invested her modest savings in a few acres of Arlington. With materials gleaned from a demolished building on Jefferson Street, she constructed her first small, single-family home in a desirable location near Vassar College. When she was finished developing, she had created a neighborhood and a reputation for getting things done.

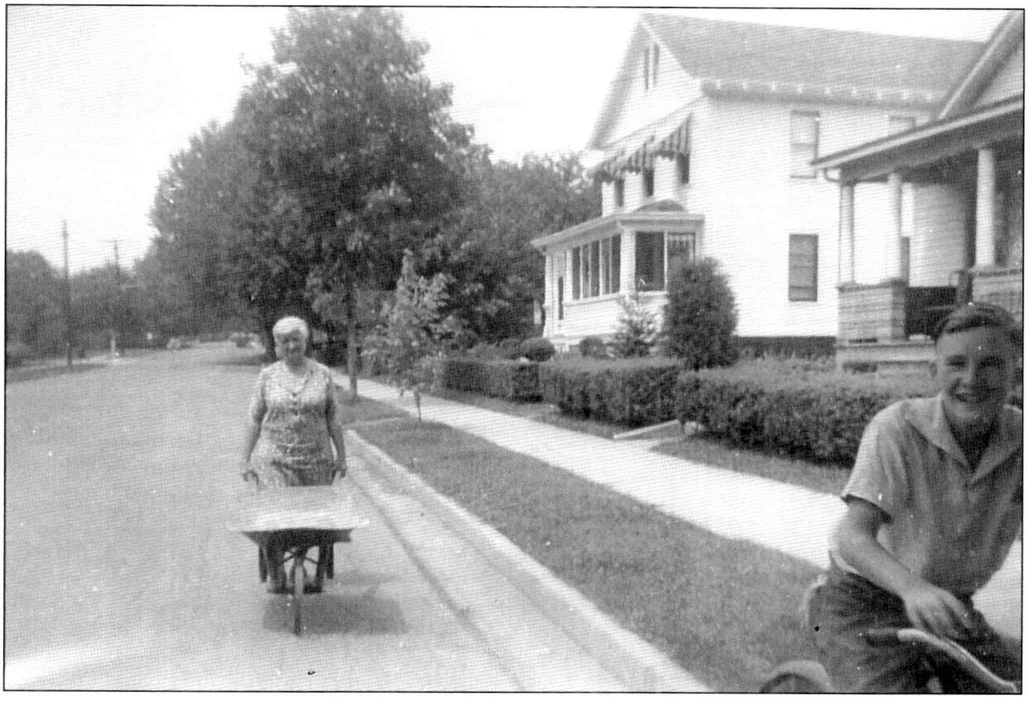

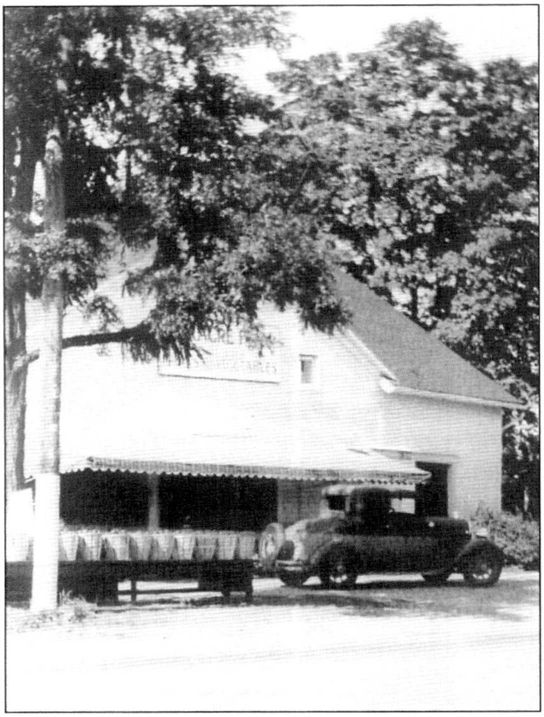

The Adams Farm Market. (Mark Adams.) Brickyard Hill used to divide farms from suburbs. The Adams farm on Pleasant Valley Road beyond the hill grew fine vegetables and even before World War II opened a stand to sell its own harvest. Business was so good that the family began renting fields from other farmers to keep up with demand for popular produce. An unbeatable combination of business acumen, green thumbs, and commitment to long hours turned a modest vegetable stand into a major Mid-Hudson agri-business employer.

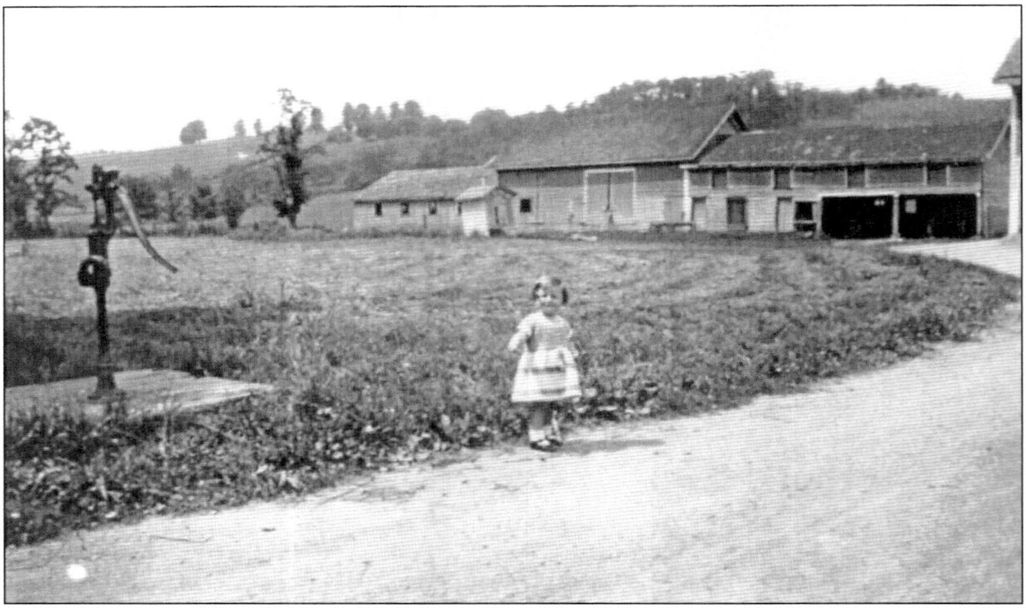

The Frank Farm. (Elinore Frank Haverkamp.) The farmer's little daughter grew up within walking distance of suburban Arlington after Frank Brothers, who had come from Germany, bought 200 acres on Pleasant Valley Road (Dutchess Turnpike) in 1929. The David Barnes homestead, built in 1827 with 1,000 feet of prime state road frontage, was sold to settle an estate. Otto Frank turned the land into a successful cattle farm providing both dairy products and beef for local meat-packing plants like Knauss Brothers in Fairview.

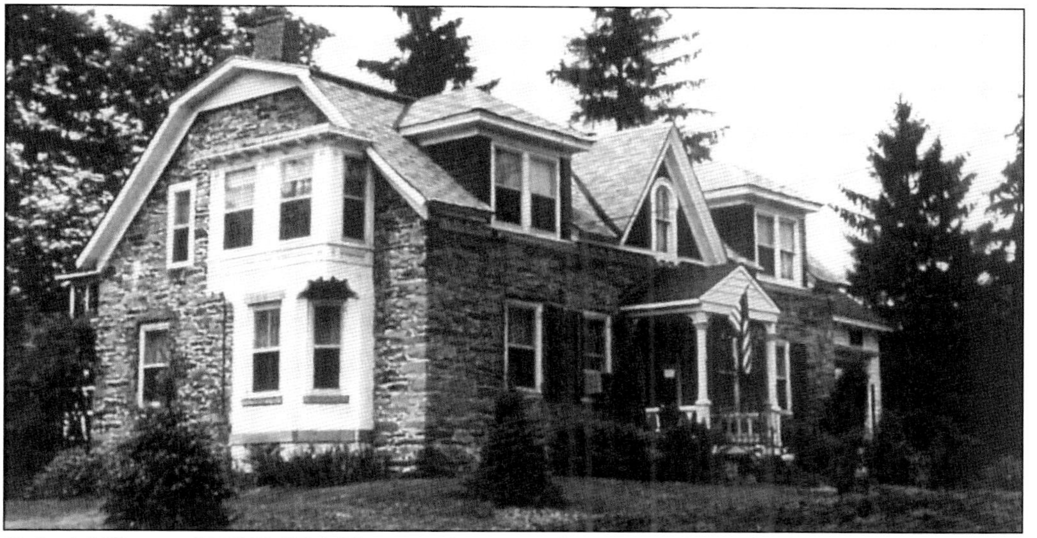

Colonial House. (DCHS, JG.) The stone house on the corner of Hornbeck Road, known locally as "Colonial House," has watched the passing parade on Route 44 for about two hundred years and has thus far resisted the road's continuing encroachment on the former farm. Mrs. C.A. Smith, mother-in-law of present owner Frank Hanlon, moved from farming to development in the 1930s, sketching her own plans for the orchard across the street which would become Colonial Knolls residences.

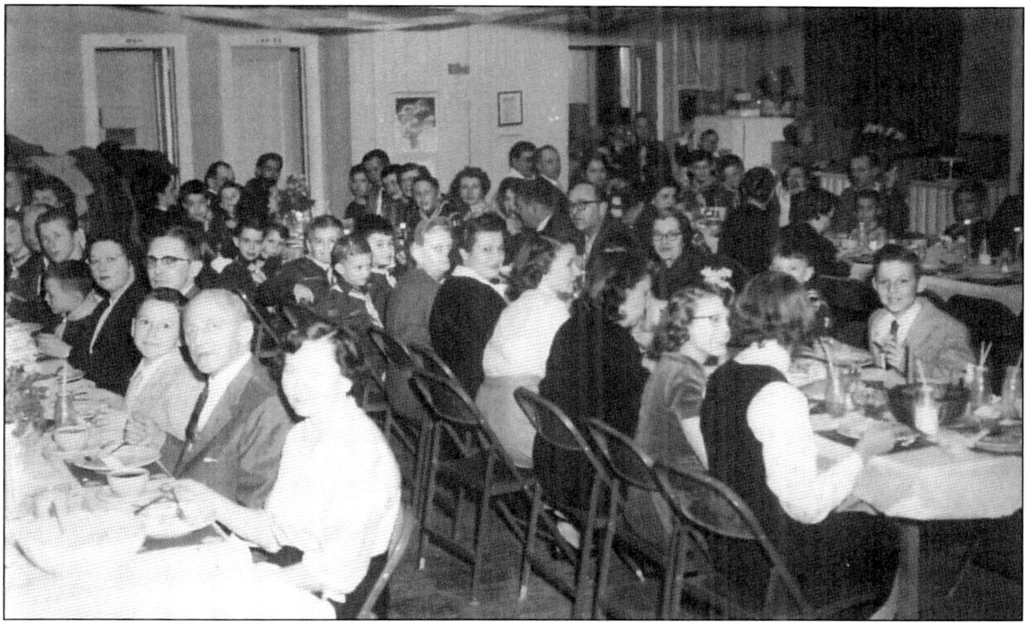

A Rochdale Cubs Dinner. (Frank Hanlon [FH].) The hamlet of Rochdale is tucked away, hidden on a meandering country road that circles from Pleasant Valley Road down to the Wappinger Creek and back again to the main road. Rochdale dates to the early nineteenth century when housing for workers was built around a milling industry. The hamlet has resisted commercial growth, remaining a small residential community with strong neighborhood ties. A c. 1950 Cub Scout dinner brought out everyone.

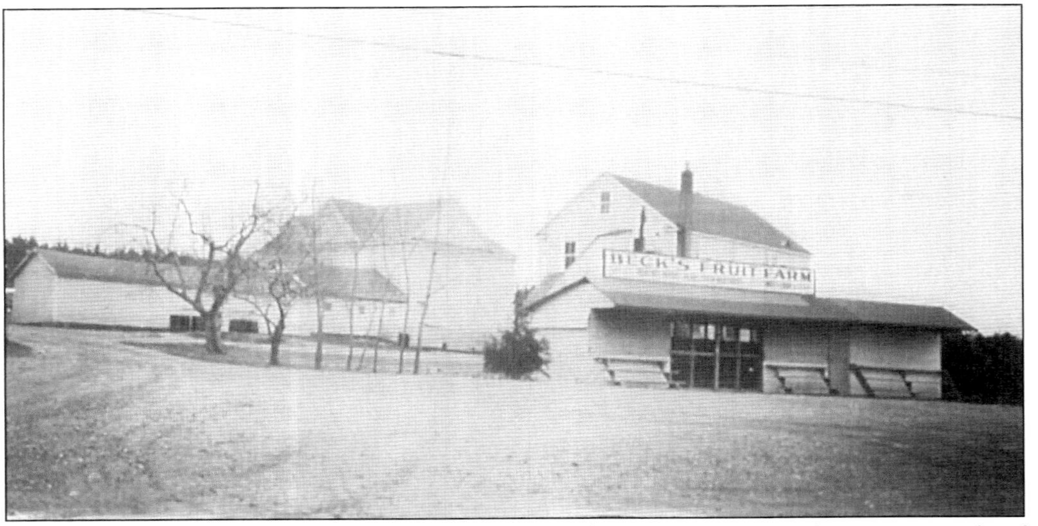

Beck's Farm. (WH.) Half a mile beyond the Poughkeepsie Grange on the opposite side of Manchester Road (Route 55), the Charles Beck family apple orchards spread out over the hillsides near the Wappinger Creek. Every fall, the Beck roadside stand blossomed with ripe apples and fresh pressings from the family's cider mill. Like Kimlins' on Cedar Avenue, this was a favorite fall destination for hikers and bikers from Vassar and Arlington.

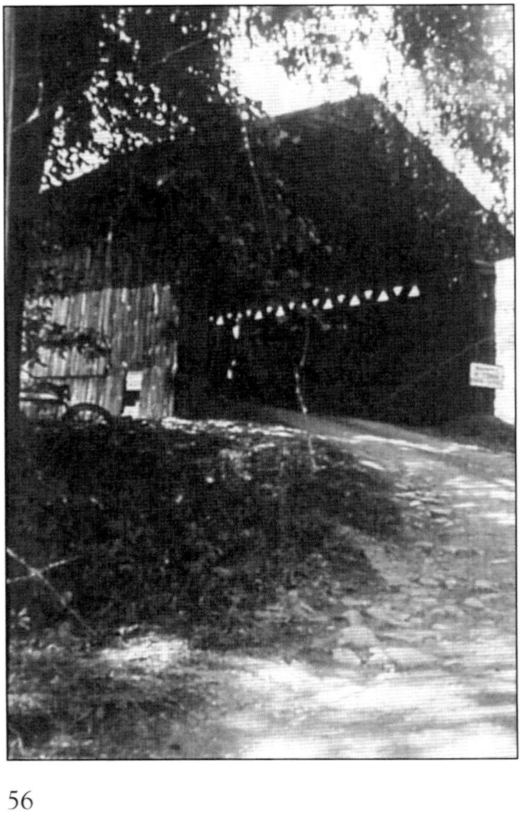

Manchester Bridge. (MT.) The Wappinger Creek becomes shallow at Manchester, making it a good fording place in the days before bridges, and a good place for a bridge when population and road travel increased to the point where one was needed. The old wooden bridge, seen here in a nineteenth-century photograph, was long ago replaced by a tangle of bridges accommodating Central New England, Poughkeepsie, and Eastern rail lines (c. 1880), as well as auto traffic.

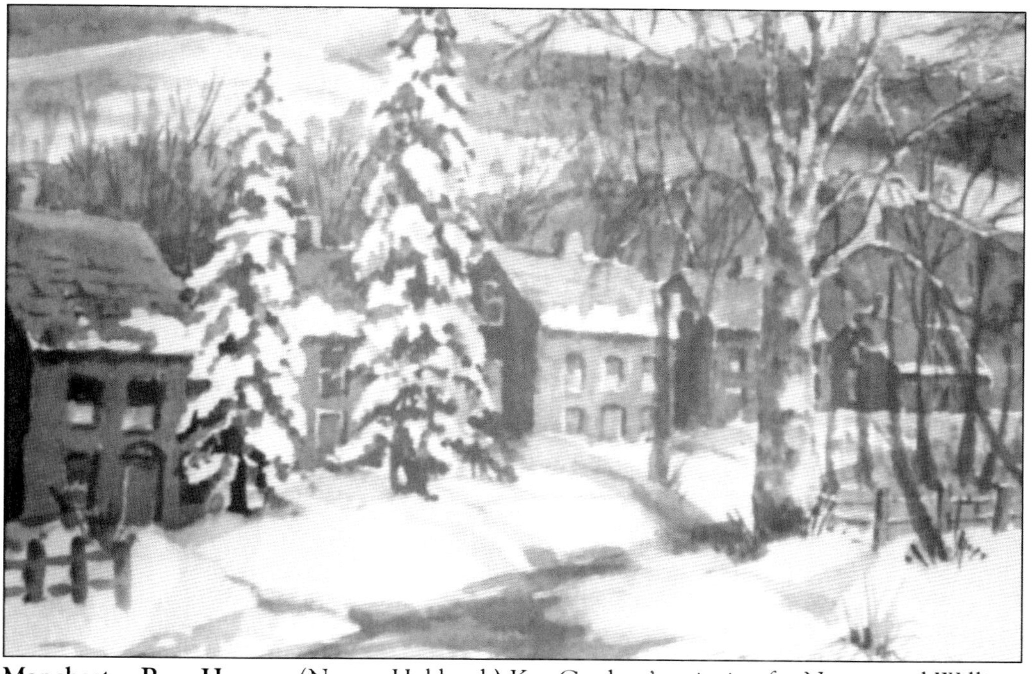

Manchester Row Houses. (Norma Hubbard.) Kay Gardner's painting for Norma and William Hubbard shows the old brick row houses that formerly nestled in a hollow north of the Manchester Road (Route 55) bridge/railroad intersection. Two family houses with generous porches originated as factory housing built c. 1875 for mill hands at the Bradbury, Priestly and Robinson Paper Mill. In a 1968 *Poughkeepsie Journal* interview, Henry Page Jr. said that Manchester had long supported large industries: a cotton mill in 1812 and the paper mill supplanting it in 1837.

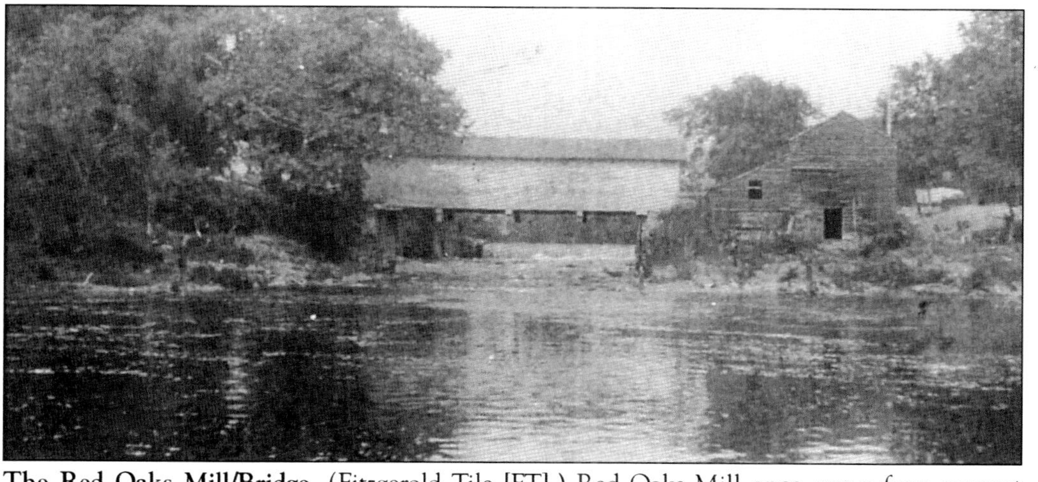

The Red Oaks Mill/Bridge. (Fitzgerald Tile [FT].) Red Oaks Mill once was a farm support community named for a gristmill here on the Wappinger Creek where falls and a curve in the creek's course were perfect for a dam. A wooden bridge built in the nineteenth century made the mill accessible year-round. The covered bridge, replaced several times since 1900, and the decaying mill seen here are gone, but commerce has thrived near the dam where a popular roadhouse/restaurant was built in the 1930s.

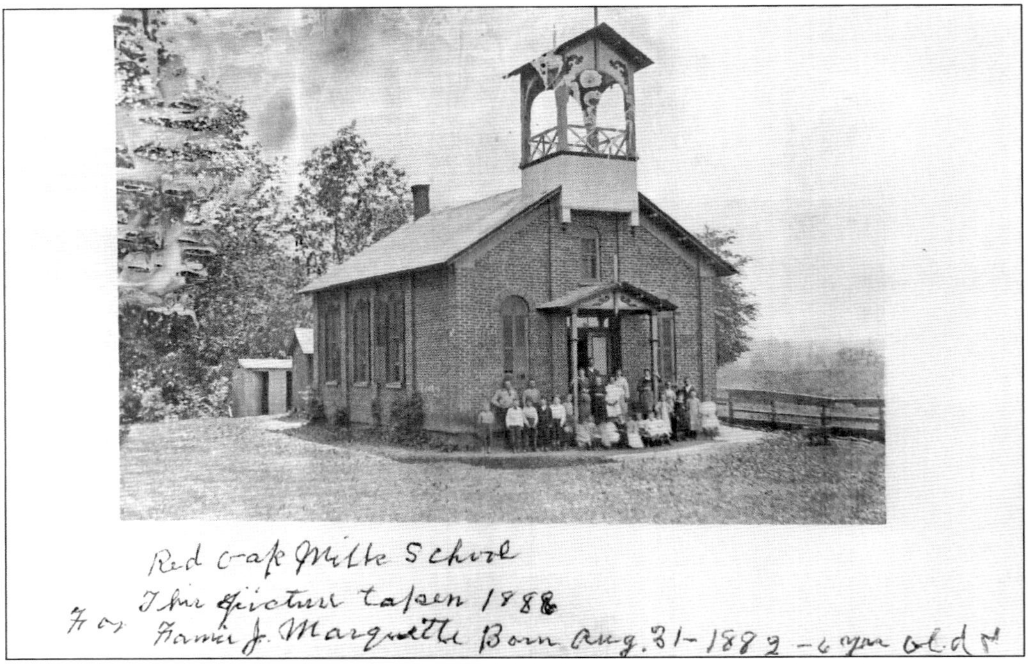

The Red Oaks Mills Elementary School. (FT.) Small independent school districts around hamlets or neighborhoods abounded from the mid-nineteenth century throughout the town. The extent of schooling, type of edifice, and quality of teaching depended upon the generosity of residents and state aid. Single-room structures were the norm and eight grades the limit. The brick Red Oaks Mill School attended by six-year-old Fannie Marquette in 1888 was a substantial building that today houses Fitzgerald Tile.

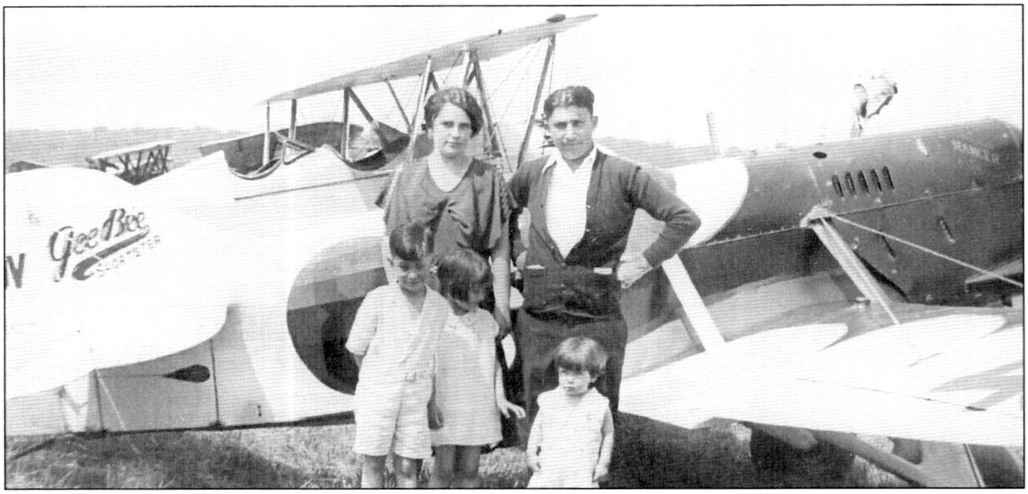

Poughkeepsie Airport. (Mary Lou Sotanski [MLS].) A few years after Glenn Curtiss made his dramatic 1910 flight down the Hudson, the airfield known locally as the "Red Oaks Mill Airport" opened. Its metal hangers sat on a flat lot west of Vassar Road at the Route 376 intersection. Mary Lou Sotanski's grandparents and their children were among early callers in the 1920s and '30s, attracted by a chance to see barnstormers in single-engine racing planes. The bravest visitors were talked into a "spin" or lessons given there.

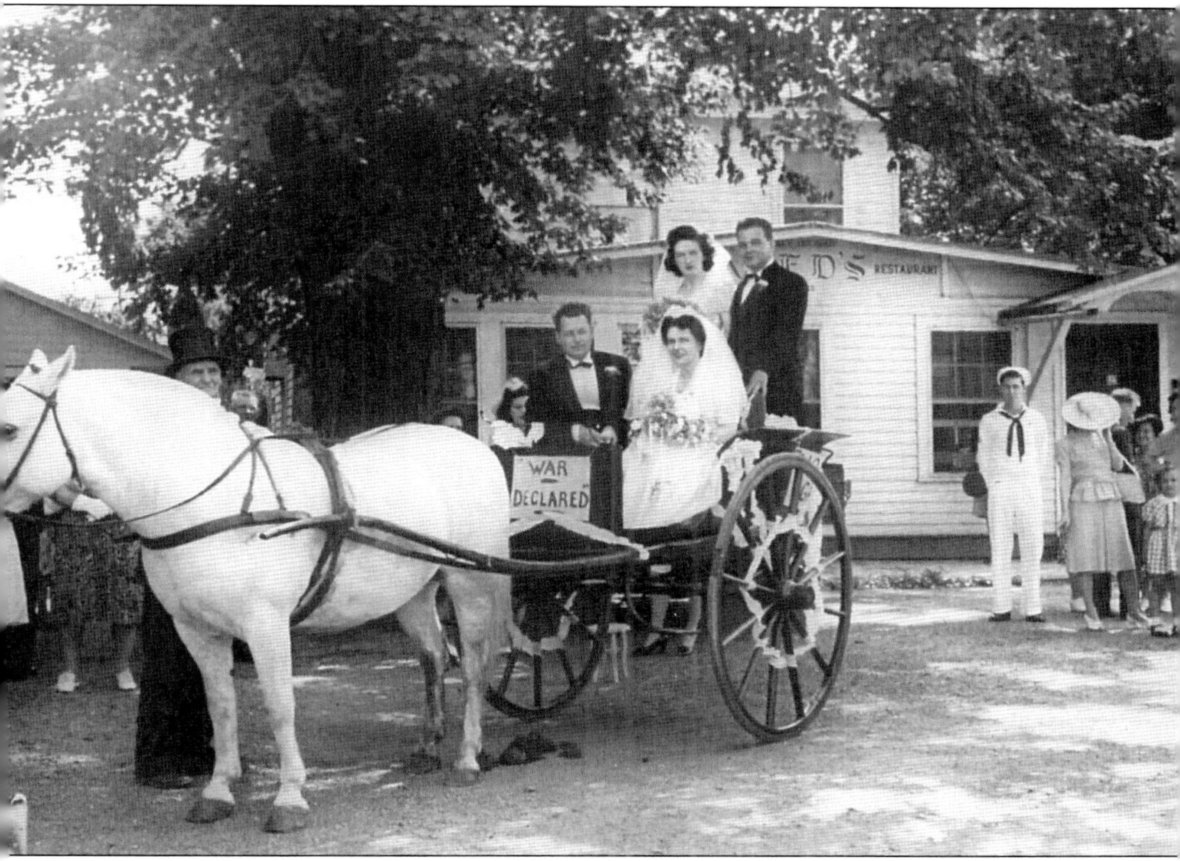

A Pascoe Wedding. (Mary Kaye Dolan [MKD].) World War II brought many couples together as concern for the future pressed romance to its ultimate conclusion. William Nied's Restaurant on the corner of Cedar Avenue hosted the reception for the festive wedding of Frank and Betty Pascoe on July 8, 1945. The war had ended in Europe, but still raged in the Pacific. The sailor guest and the sign about potential marital wars indicate that this was a period when patriotism was fed by volunteer spirit and attempts to be lighthearted about a very scary future.

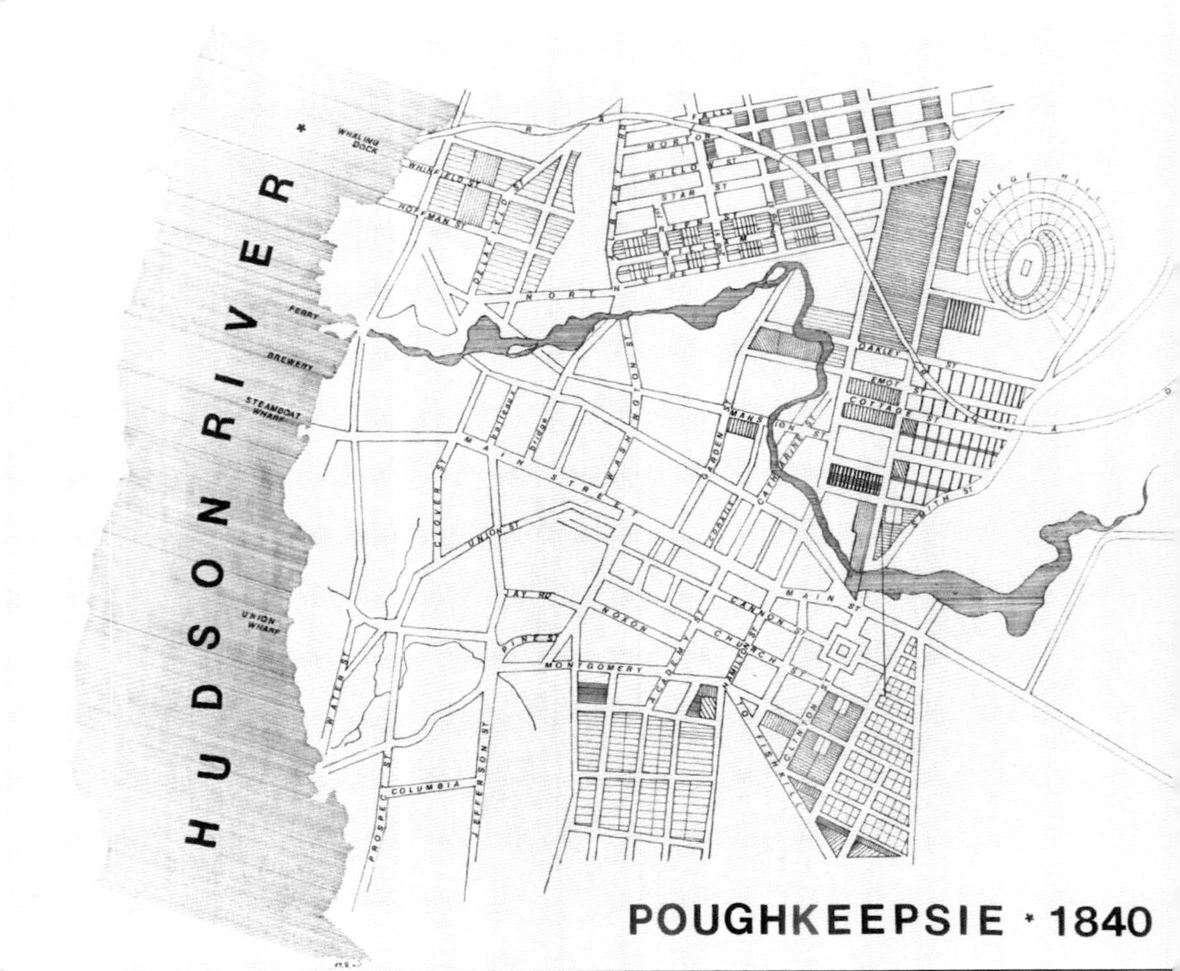

A Map Variously Dated 1835, 1837, and 1840. (DCHS, Mrs. James Key, PK.) This map of the village of Poughkeepsie shows where development had already occurred and the then-contemporary vision of potential development. Note the presence of the winding Fallkill Creek and its ponds as well as the sizeable tracts laid out for development on the north side, especially around College Hill.

Three

Stretching Northward

Prosperous mills, businesses, and farms grew the length of the Fallkill Creek throughout the eighteenth century. A path northeast off the Filkintown Road used by drovers became the Salt Point Turnpike. In the nineteenth century, farms close to the village of Poughkeepsie gave way to larger water-powered mills and planned upscale residential development along the newly constructed Mill Street and Mansion Square Park. By mid-century, numerous private academies dotted the north side and College Hill, giving Poughkeepsie the name "City of Schools."

North along Post Road overlooking the river, country estates stretched to the Clinton/Hyde Park border. Because it was "geographically central, easily accessible," the James Roosevelt estate was selected in 1866 as the site of the new State Hospital for the Insane, the first of several major public institutions to be built in the area. The completion of the railroad bridge in 1888 and rail lines from Poughkeepsie and New England fed industrial development. By the twentieth century, the estates had became part of either institutional or industrial development, the locations of what would become Marist College, St. Francis Hospital, FIAT/Western Printing, Schatz Federal Bearing, and other smaller factories.

The Fairview Improvement Company in the 1920s promoted planned, middle-class, suburban residential development close to the factory and institutional jobs, erasing all but a handful of remaining farms.

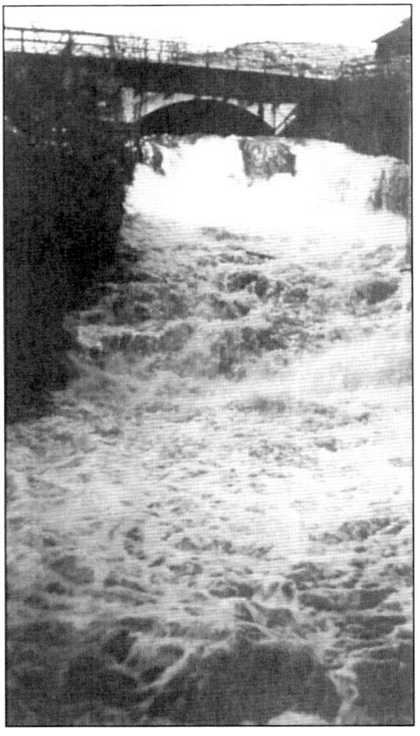

Fallkill Creek. (Mylod family album.) The Fallkill Creek was for many years the source of power for a variety of mills—grist, flour, dye, wood, and saw, for example. Its energy was also harnessed for factories along its banks. However, by 1870 steam had become recognized as the only reliable force for driving machinery, and the city undertook the Fallkill improvement project, a public health initiative, which drained and filled in the mill ponds.

The Innis Dye Works on Fallkill, 1899. (DCHS.) The Innis Dye Works were located on the Fallkill Creek after it had ceased to be the source of power. The railroad bridge indicates that, as proximity to water had once been of paramount importance, the location of industries near the railroad would become increasingly desirable.

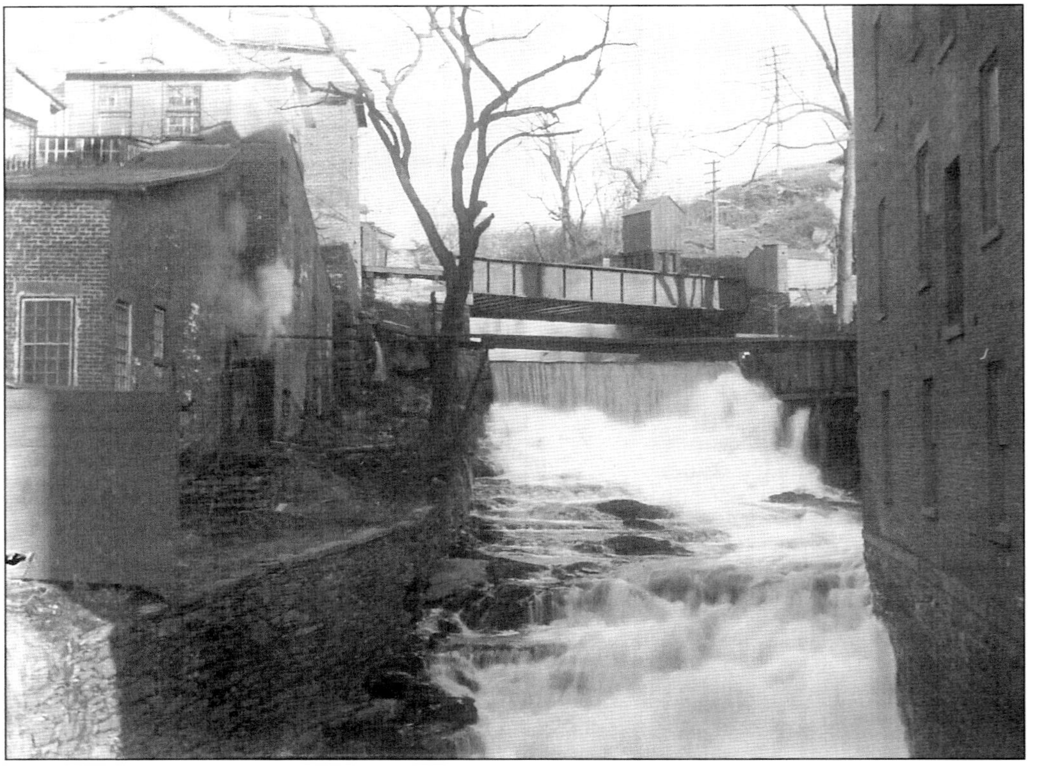

St. Paul's Church. (DCHS.) The present church, an example of Gothic Revival architecture, opened in 1872 replacing the first church building. The church's original construction was part of the grand scheme of the Improvement Party to establish a neighborhood around Mansion Square. Members of the Improvement Party, which flourished from 1830 to the panic of 1837, were also active in promoting municipal improvements such as new streets, pavements, and schools.

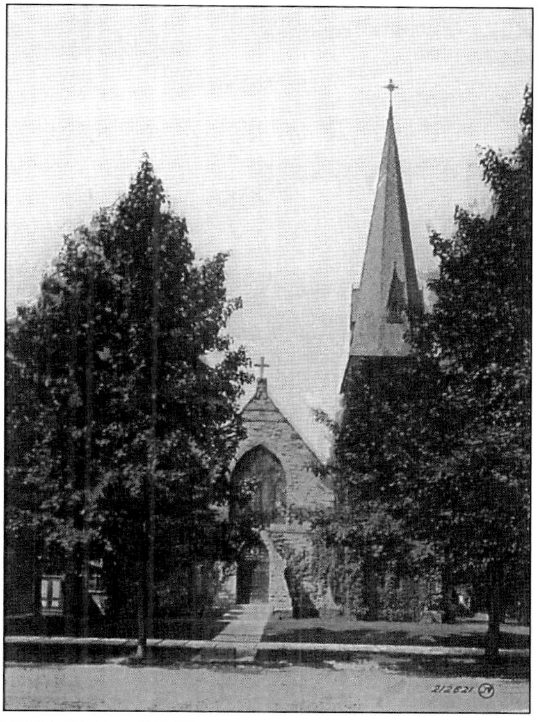

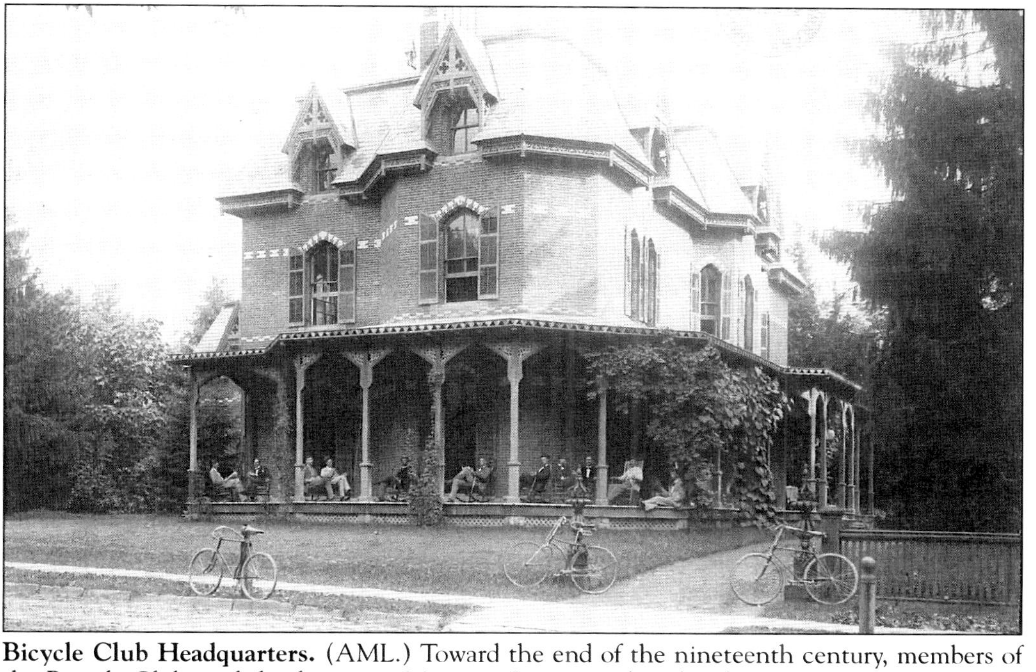

Bicycle Club Headquarters. (AML.) Toward the end of the nineteenth century, members of the Bicycle Club used this house on Mansion Square as their headquarters. The mansion was once owned by Thomas L. Davies, an active member of the Improvement Party, first president of the Poughkeepsie Bank, an organizer of the Poughkeepsie Whaling Company, and an original trustee of the Poughkeepsie Rural Cemetery.

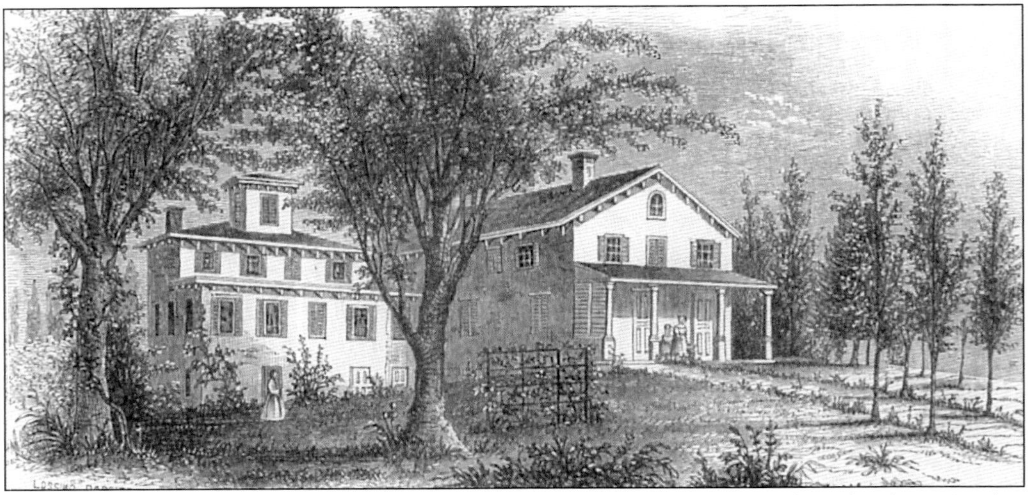

Cottage Hill Seminary. (DCHS.) This early Lossing engraving shows the school on Garden Street that was run in the 1830s by Miss Lydia Booth, step-niece of Matthew Vassar, and was instrumental, it is said, in turning her uncle's attention to the issue of women's education. This school and the many others around town attracted pupils from all over the state and county, and gave Poughkeepsie its name, "City of Schools."

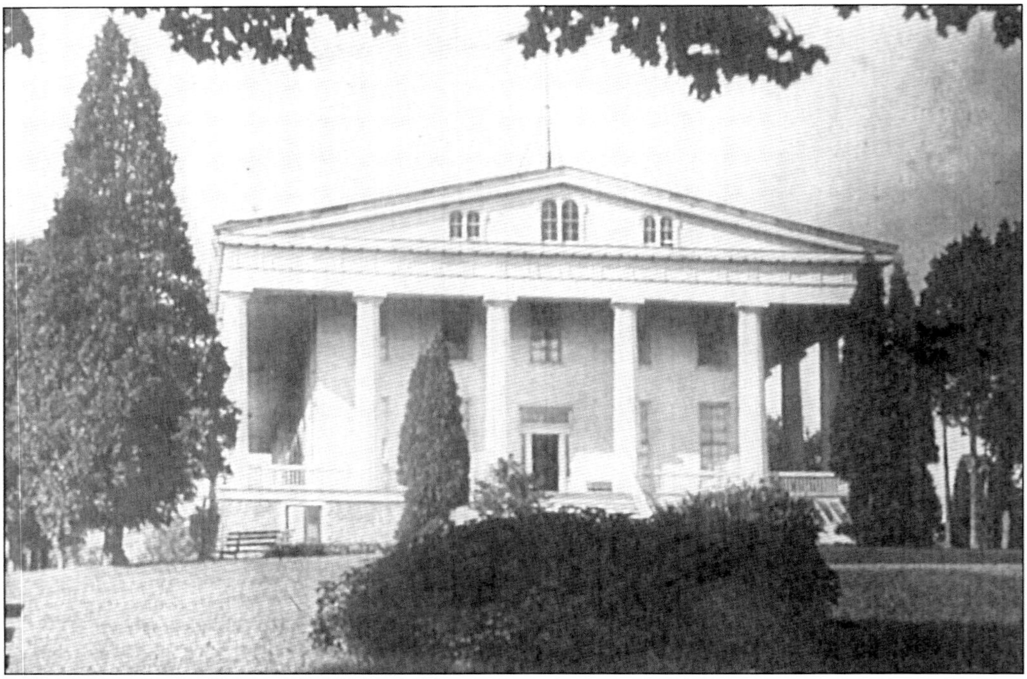

Poughkeepsie Collegiate School on College Hill. (DCHS.) Erected originally by the Improvement Party in the style of the Greek Parthenon, the Poughkeepsie Collegiate School was founded in 1835 and opened the following year. The school continued until the late 1860s, when the building was acquired by George Morgan and converted into a hotel. Successor schools were the Poughkeepsie Military Institute on Smith Street, headed by Charles B. Warring, and the Riverview Academy, directed by Otis Bisbee.

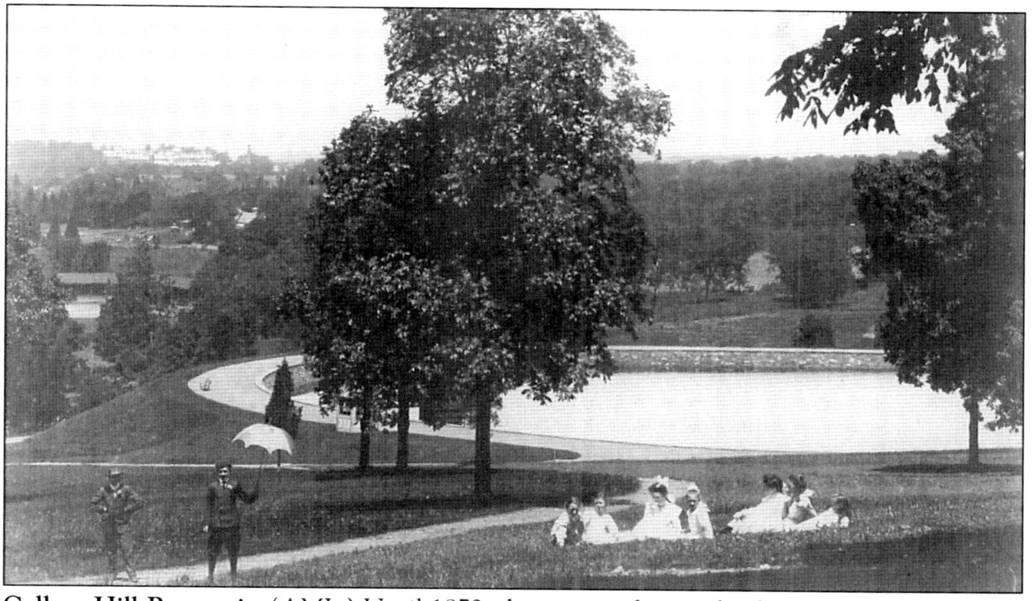

College Hill Reservoir. (AML.) Until 1872, the source of water for domestic use was cisterns and wells that were often located next to privies, contributing to Poughkeepsie's reputation for being "sickly." In 1870 after lengthy study, the Hudson River was chosen as the supply for the city water system and the reservoir was built on College Hill. The area around the reservoir became a favorite place for picnics.

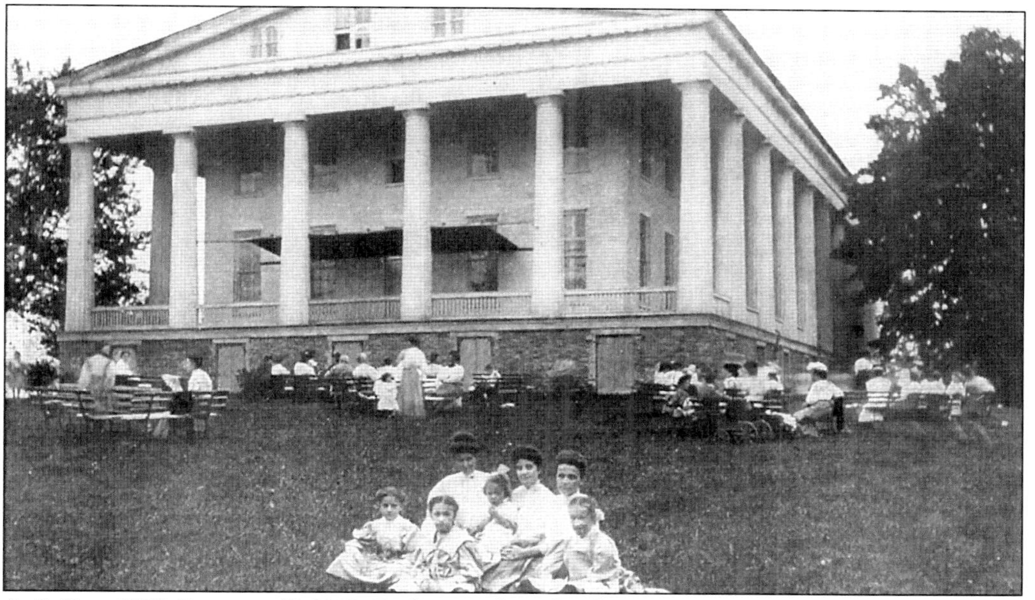

A College Hill Concert. (DCHS, Barbara Velletri [BV].) People also enjoyed concerts held on College Hill. After the hotel had closed, and John Guy Vassar's plans to build an orphanage there had failed to materialize, W.W. Smith purchased the property in 1892 and gave it to the city with plans for its improvement as a public park. The Parthenon-like structure burned in a spectacular fire in 1917. Its successor, the Dudley Memorial, burned in 1944, and was later rebuilt.

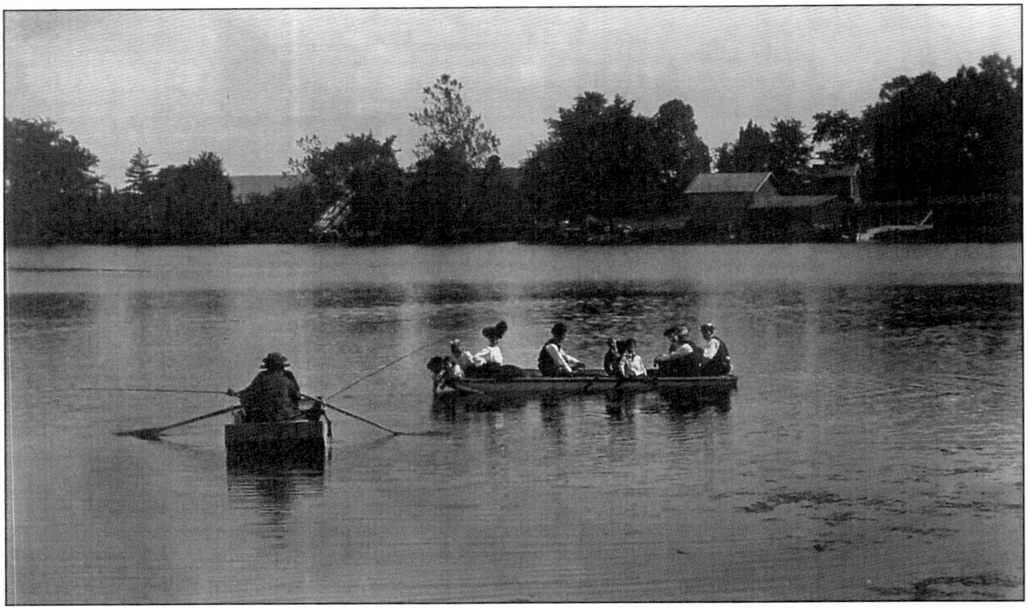

Morgan Lake Boaters. (AML.) George Morgan, once owner of the College Hill Hotel and mayor of the city of Poughkeepsie, constructed the lake on the east side of College Hill, hoping at the time, perhaps, that it would become part of the city's water system. However, it did not. Instead Morgan Lake became a source for ice and a popular place for boating and fishing.

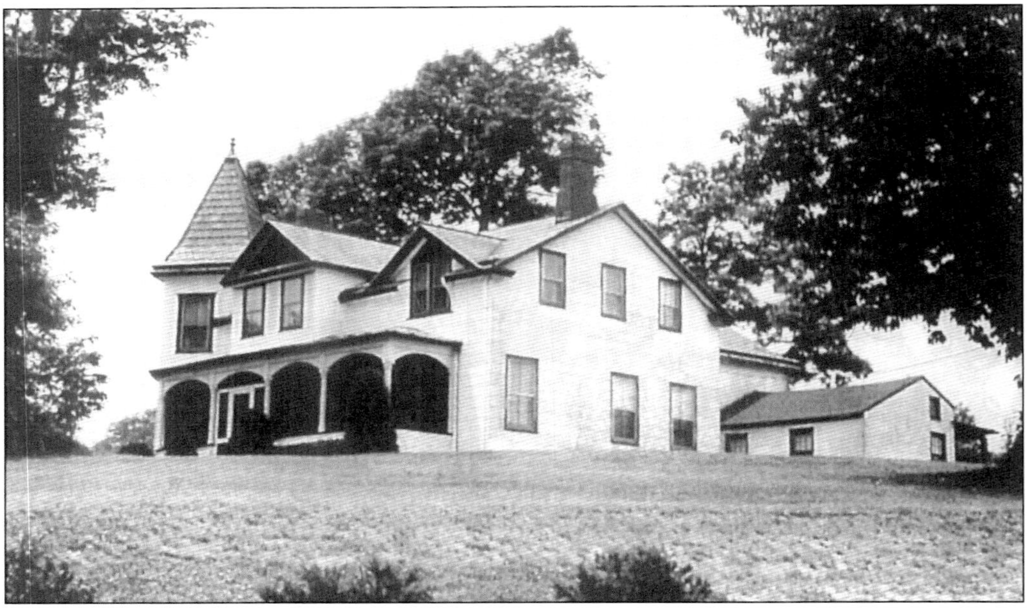

Amato's Farm. (Dutchess County Department of Planning and Economic Development [DCPED].) The Amatos were among the earliest Italian families who came to Poughkeepsie before the turn of the century. They originally settled near what is now Mt. Carmel Square; later George Amato moved near Morgan Lake to grow fruits and vegetables to market. The business continued for many years, but some of the acreage gave way to residential development.

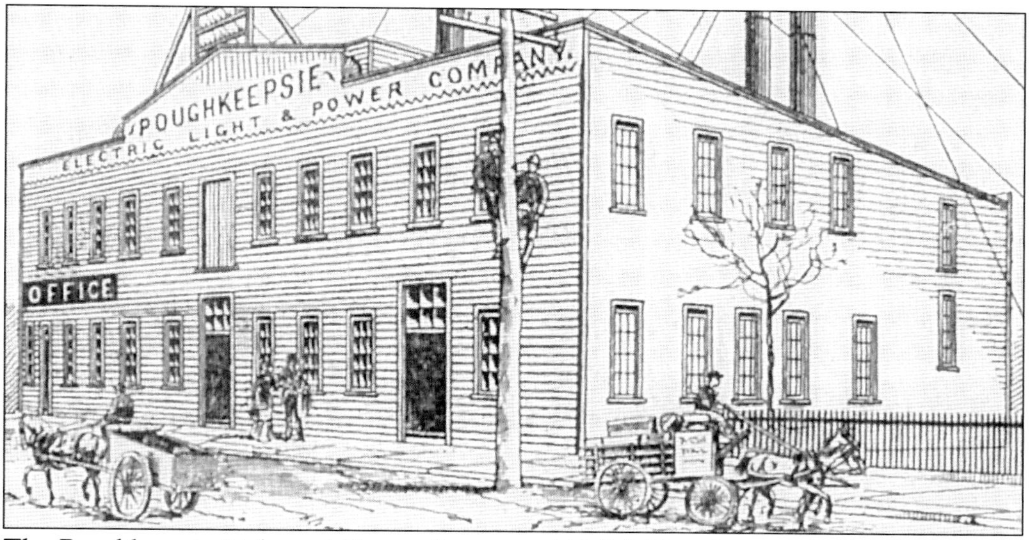

The Poughkeepsie Light and Power Company. (AML.) This drawing of the Poughkeepsie Light and Power Company on Winnikee Avenue appeared in a turn-of-the-century booklet advertising businesses and homes in Poughkeepsie. In 1886, just two years after the first electric lights were put up in Poughkeepsie, the company secured the contract for lighting the streets for $18,000. It also provided light and power for small machinery, which enabled companies to manufacture a variety of products from buttons to cough drops.

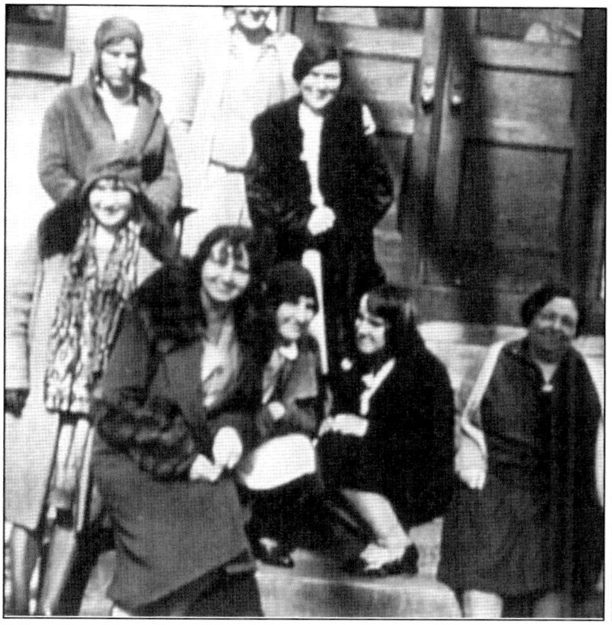

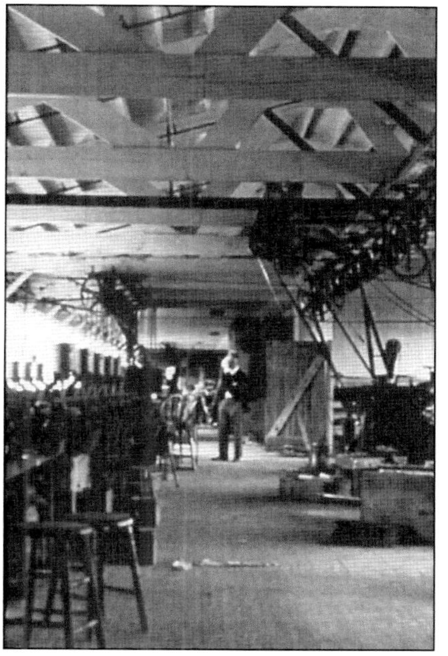

The Pioneer Pearl Button Factory. (Patsy Newman Costello.) **The Seneca Button Factory.** (MMB.) Margaret Andros Newman and her twin sister Elisabeth Andros, mother and aunt of Patsy Costello, are among the women who worked at the Pioneer Pearl Button Factory on Mansion Street in the 1920s and '30s. The Seneca Button Factory was located on North Hamilton Street and was mentioned in the 1910 city directory as one of the inducements of the Fairview Improvement Company.

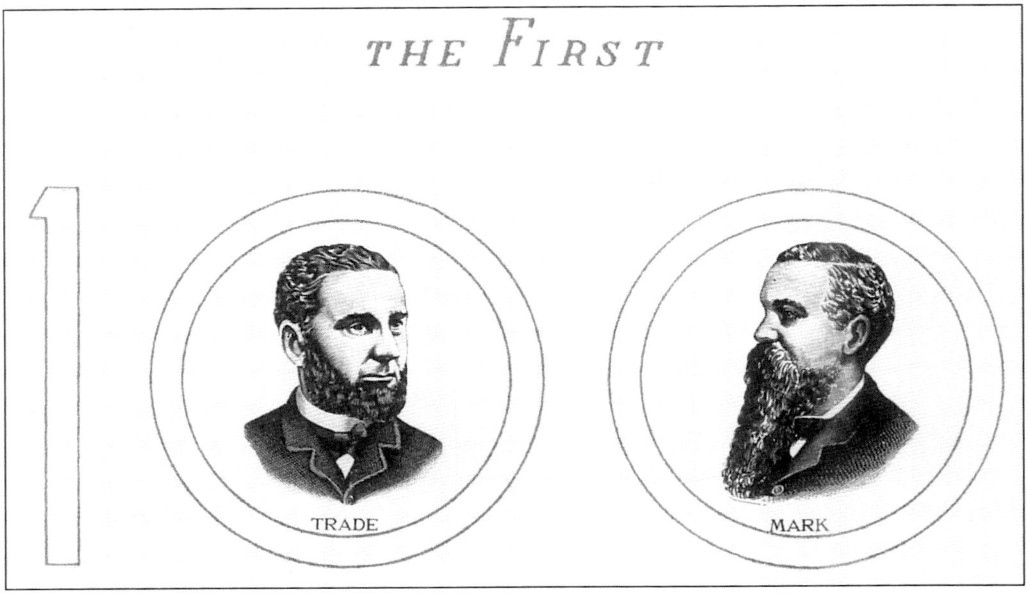

Smith Brothers, 1947. (Arthur B. and Ruth McComb [ABRMcC].) This program, which is from the 1947 celebration of "The First Hundred Years" of Smith Brothers, shows the famous "Trade" and "Mark." When James Smith, the father of the original Smith brothers, arrived in Poughkeepsie by steamboat in 1847, he could see a thriving village of ten thousand people that he knew was already connected by telegraph to New York City and would soon have a railroad. The cough drop factory was located on Church Street and was moved to North Hamilton Street in 1914.

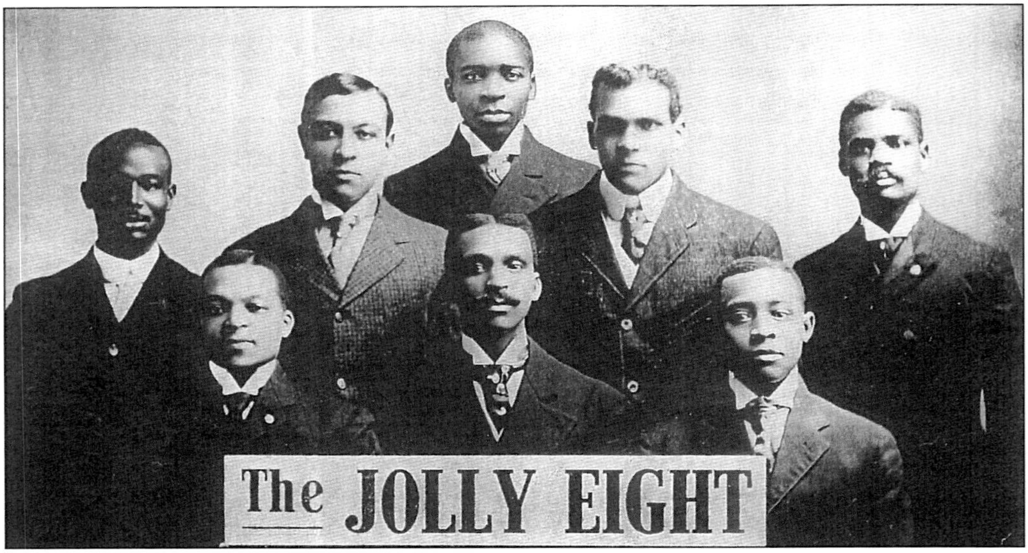

The Jolly Eight, 1910. (Walter Patrice [WP].) The Jolly Eight was a social club of entrepreneurs. Their businesses included catering, contract painting, running the concessions at the Driving Park, ash collection, furniture moving, a bakery, and a restaurant. Pictured are (front row) Walter Jackson, Yarborough Chapman, and Edward Quick; (middle row) Oscar May, Charles Francis, Tom Yancey, and Paul Paskler; and (back row) Ben Westen.

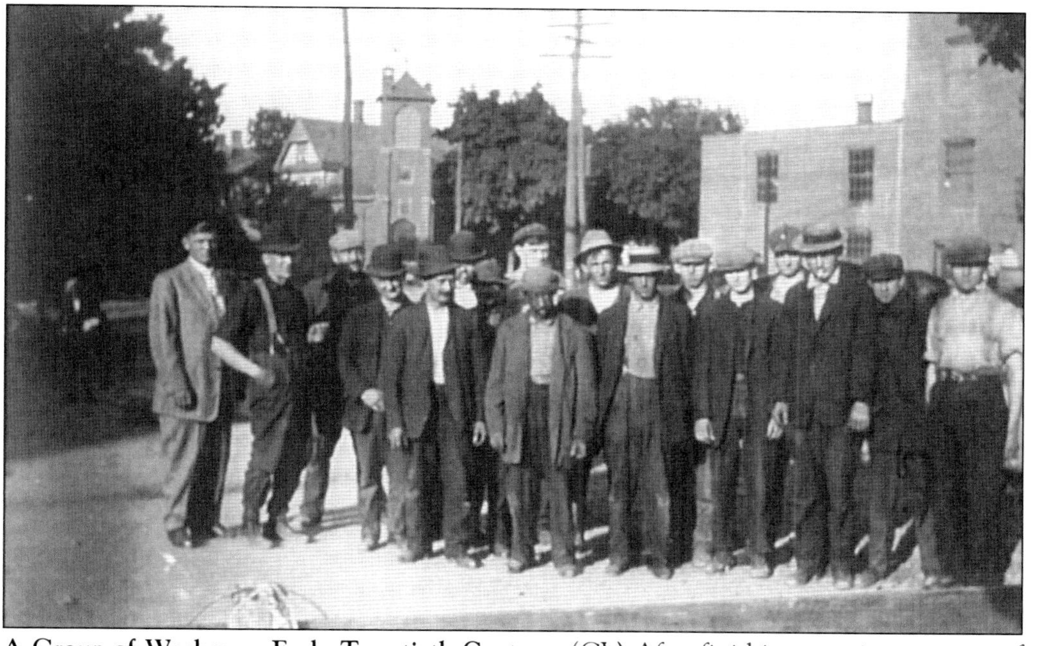

A Group of Workmen, Early Twentieth Century. (CJ.) After finishing a project, a group of plumbers wearing a variety of hats posed for this photograph at Clinton Square. Ebenezer Baptist Church is in the background. This congregation was organized in 1891, and the building erected in 1905. There was a horse water trough on the square for many years, but, as the automobile replaced horsepower, the trough became a flower planter and eventually was removed to ease traffic congestion.

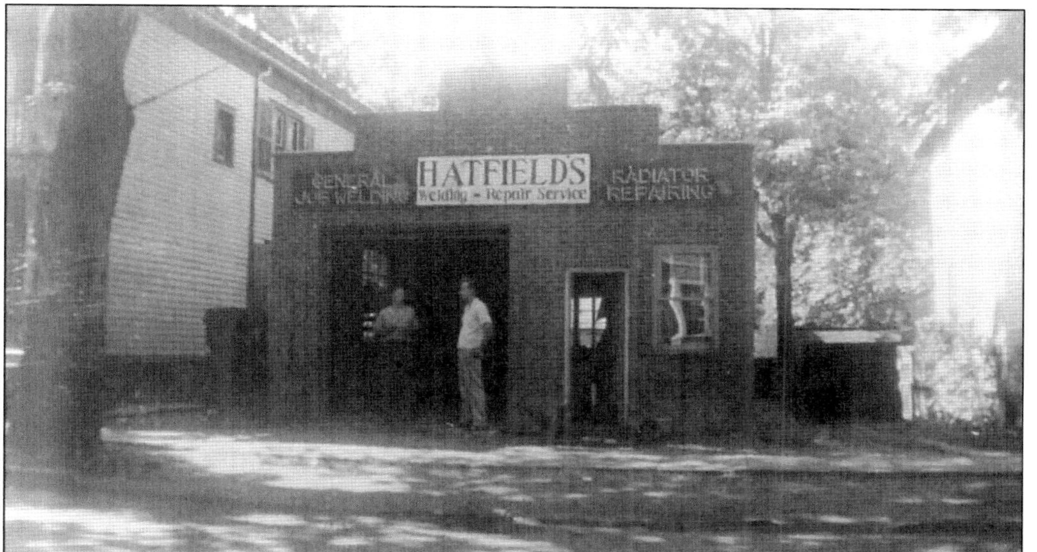

Hatfield's Welding Business, 1947. (Ann Hatfield.) One hundred years after the establishment of Smith Brothers, Ted Lafko and L. Howard Hatfield are seen in front of Hatfield's Welding business, which began on Winnikee Avenue in 1947. Hatfield Metal Fabrication, as it was known then, was founded by Henry Howard Hatfield.

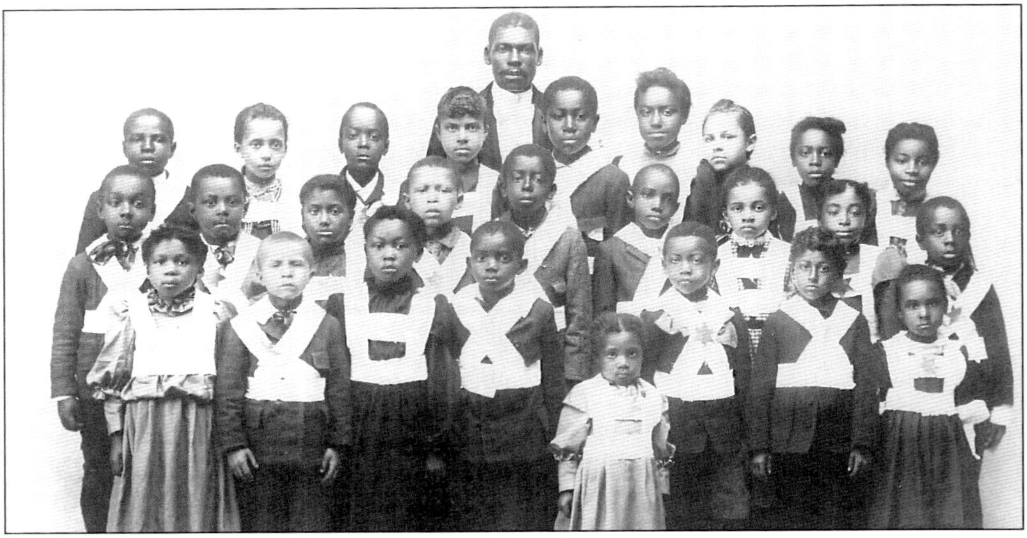

An AME Zion Youth Group, 1890. (W.P.) This photograph that belonged to Unetta Patrice was taken when she was only a year old, and too young to be a member. Her sister Leila, however, was part of the group that visited other churches. After separating from the Methodist church on Washington Street in 1836, Poughkeepsie AME congregants held their first service in the old Lancaster Schoolhouse on Church Street. The first church building was a former school for "colored" children (the term used then) and in 1843, after a fire, the church was rebuilt on the same site on Catharine Street.

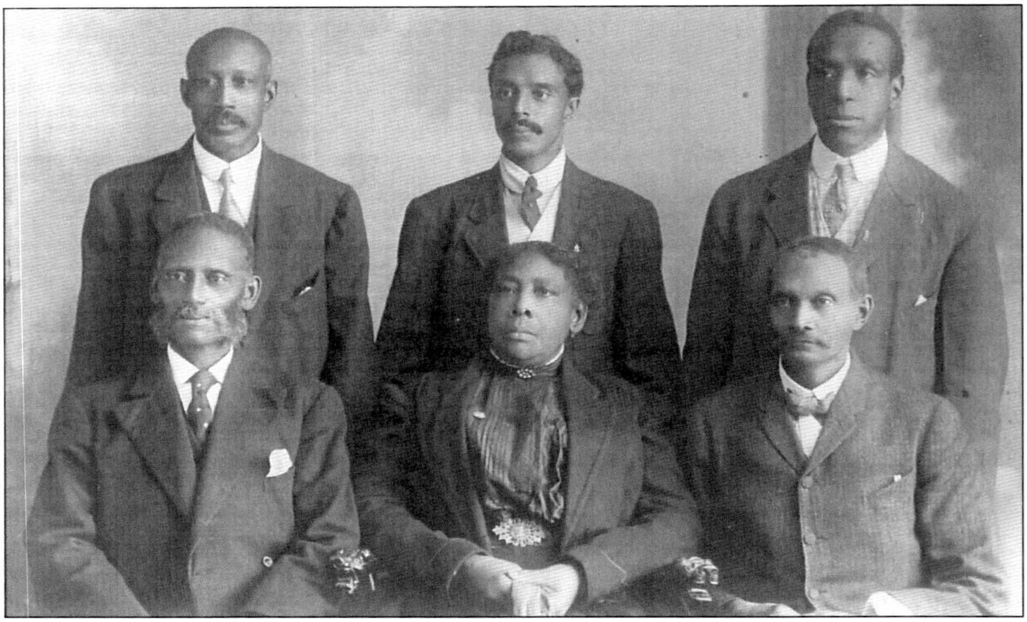

AME Zion Trustees, 1911. (W.P.) The trustees shown are (front row) William Deyo, Mary J. Colden, and Jasper Jackson (president of the board and grandfather of Walter Patrice); (back row) Andrew Johnson, George Taylor, and John Miller. It is noteworthy that a woman held a leadership position at that time. Having outgrown its building on Catharine Street, the congregation bought property on Smith and Cottage Streets upon which to erect a new church.

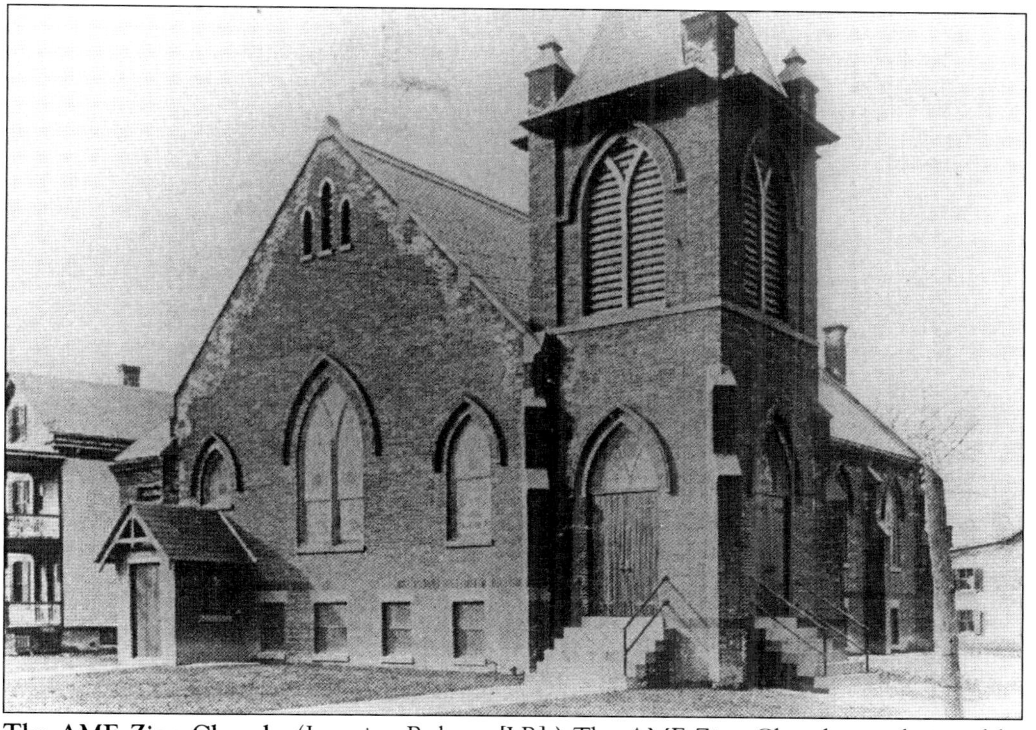

The AME Zion Church. (Lorraine Roberts [LR].) The AME Zion Church was designed by DuBois Carpenter and built in 1911 on the property previously purchased. W.W. Smith, a local philanthropist, provided $20,000 to augment the contributions of the congregation and the funds raised by selling the building on Catharine Street.

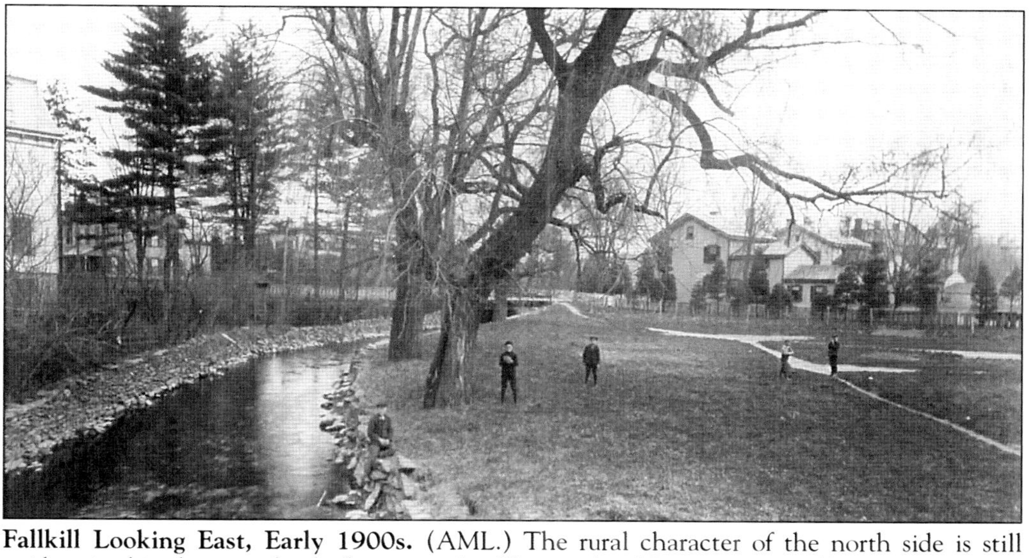

Fallkill Looking East, Early 1900s. (AML.) The rural character of the north side is still evident in this photograph which appeared in *Illustrated and Descriptive Poughkeepsie*, *1906*. The caption read: "Sanford's ball fields and the Fallkill creek." The creek, a major source of power in earlier days, had become a favorite swimming and fishing spot despite heavy industrial use farther upstream.

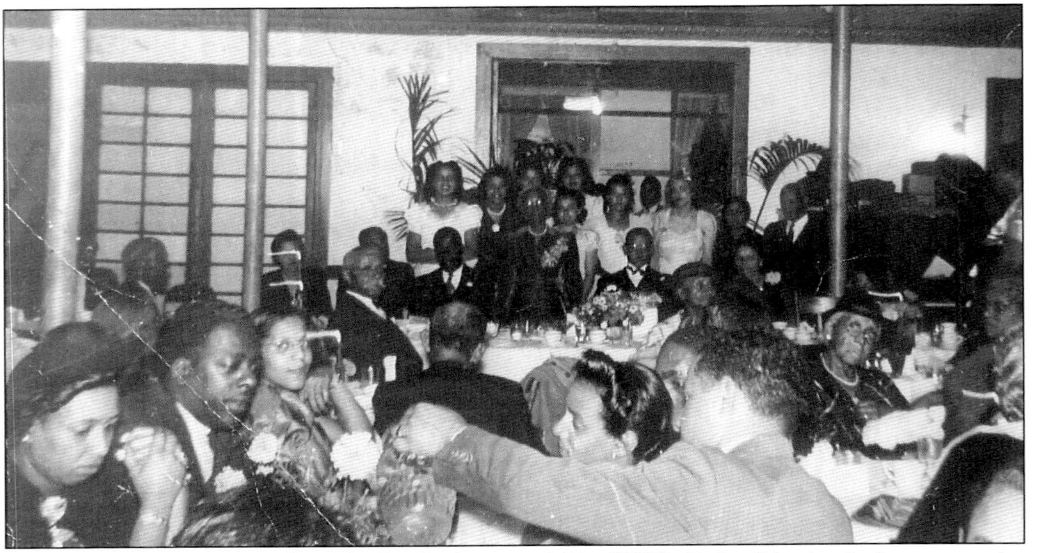

A Dinner Honoring Sadie Rhodes Lefevre, 1941. (WP.) Sadie Rhodes Lefevre was the organist of the AME Zion Church for sixty years. According to Walter Patrice, she may also have been one of the first minority children to attend the formerly segregated public schools in Poughkeepsie. In 1873, Joseph Rhodes and his wife had insisted that their children attend the city's public schools, presenting a test case of the federal civil rights law. The children were finally allowed to attend public school and in 1874 the New York State Legislature passed legislation to abolish segregation in public schools.

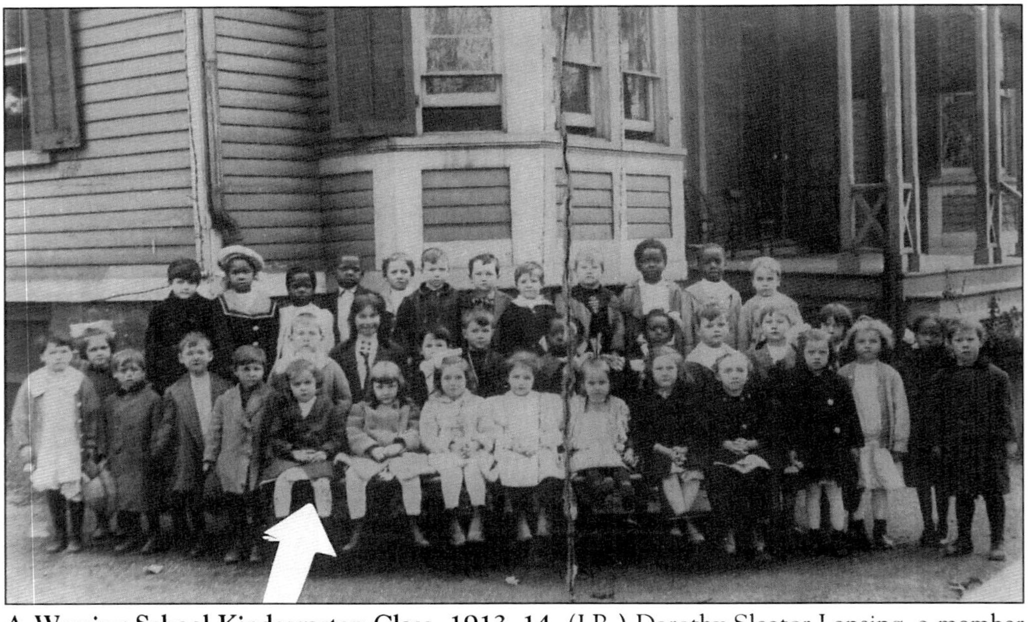

A Warring School Kindergarten Class, 1913–14. (LR.) Dorothy Sleator Lansing, a member of this kindergarten class, seated above the arrow, provided this photograph to Lorraine Roberts. Warring School was originally a military academy on Smith Street, directed by Charles B. Warring. After some years, the military academy failed and the original building was purchased by the City of Poughkeepsie in 1902.

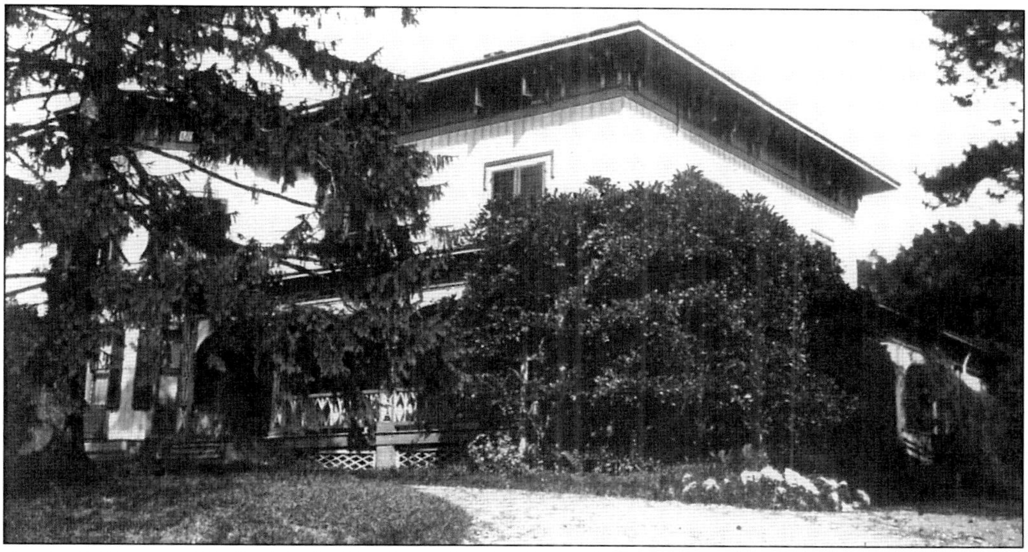

Sanford House, 1912. (AML.) Robert Sanford's residence at 29 North Hamilton Street was described by Edmund Platt as "surrounded by nearly six acres of lawn and beautiful shade trees, with winding walks and the bubbling water of the Falkill flowing through its grounds." Shortly after the photograph was taken, the house was torn down and Poughkeepsie High School was built.

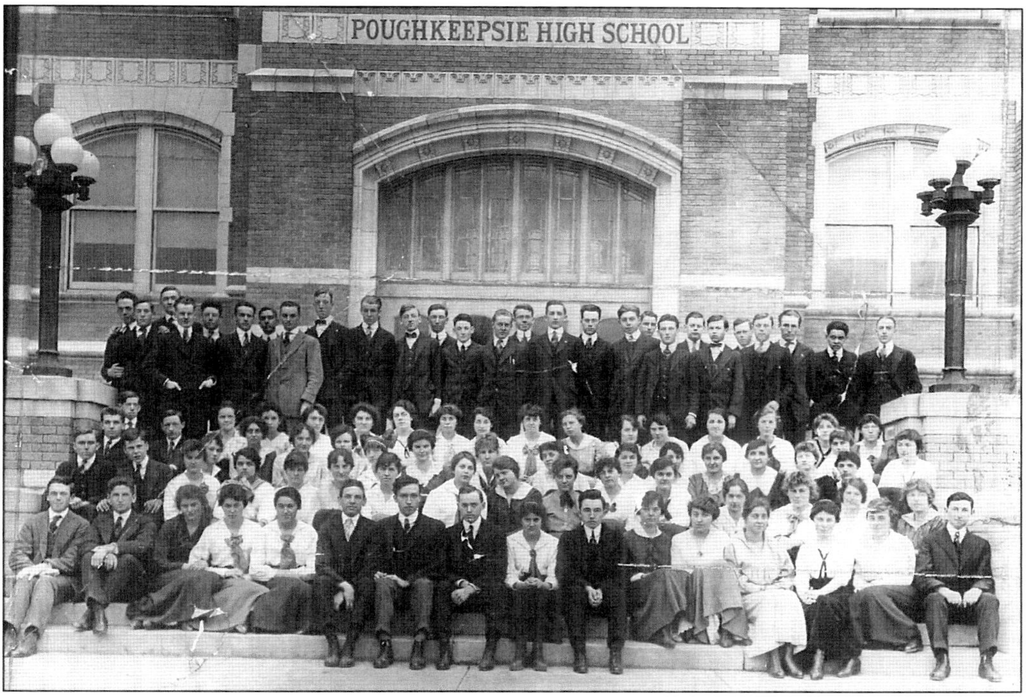

The Poughkeepsie High School Graduating Class of 1916. (DCHS.) The class of 1916 was one of the first to graduate from the new high school on North Hamilton Street. At that time students came from surrounding communities to attend high school in Poughkeepsie, some boarding with Poughkeepsie families during the week.

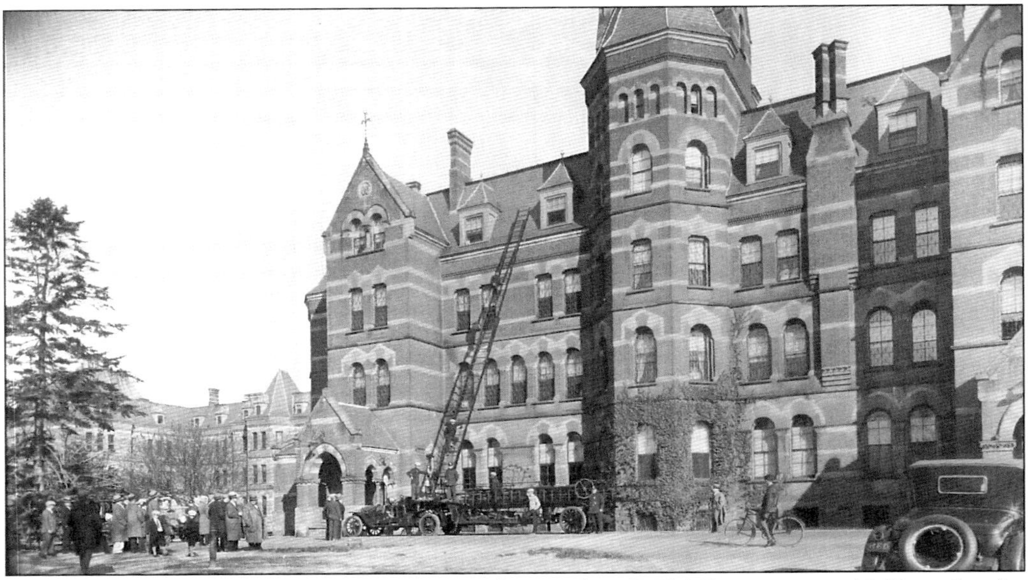

The Hudson River State Hospital, 1930s. (Len Peluso [LP].) Beginning in 1867, under the direction of Calvert Vaux and Frederick Withers, the Hudson River State Hospital was designed and built on what had been the James Roosevelt estate. This was the first such institution designated as a "hospital" rather than an "asylum." Frederick Law Olmsted of Central Park fame helped to draw up plans for the grounds. Safety of the inmates was a primary concern as evidenced by this fire drill.

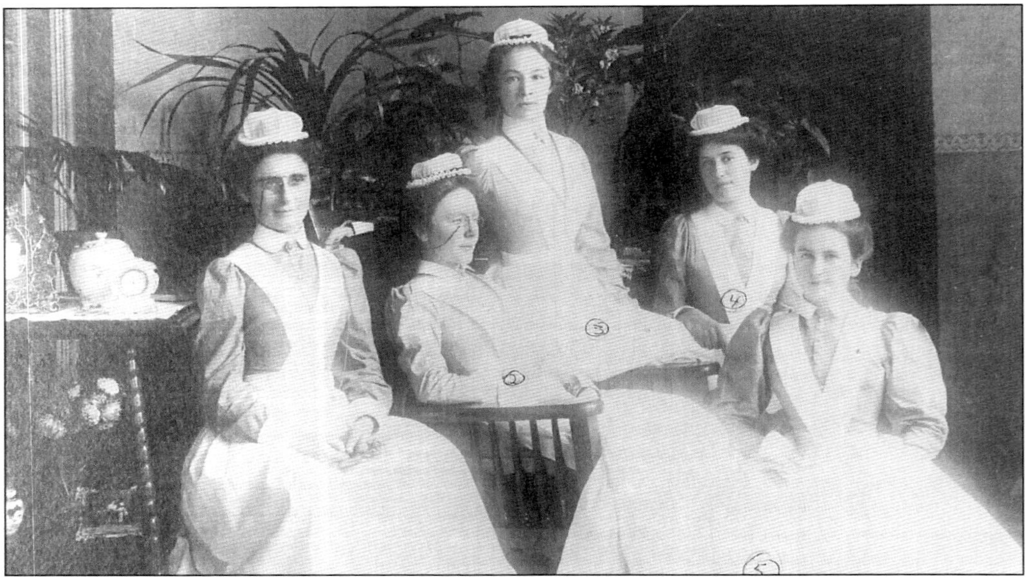

Nurses, Class of 1898. (Hudson River Psychiatric Center [HRPC].) In 1886 the Hudson River State Hospital established the first school of nursing in Dutchess County. It was not until 1903 that nursing was recognized as a profession in the United States. From its beginning both men and women were admitted to the school. Nursing was seen as a "calling" which required total dedication.

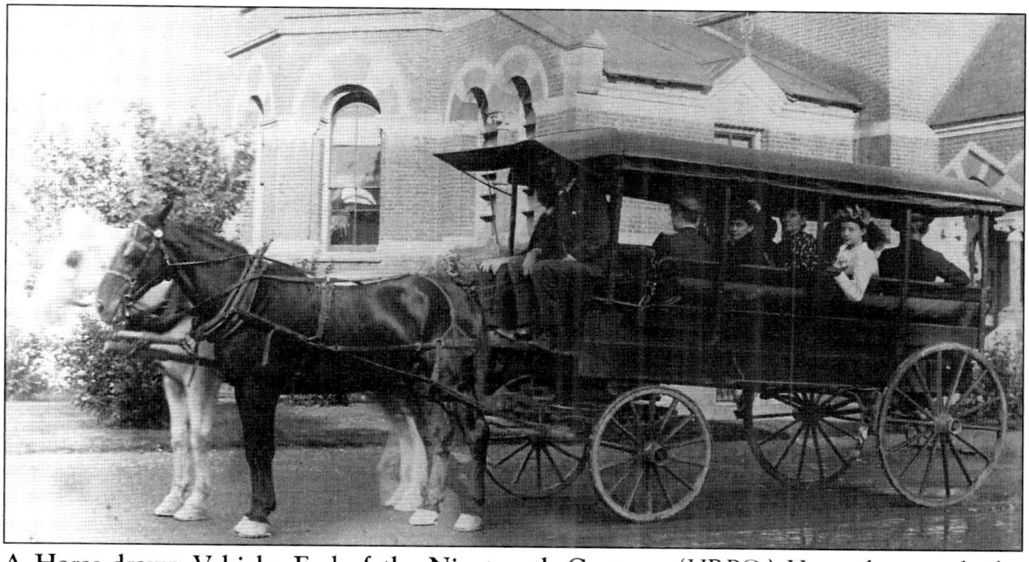

A Horse-drawn Vehicle, End of the Nineteenth Century. (HRPC.) Horse-drawn vehicles were used until the advent of electric trolleys and later of buses and cars to bring visitors and prospective employees to the Hudson River State Hospital. For many years the hospital was a self-contained community with nearly all the employees living on the grounds. Many worked twelve hours a day, six days a week until about the early 1930s.

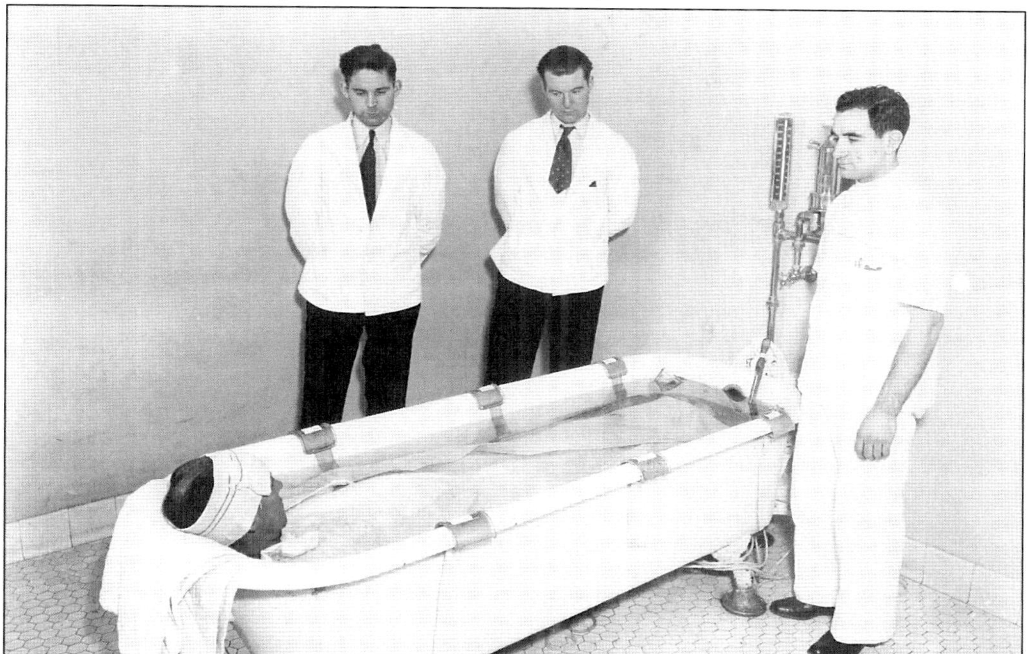

Len Peluso and Hydrotherapy, 1930s. (LP.) Len Peluso (on the extreme right), a male nurse, and two attendants are administering hydrotherapy to a patient. The history of various innovative treatment modes can be traced at the Museum of the Hudson River Psychiatric Center Historical Association, housed in the former patient library at HRPC.

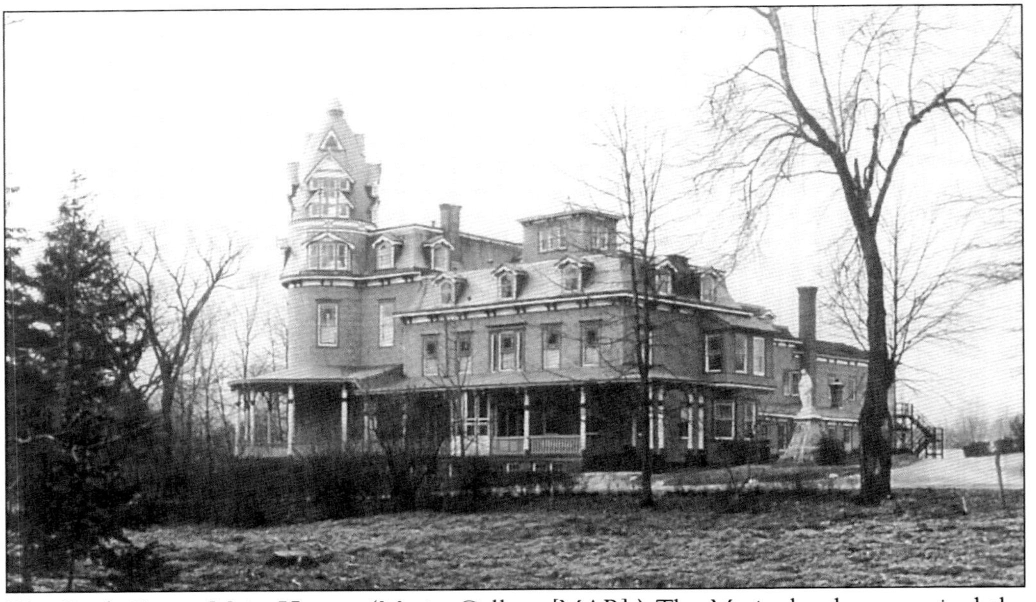

The Bech Estate Main House. (Marist College [MAR].) The Marist brothers acquired the Hudson River estate of Edward Bech in 1905 and renamed it St. Ann's Hermitage. Bech was a Danish immigrant, later Danish consul, and owner of the Poughkeepsie Iron Company and Fallkill Iron Works. After he purchased Hickory Grove, a farm on the Hudson River, he engaged the Danish architect Detlef Lienau to design a gatehouse, gardener's cottage, carriage house, and a main house that was never built.

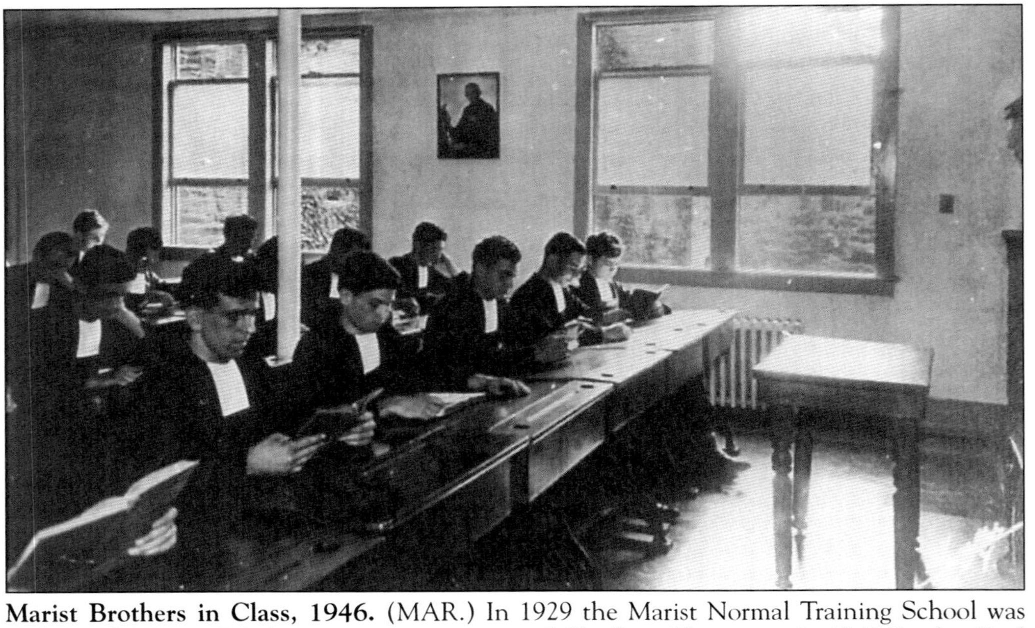

Marist Brothers in Class, 1946. (MAR.) In 1929 the Marist Normal Training School was authorized to grant BA degrees in conjunction with Fordham University. In 1943 Brother Paul Ambrose Fontaine, FMS, was appointed president of Marian College which received its charter as a four-year college in 1946 and continued its mission to train Marist brothers as teachers. In 1950, sixty-six students were enrolled.

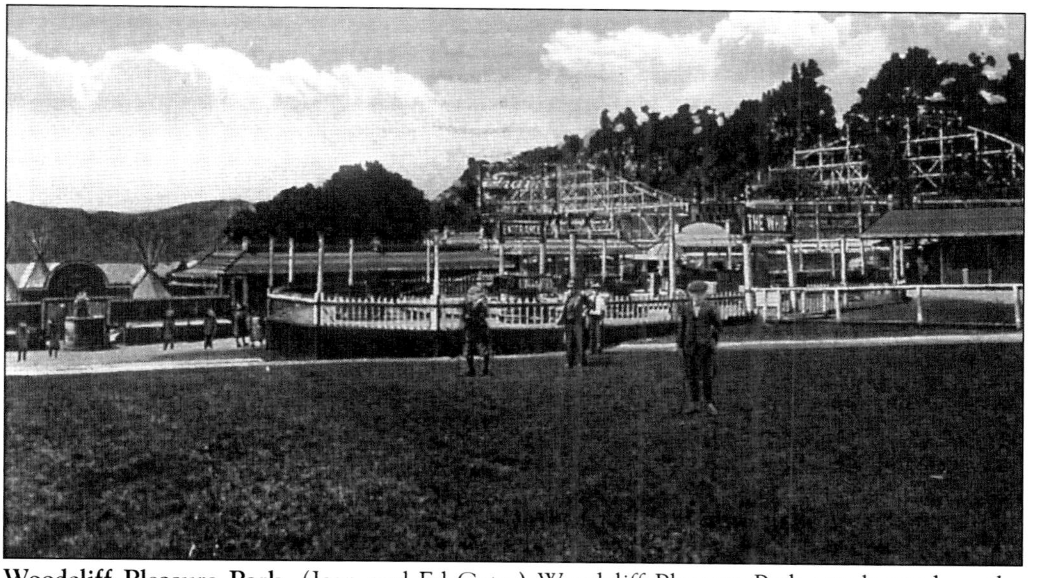

Woodcliff Pleasure Park. (Jean and Ed Cote.) Woodcliff Pleasure Park was located on the present-day site of the Marist College townhouses. Once the estate of John L. Winslow, holder of the first American rights for the manufacture of Bessemer steel, Woodcliff became "the principal playground of Poughkeepsie" according to the 1937 American Guide Series book on Dutchess County.

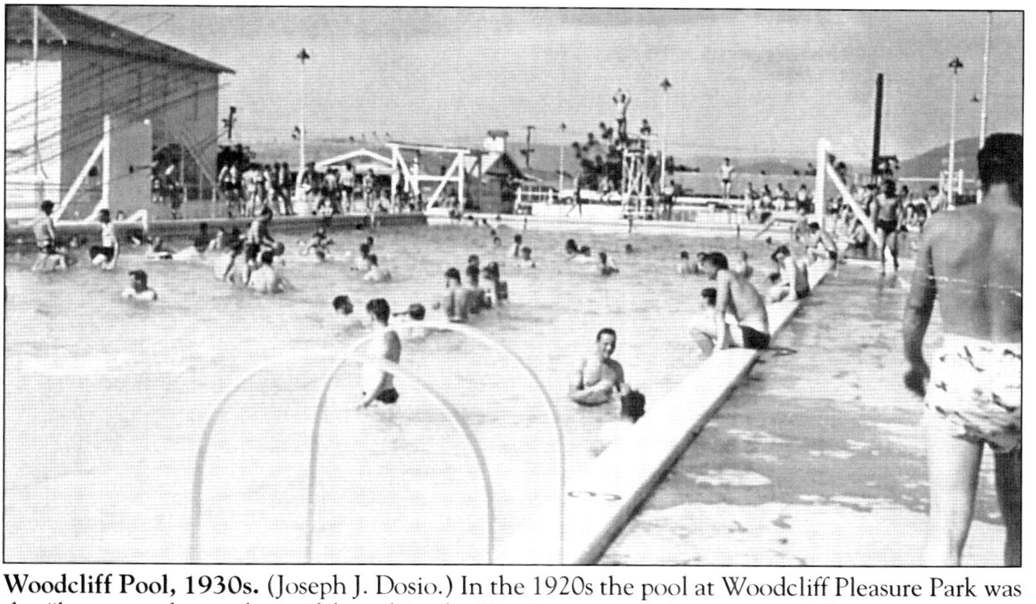

Woodcliff Pool, 1930s. (Joseph J. Dosio.) In the 1920s the pool at Woodcliff Pleasure Park was the "largest and most beautiful pool in the East," constructed at a cost of almost one quarter million dollars for use by three thousand bathers at one time. The water was "scientifically treated and made as pure and crystal as the water you drink." Joseph J. Dosio (far right) at age sixteen is shown here enjoying the pool.

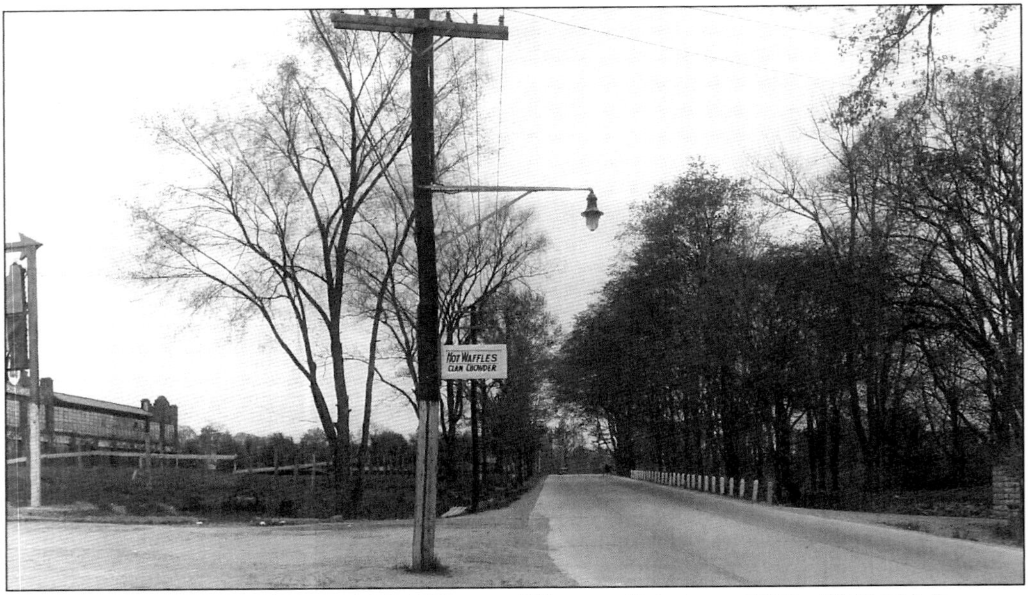

Albany Post Road in front of FIAT/Lancia/Western Printing, 1929. (DCHS.) Between the Marist Normal Training School and the FIAT factory was Albany Post Road, a narrow two-laned road. According to the 1910 city directory, the FIAT Automobile Works employed 350 skilled workmen with plans to hire a thousand. During World War I munitions were manufactured there. Later the factory became the Western Printing and Lithography Company, which prepared maps for invasion troops during the World War II.

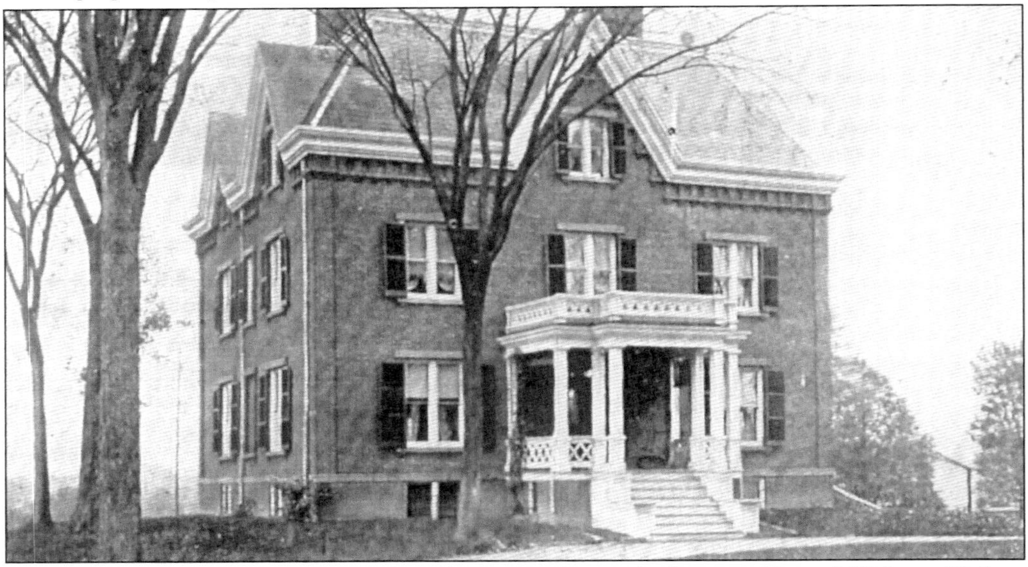

Hill Crest, pre-1914. (DCHS, BV.) Hill Crest Park was the home of Daniel Webster Wilbur. In 1913 local physicians requested Reverend Joseph F. Sheahan, pastor of St. Peter's Catholic Church, to secure a nursing order of sisters to establish a hospital in Poughkeepsie. While the Benedictines declined, the Franciscan order agreed. The site was selected for St. Francis Hospital because of its convenient location on Albany Post Road, midway between New York City and Albany.

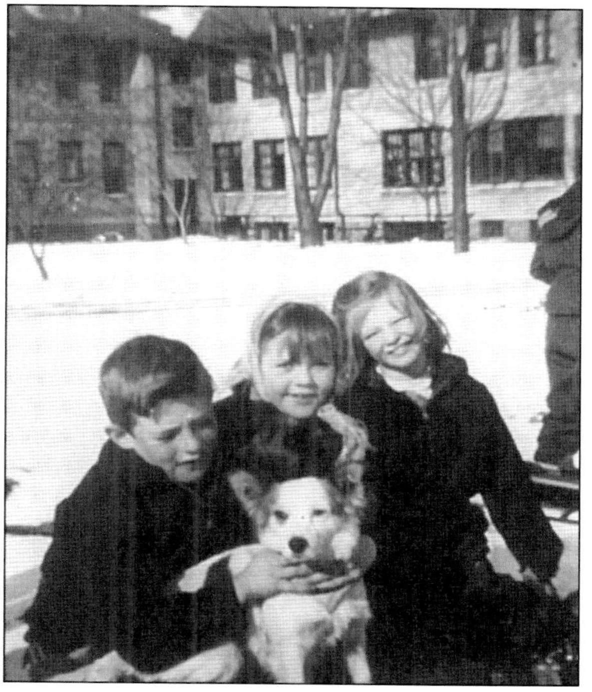

Children with Dog in Front of the Children's Home. (Children's Home [CH].) The building dates this photograph to after 1922, when the home had relocated from the city of Poughkeepsie to a 25-acre site in Fairview. It was in 1847 that a group of women in Poughkeepsie had decided that saving the children was the "only true way to arrest the evil of poverty." With determination and commitment, they founded the Poughkeepsie Orphan Home and Home for the Friendless, acquired land, constructed a building, and created an endowment—all within ten years.

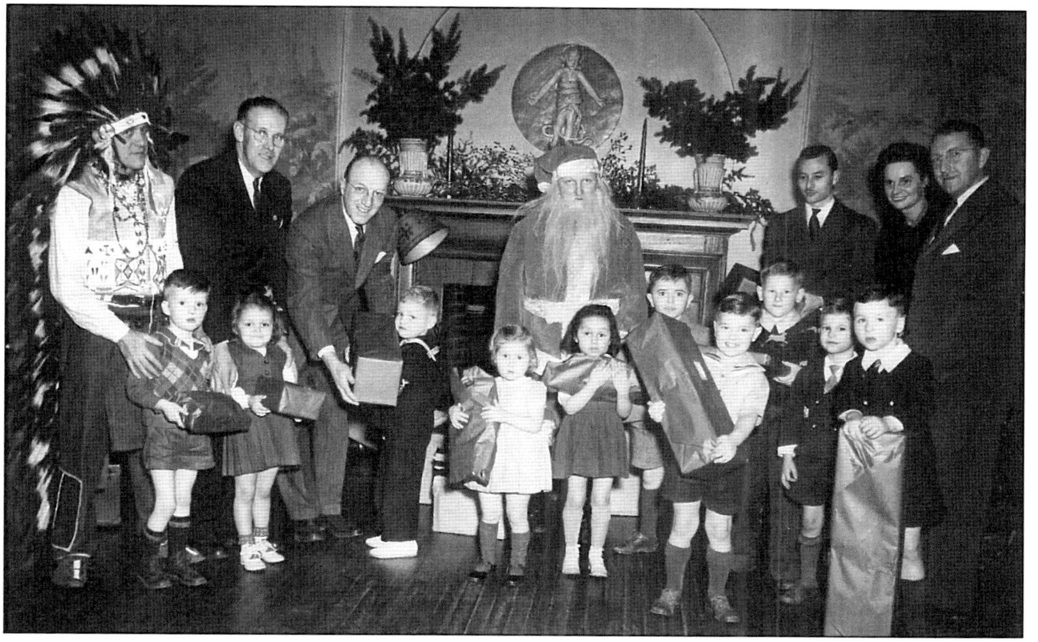

A Christmas Party at the Children's Home. (CH.) Miss Margaret Garrison (later Mrs. Austin Race), the beloved director of the Children's Home for more than thirty-five years, is seen here at the annual Christmas party. In 1919 the charter of the organization was revised, changing the name to the Children's Home of Poughkeepsie, New York. The cornerstone of the new building was laid in 1921 and in 1922, forty-seven children settled down in the home-like environment.

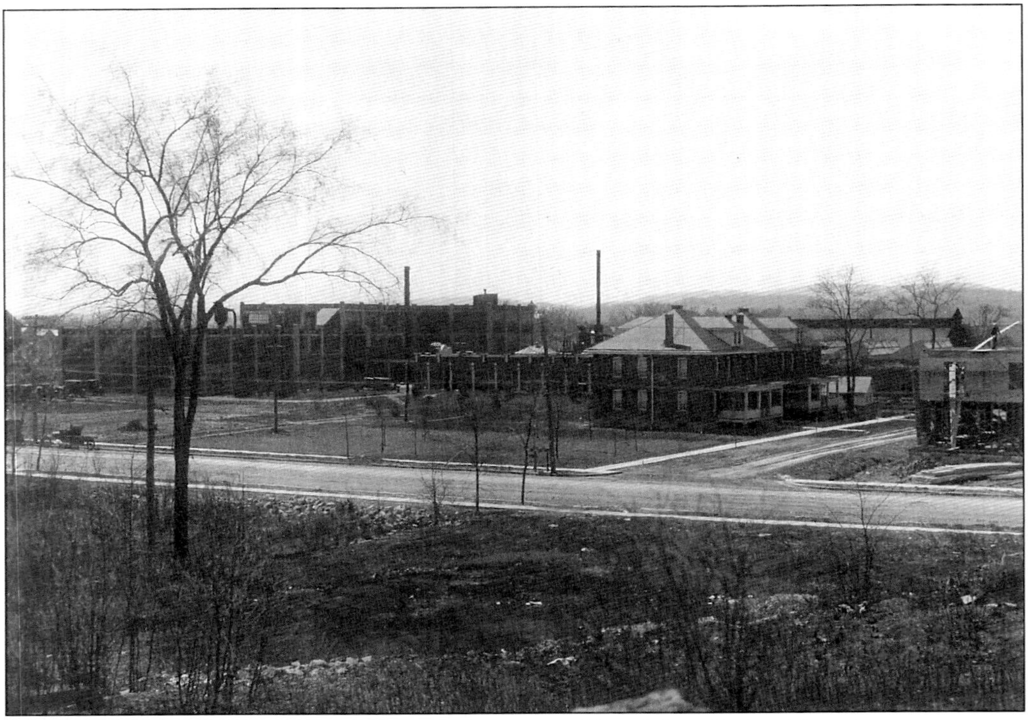

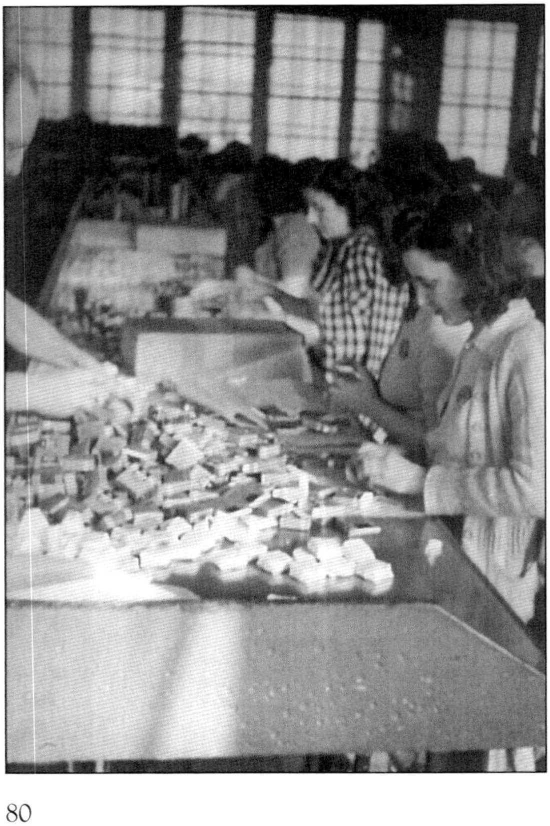

The Schatz Federal Bearing Corporation. (AML.) To the left in the photograph is the factory and in the center are the offices of the company that began as Schatz Manufacturing Company, manufacturer of punching and shearing machines. In 1910 proximity to the factory was a selling point of the Fairview Improvement Company, a planned development venture that had acquired land between "the main thoroughfare between Albany and New York" (Route 9) and Violet Avenue (Route 9G).

The Packing Division at Schatz. (AML.) Schatz later began to manufacture ball bearings and it played an important role in World War II. The packing division of Shatz Federal Bearing Corporation in this photograph was composed solely of women workers. The entry of women into the labor market as the result of World War II was to have far-reaching consequences.

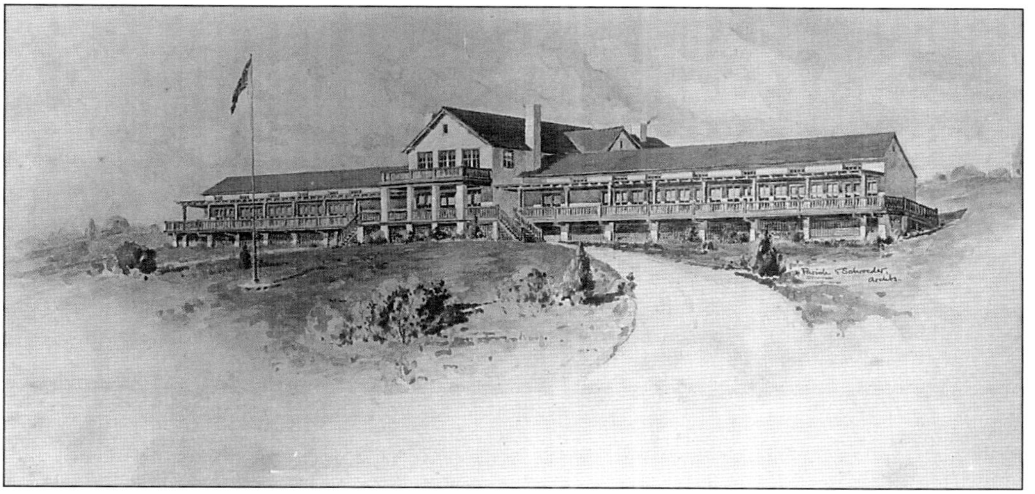

Bowne Memorial Hospital. (DCHS.) The city had opened a sanitarium in 1909 for those suffering from tuberculosis and in 1911 Mrs. Bowne, widow of Samuel W. Bowne, erected this building in memory of her husband. Medical advances made the treatment of getting sun and fresh air obsolete. After the hospital had been closed for a number of years, it became part of the site of Dutchess Community College.

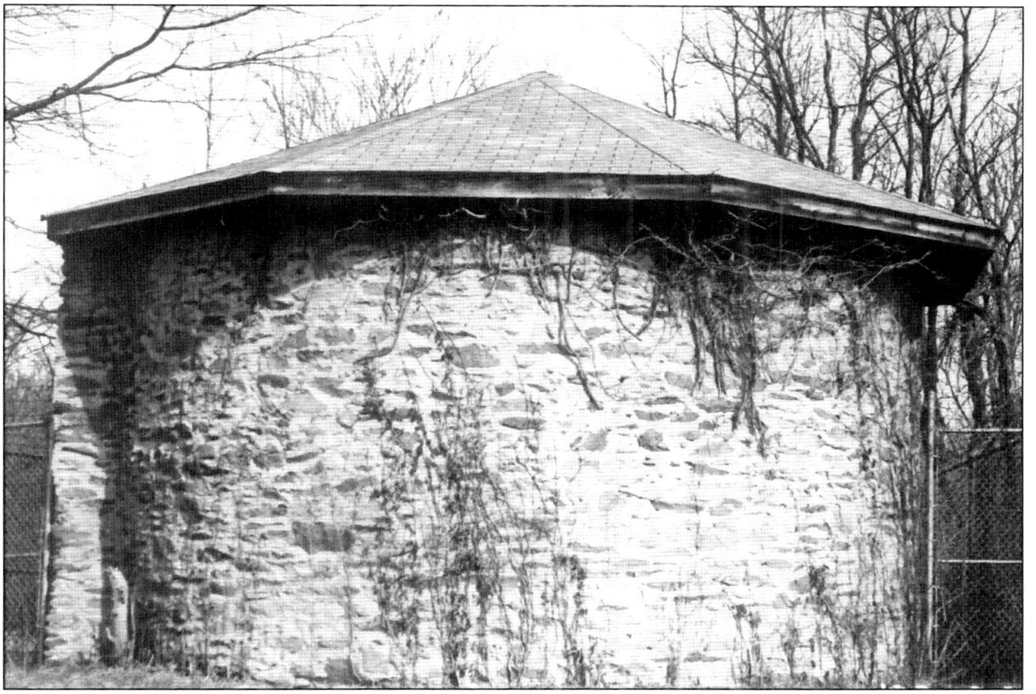

Morello's. (DCHS, JG.) Morello's was a favorite spot to relax and have fun. Originally a farm, it became a place where young people especially could come together to swim and have a good time. Eventually, it, too, was to become part of the site of Dutchess Community College. This silo remains in the parking lot across from Hudson Hall.

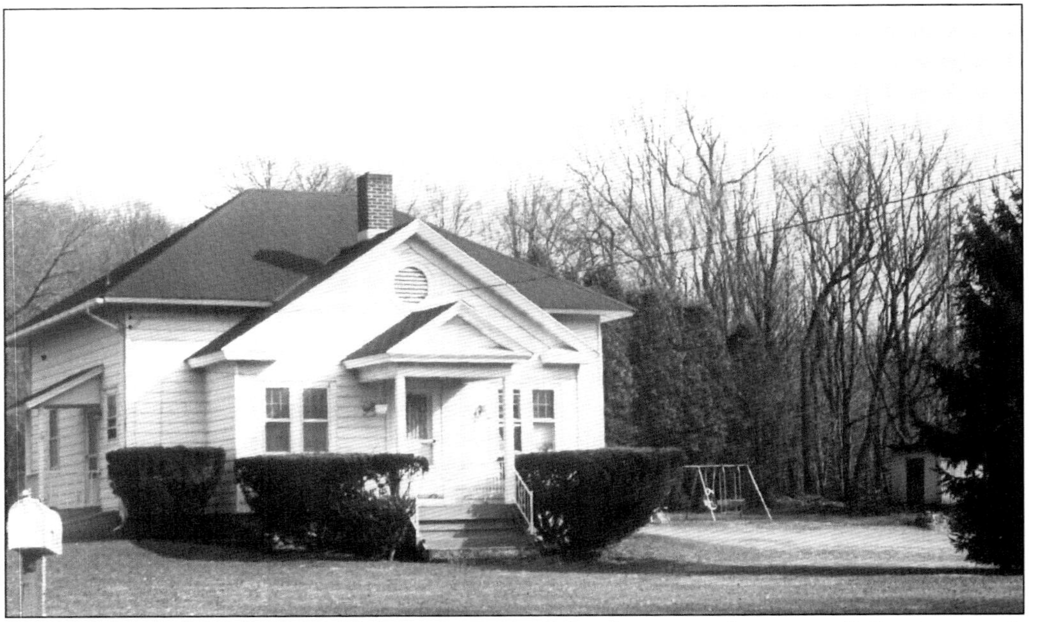

Maple Grove School. (DCHS, JG.) Maple Grove School was one of many small district schools that dotted the landscape. Located on Salt Point Turnpike, its pupils came from the surrounding farms. However, by the end of the 1930s, the Hyde Park Central School District had been organized, and students from this area traveled to the new Violet Avenue School. The building pictured here became a residence.

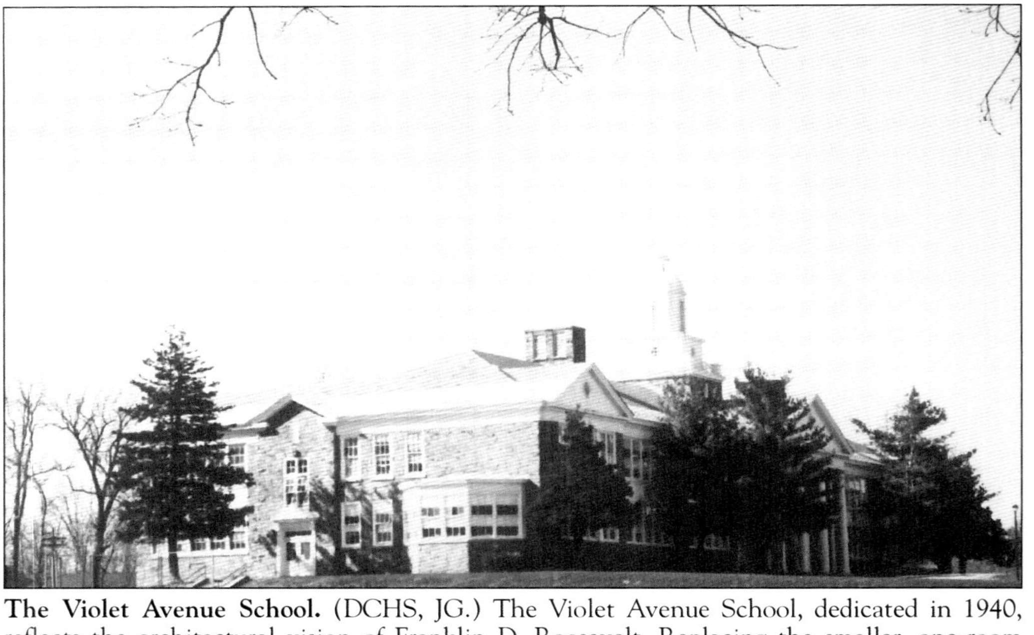

The Violet Avenue School. (DCHS, JG.) The Violet Avenue School, dedicated in 1940, reflects the architectural vision of Franklin D. Roosevelt. Replacing the smaller, one-room schools such as Viola, Fairview, and Maple Grove, the building was constructed of native stone. Its style was influenced by the American Colonial Revival architecture favored by the president. Its enrollment increased as the Fairview area continued to grow in population.

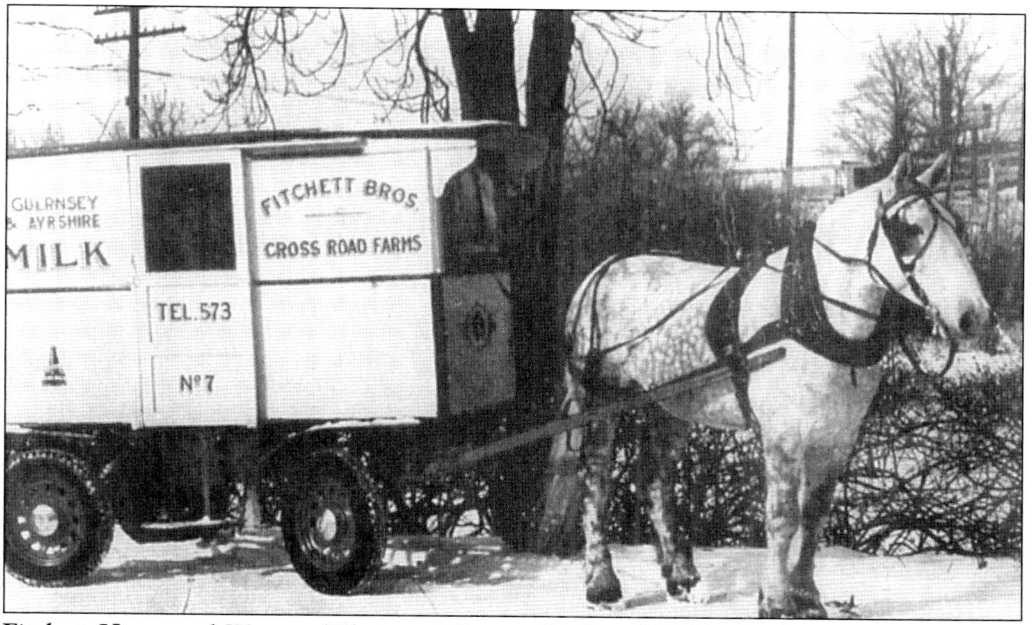

Fitchett Horse and Wagon. (Edwin and Bernice Fitchett [EBF].) This horse and wagon were used to deliver milk in the early days of the dairy that began operation in 1904. The Fitchetts grew the fodder for the cows, raised the livestock, milked them, bottled the milk, and delivered it. By 1944 the farm had 350 acres and a herd of two hundred cows. A processing plant by the railroad was acquired in 1926 to eliminate the bottling of the milk by hand. The milk was sold at retail.

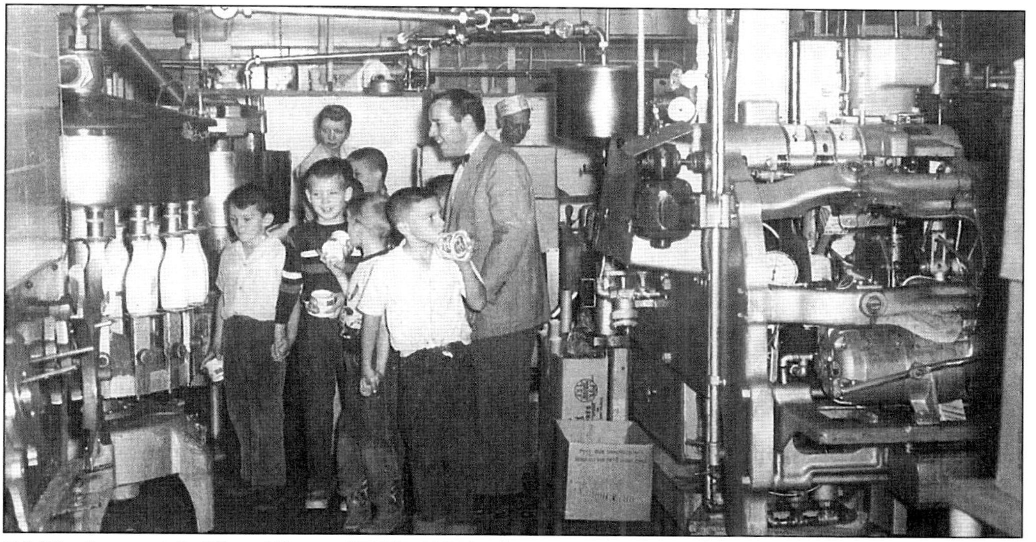

Ed Fitchett with New Plant. (EBF.) Ed Fitchett, an occasional volunteer magician, is seen here practicing another version of his "magic act" for schoolchildren visiting the new plant, which replaced the original plant after it burned in 1943. Fitchett's Dairy was a very popular destination for school field trips and the business continued until 1987. However, as early as 1944, Governor Dewey, while visiting the Fitchett Brothers farm, had predicted with some foresight "more difficult times ahead for farming and farmers."

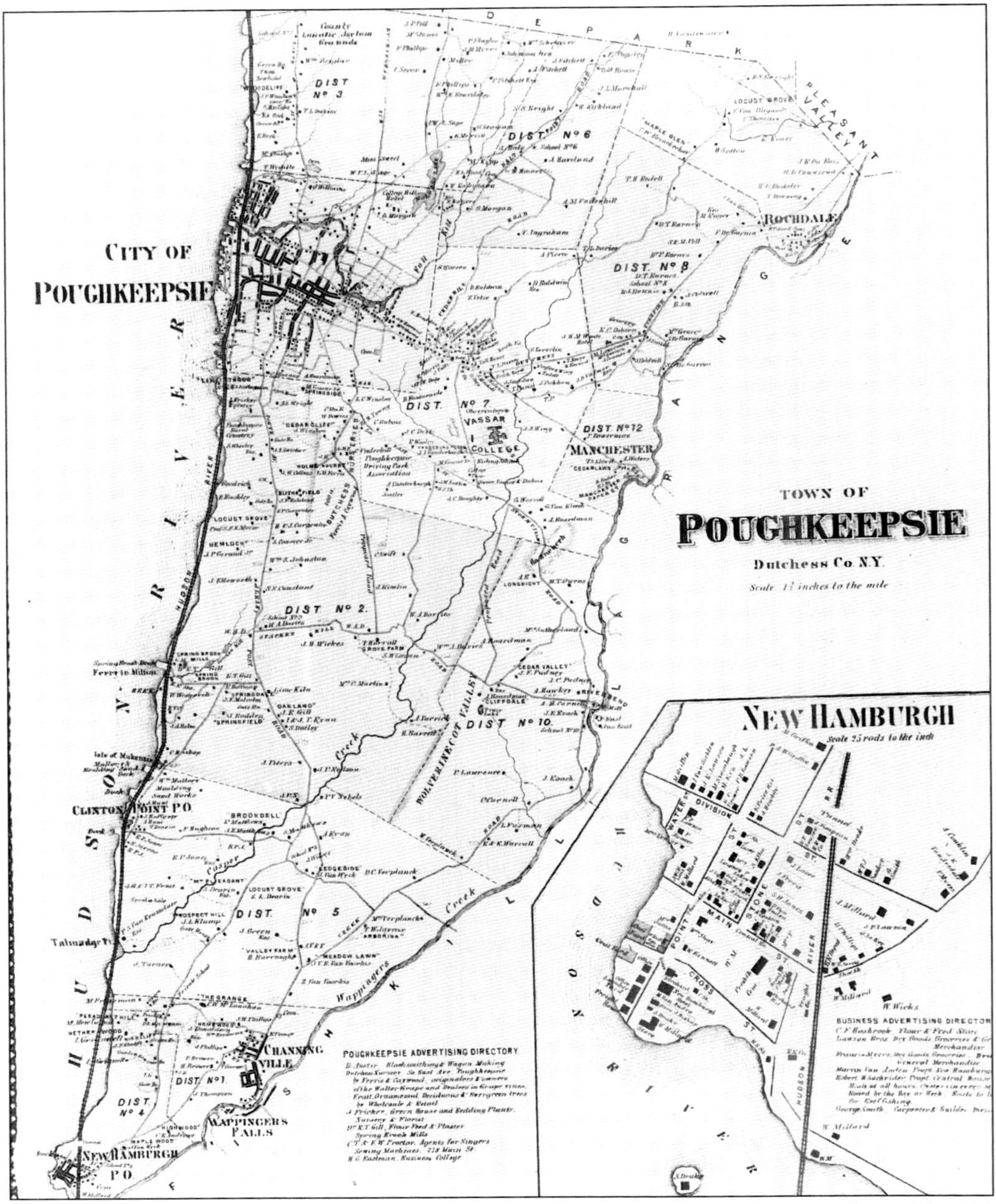

A Map Dated 1868. (Bowdoin Park Historical and Archaeological Association [BPHA], PK.) Emerging growth patterns in the city and town are clearly related to improved transportation corridors. The railroad spurred growth in New Hamburgh, Clinton Point, and the city. Milling operations on both sides of the Wappinger Creek turned Channingville into a busy hamlet. New estate entrances lined Albany Post Road, but the interior farmlands remained relatively unpopulated. Free school districts were delineated throughout the town.

Four

Outlining a Town and City to the South

The area of Poughkeepsie that lies south of the city was for many generations the least populated. River frontage by way of "water lots" was prized by colonial patentees as the key to fortune when the Hudson was the main transportation artery. Indeed, all early settlements were water-related. The Wappinger, Spackenkill and Casparkill Creeks were valued as sources of waterpower and occasional small boat ports. The siting of mills, landings, and ferry points to Orange and Ulster created communities such as New Hamburgh and Channingville and defined the easterly direction of the internal road system connecting inland farms and mills to the river.

The vast landholdings of the first families between public points barred most residents from the river, and in the nineteenth century large estates flourished along it. On the south side of the city, handsome residences were built as woodlands gave way to houses. Small clusters of development around business and industry grew along King's Highway/Albany Post Road on its circuitous northerly course roughly parallel to the river. The various rail and trolley lines after 1849 made interior travel easier, but it was the Hudson River Railroad that was the key feature of nineteenth-century development. After 1900 the automobile slowly began to replace horses and wagons, but little change was seen in the rural nature and slow pace of growth in this area until World War II and the coming of IBM. Then change was rapid and world-shaking.

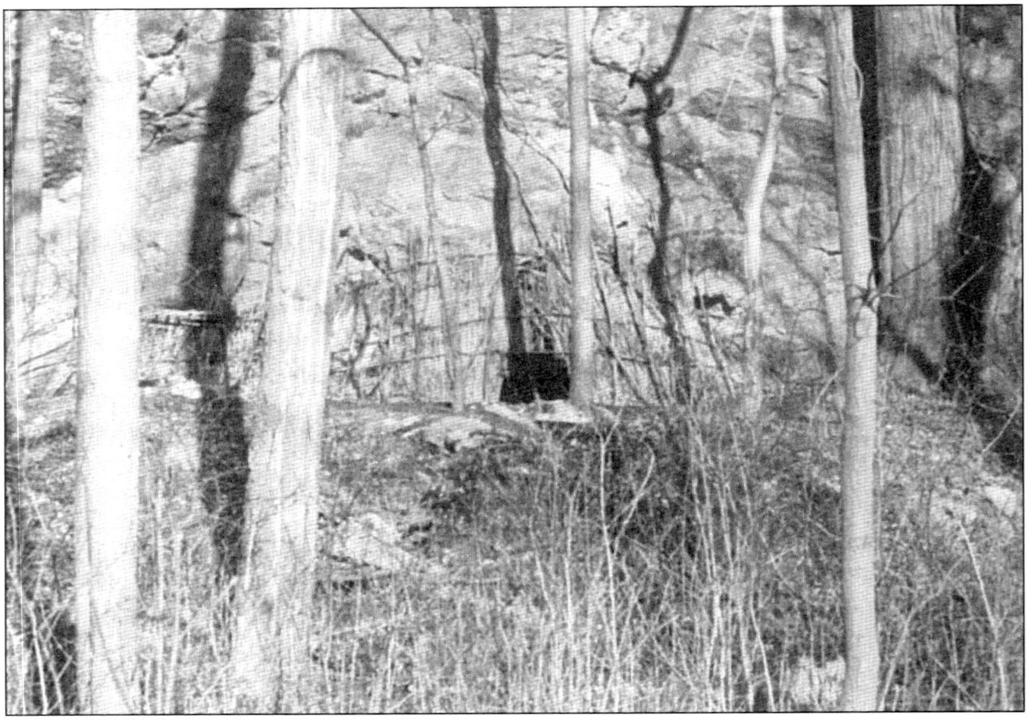

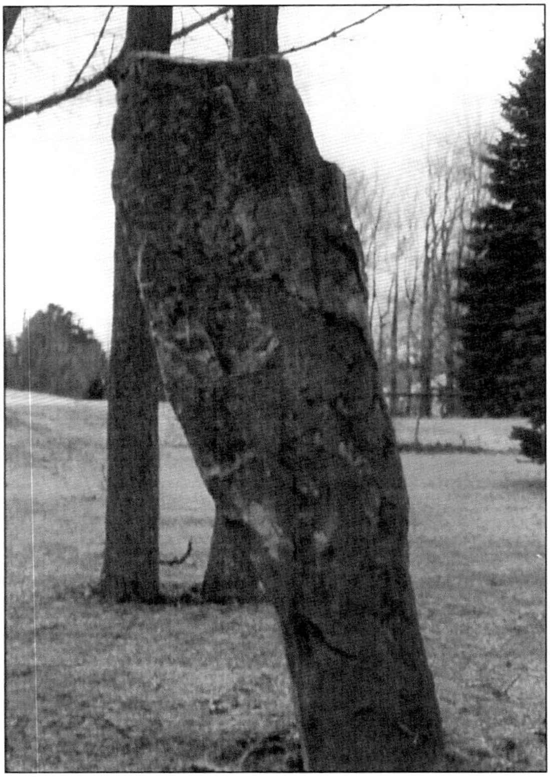

Rockledge Shelter. (BPHA.) This is one of several caves in the present Bowdoin Park that were used by the native peoples before the arrival of Dutch and English settlers. Archeological studies have documented the presence of prehistoric native peoples at least ten thousand years ago. Easily accessible from the Hudson River, the caves provided shelter and an unobstructed view of intruders.

The Standing Stone. (DCHS, JG.) This rectangular slab of limestone has been standing in the southern part of Poughkeepsie since before recorded history. Its base shows that it was shaped and that it is not the result of natural weathering. Visually similar to isolated standing stones (menhirs) found in Europe, theories about its significance range from its being part of pre-Christian fertility rites and/or other ceremonial activities to serving as a prehistoric road sign.

Wappinger Creek, 1905. (DCHS, Margaret DeMott Brown.) The Wappinger Creek has been the eastern and southern border of Poughkeepsie since the earliest patents. It flows through Wappinger Lake and divides the village of Wappingers Falls into the part which is in the town of Wappinger and the part once called Channingville in the town of Poughkeepsie. At its mouth, New Hamburgh (the "Hoek") became a thriving community.

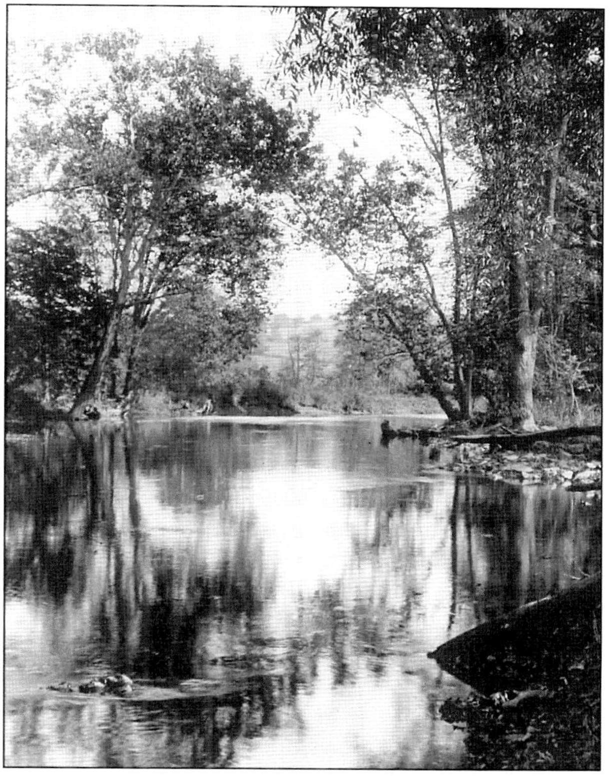

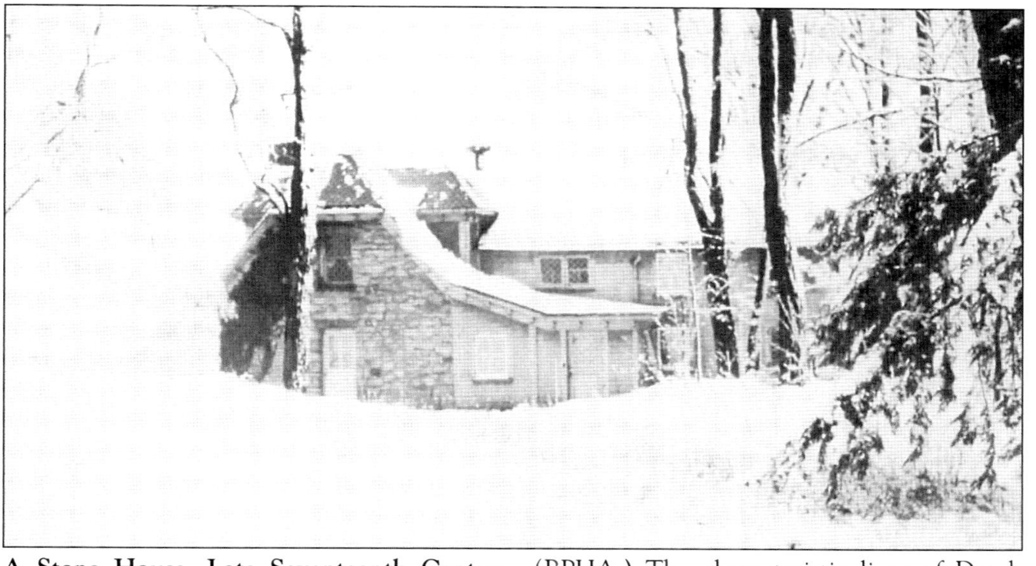

A Stone House, Late Seventeenth Century. (BPHA.) The characteristic lines of Dutch vernacular architecture are seen in this stone house which may date from the time of Peter Lassen, Dutchess County's first documented settler. Having arrived in Albany from Amsterdam in 1659, he was living on land above the "Hoek" (New Hamburgh) by 1688. After some dispute about the property title, Lassen was granted a patent in 1704 and established a homestead in the area which is now the site of the Tri-Municipal Sewer Plant.

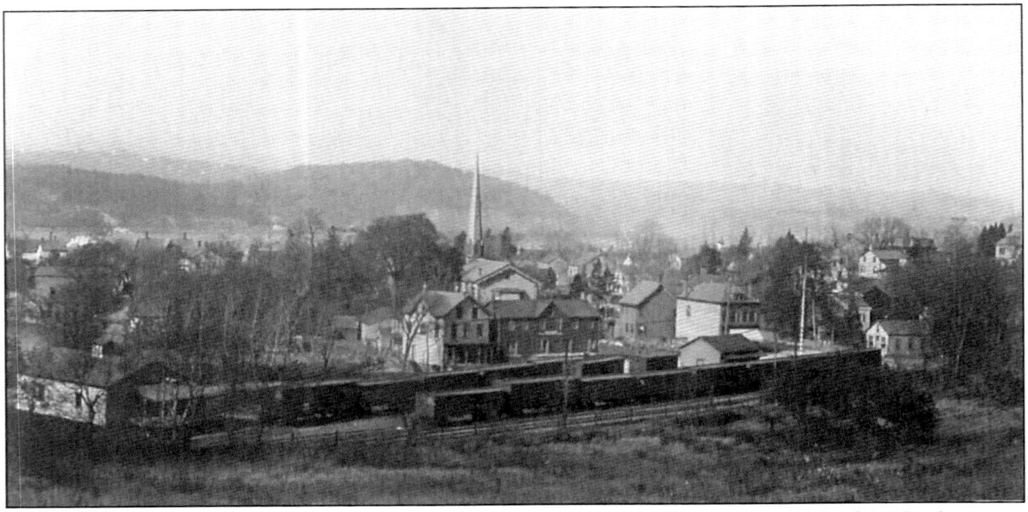

A View of New Hamburgh, Turn of the Century. (Janice A. Hilderbrand [JH].) The location of New Hamburgh at the mouth of the Wappinger Creek where it flows into the Hudson River contributed to its becoming a busy river port in the mid-1800s. It was also an early ferry site and a freight and passenger port, transporting the product of nearby lime kilns across the river. With the coming of the railroad, it became the station stop that served the towns to the east.

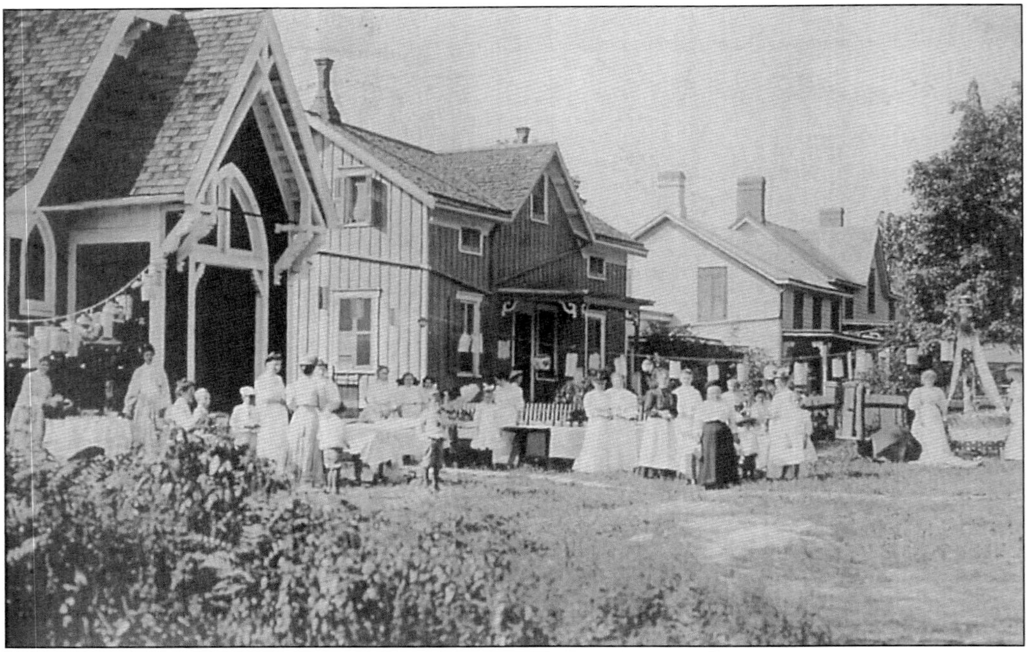

Zion Memorial Chapel (St. Nicholas-on-the-Hudson), Turn of the Century. (JH.) Zion Memorial Chapel, a Victorian Gothic style church built in 1902, was the scene of a gathering of ladies before World War I. The church was designed by Edward Lansing Satterlee, a relative of the rector of the chapel's parent church in Wappingers Falls as well as of the philanthropist who provided the major portion of the construction funds.

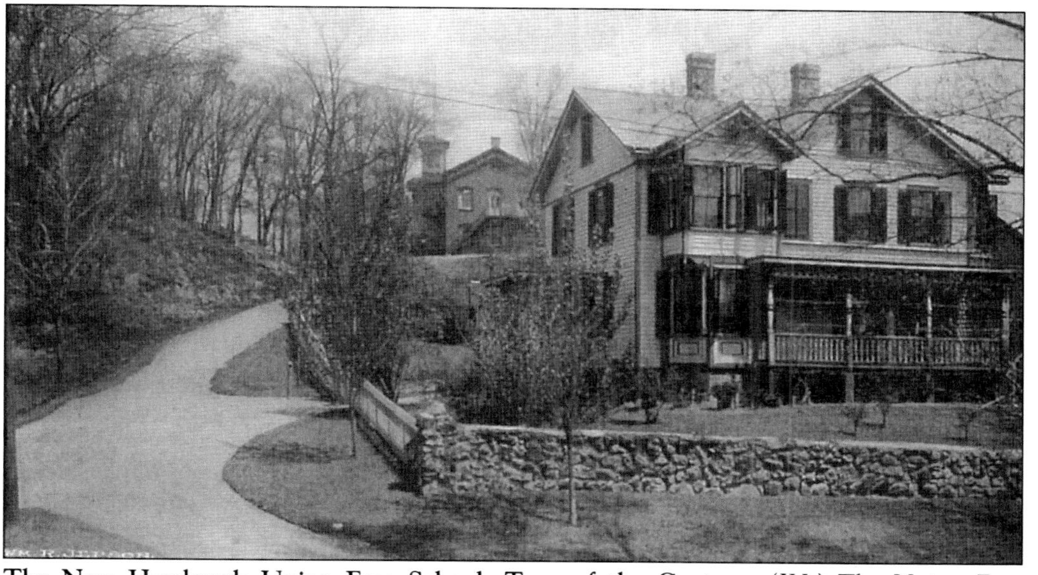

The New Hamburgh Union Free School, Turn of the Century. (JH.) The Union Free School in New Hamburgh was located on a hill overlooking the hamlet and the Hudson River. Built *c.* 1875 it is an example of late-nineteenth-century Italianate-style village schoolhouse design in the region. Its prominence and fine architecture signal the commitment of this small community to education.

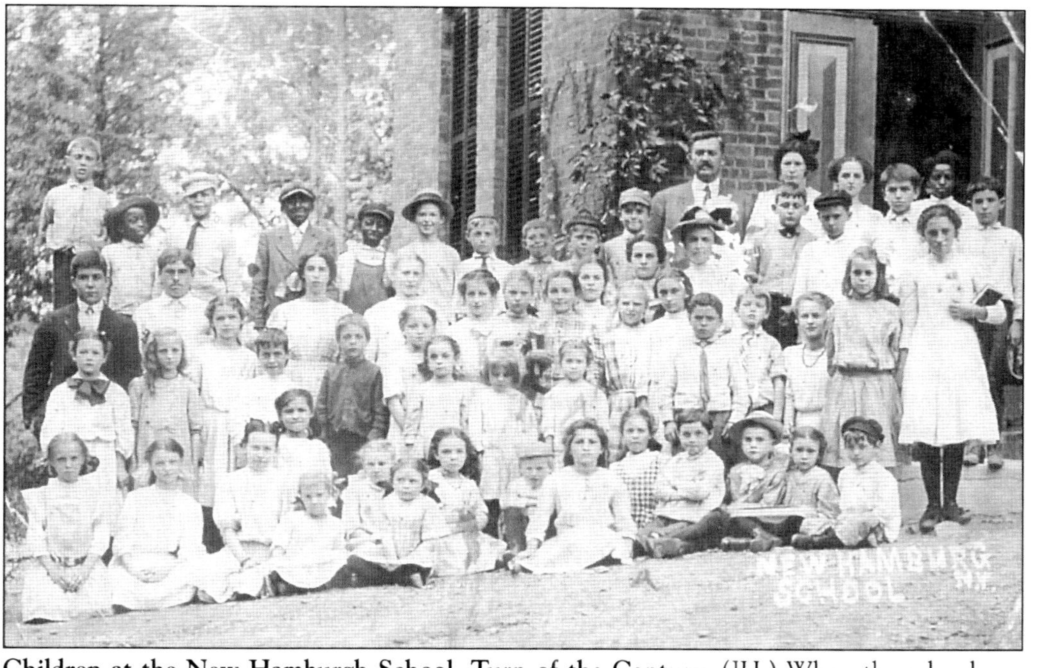

Children at the New Hamburgh School, Turn of the Century. (JH.) When the school was built in 1875, it was the hamlet's only public building, and reflected the growing prosperity of the community. At that time it was the only free school in the town of Poughkeepsie that was locally controlled with its own independent school board. Janice A. Hilderbrand's grandmother is in the front row wearing the checked dress.

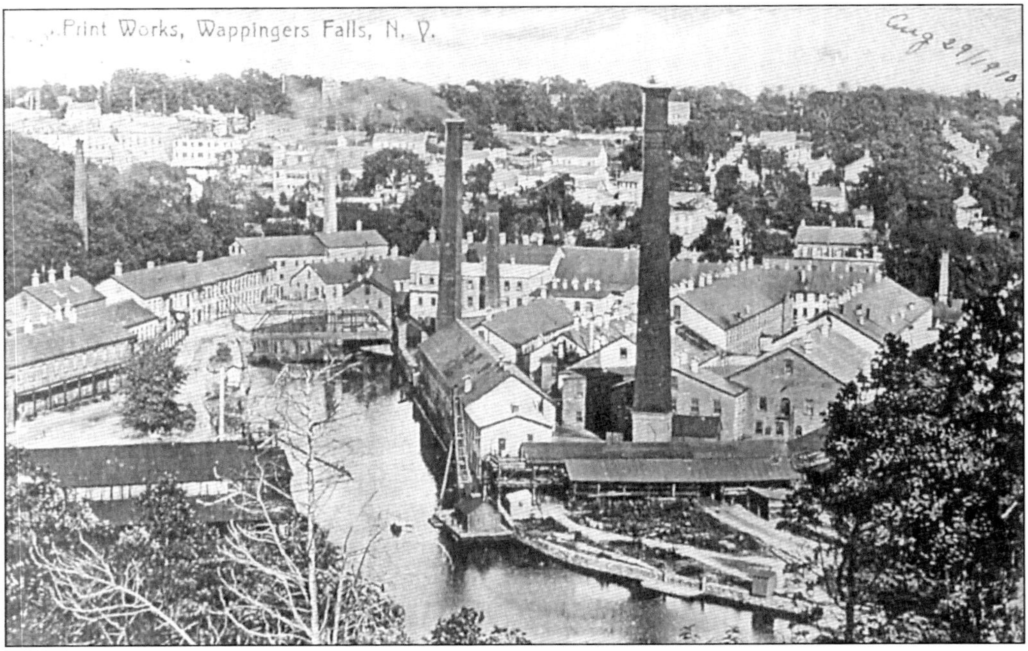

Print Works in Channingville, Turn of the Century. (JH.) The Print Works was located in Channingville, the western part of the village of Wappingers Falls that is in the town of Poughkeepsie. The village's name is derived from the fact that it was laid out on land once owned by Walter Channing of Newport. A thriving community strategically located on the Wappinger Creek, it was the site of a number of manufacturing concerns such as the Print Works.

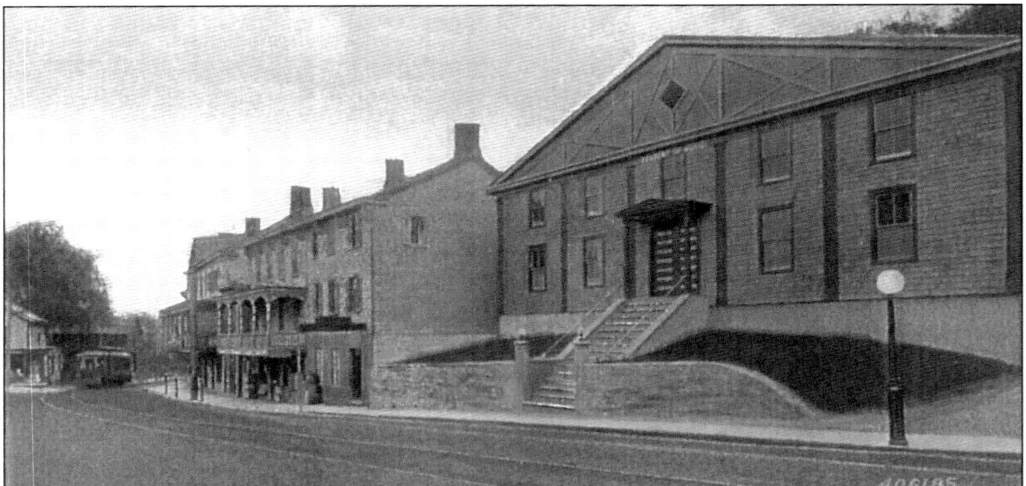

The Academy of Music, Channingville, Turn of the Century. (JH.) People gathered at the Academy of Music in Channingville for various entertainments. Later it was altered to become a movie house, but today County Players continue the theatrical tradition. The trolley tracks in the foreground show that the theater was easily accessible by the trolley lines, which were extended *c.* 1895 to Wappingers under the leadership of James W. Hinkley. At the same time electricity also arrived.

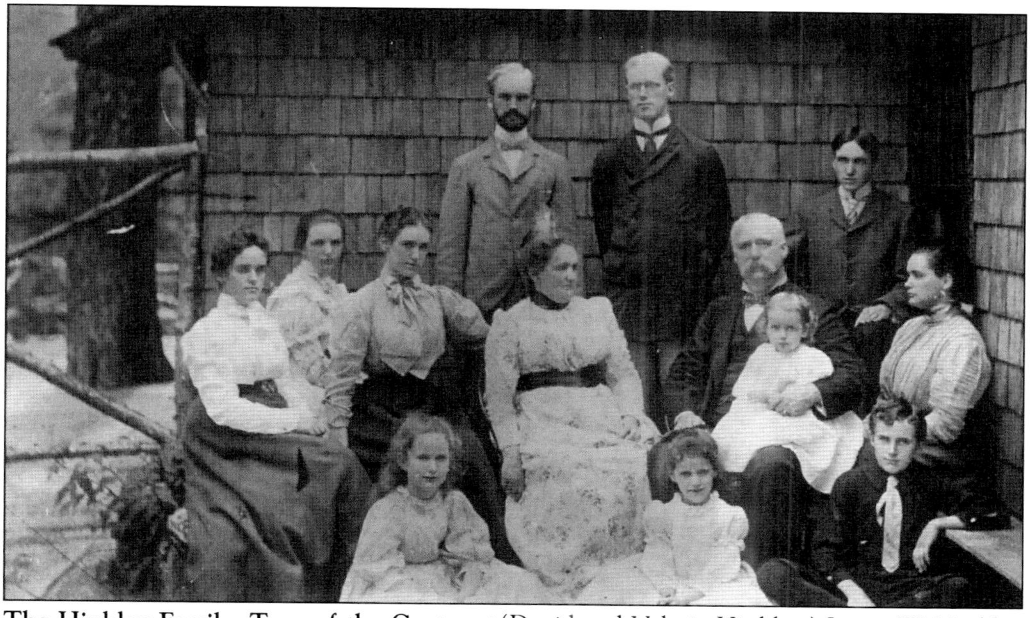

The Hinkley Family, Turn of the Century. (David and Valerie Hinkley.) James W. Hinkley and his family (Rhoda, Barbara, Edward, Anne, Josephine, Jane, Mary Margaret, baby Priscilla, Mary, Silas, "Will," and John) contributed in many ways to community life. Hinkley acquired and consolidated several newspapers. He also bought the city railroad and obtained franchises to build the north and south loops as well as the electrified trolley line to Wappingers Falls. An active Democrat, Hinkley served as chairman of the Democratic State Committee.

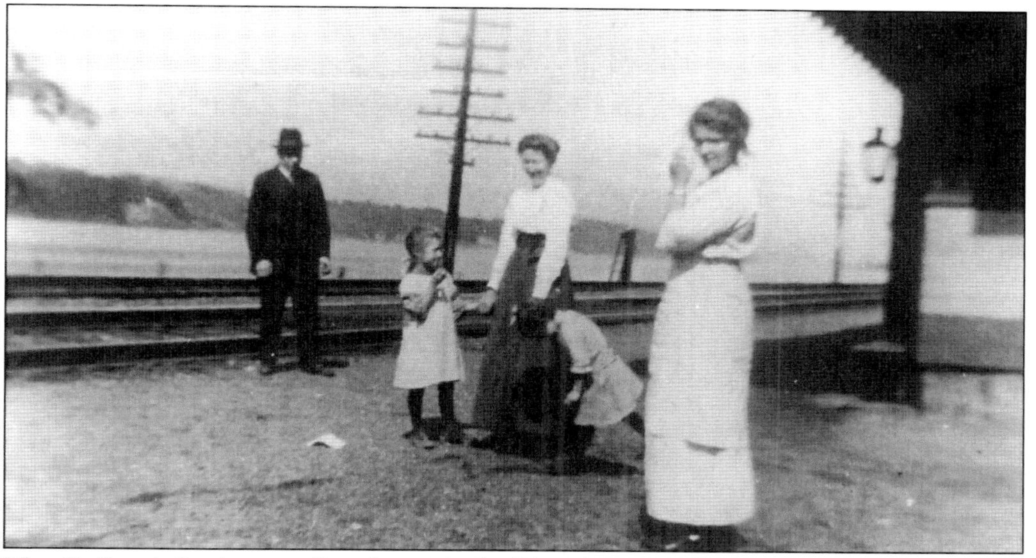

The Railroad Station at Camelot, 1915. (Timothy P. Holls [TPH].) Halfway between Poughkeepsie and New Hamburgh on the New York Central Railroad was Camelot, which was at the end of present-day IBM Road. Originally known as Milton Ferry, it was renamed by the president of the railroad in 1886 to avoid confusion with Milton across the river. The station itself was moved south to the end of today's Camelot Road about the turn of the century. The station master, A. Hyde, is shown here with his family.

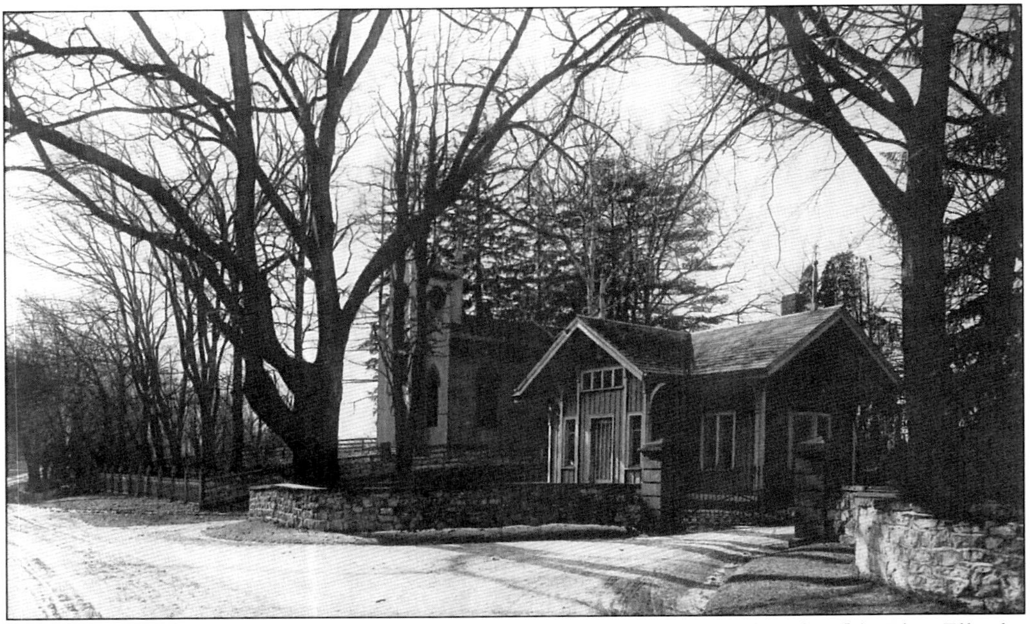

Ellesdie Chapel, pre-1903. (Lawrence Majewski/Dewey Owens [LM/DO].) The Ellesdie Presbyterian Chapel is seen here in its original setting among the trees next to the gatehouse of The Cedars estate. Built in 1844 by James Lenox who objected to hitching his horses on Sunday to drive to a more distant church, it is named Ellesdie after the families owning neighboring estates—L for Lenox, S for Sheafe, and D for Donaldson.

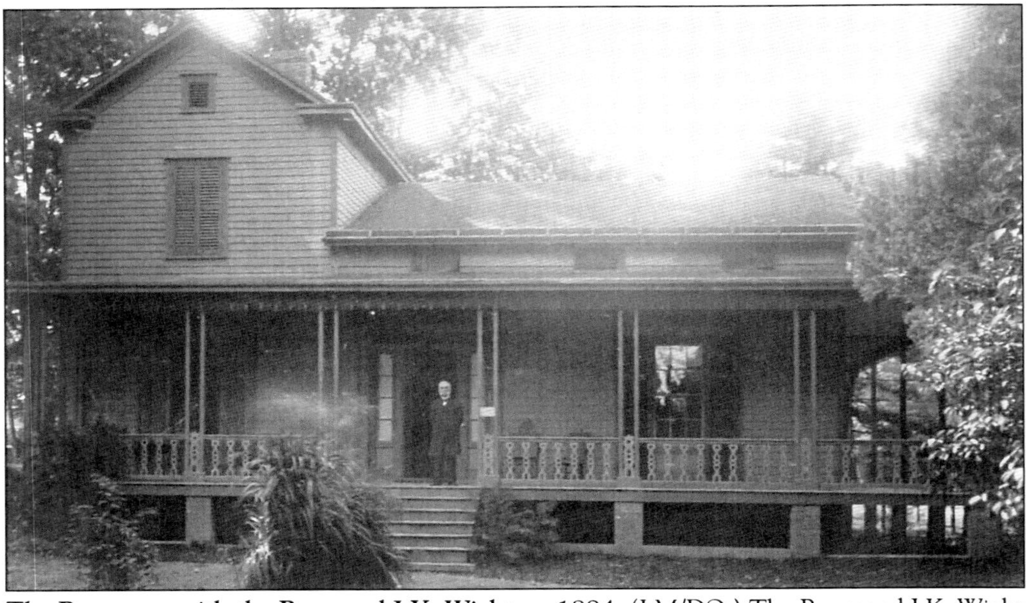

The Parsonage with the Reverend J.K. Wight, c. 1884. (LM/DO.) The Reverend J.K. Wight came from a mission in China to be pastor at the Ellesdie Chapel in 1859. The chapel was removed to the New Hackensack Reformed Church in the early twentieth century and used as a Sunday school. Wight's daughter, Julia, the youngest of eighteen children, used the house until 1959, a few years before her death at age ninety-two.

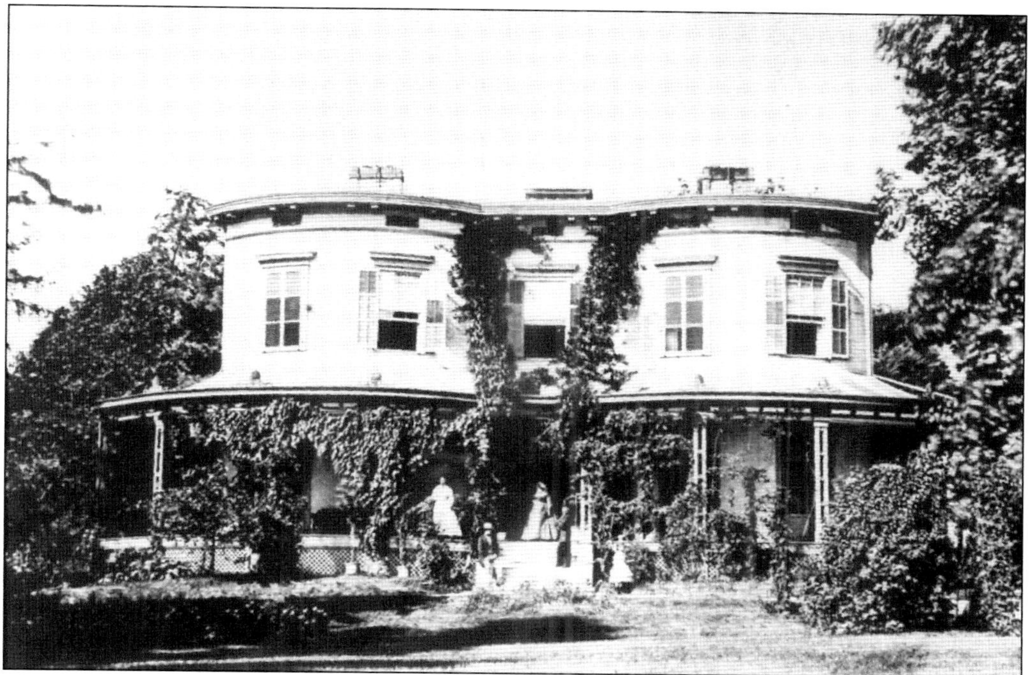

Sheafe House, pre-1872. (BPHA.) Mr. and Mrs. Sheafe are on the porch of High Cliff in this photograph taken by S.F.B. Morse, an acquaintance who owned Locust Grove, an estate to the north. Morse had helped to perfect daguerreotypes and experimented with the first cameras. The Sheafes were generous to the nearby communities of Wappingers Falls and New Hamburgh.

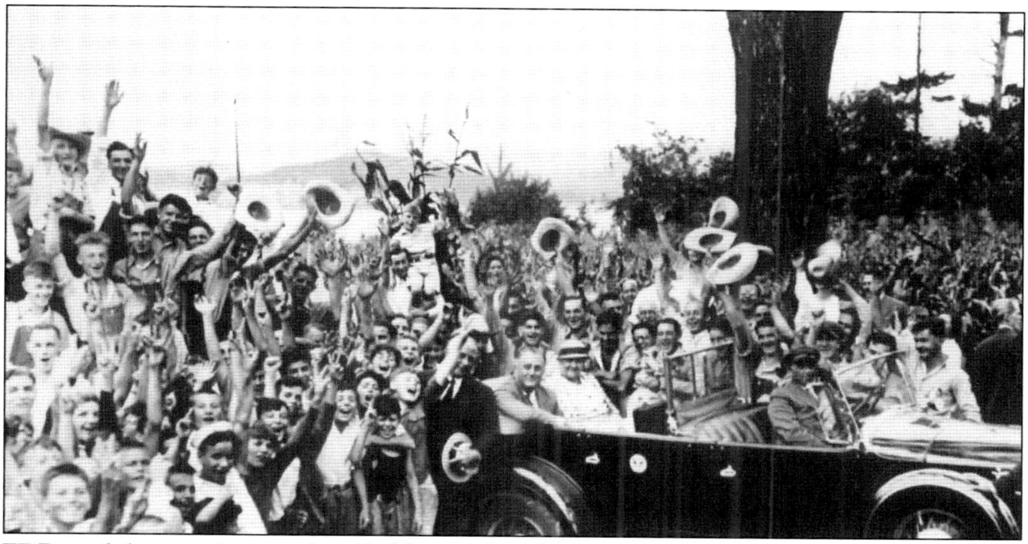

FDR and his mother at the Children's Aid Society, 1930s. (BPHA.) Franklin Delano Roosevelt and his mother are seen on a visit to the Children's Aid Society camp, which owned the area of what is now Bowdoin Park from 1928 to 1975. Eleanor Roosevelt's grandfather had served as a trustee of the Children's Aid Society for many years. Once again, as had happened to the north of the city of Poughkeepsie, an institution had replaced private estate owners.

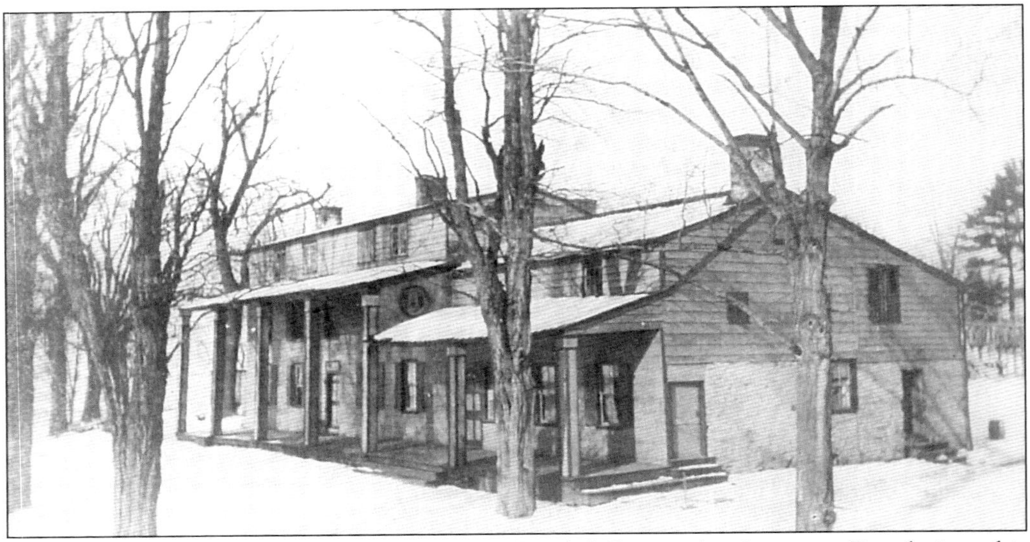

The Livingston House, 1886. (AML, Henry Booth.) During the American Revolution, this house on the Hudson River owned by Henry Livingston was struck by a shot from British ships. His son, Henry Livingston Jr., was a man of considerable wit and charm, said by some to be the author of *A Visit from St. Nicholas*. He and his wife planted the black locusts that gave Locust Grove its name, and in 1809 he gave a 60-foot-wide strip extending the whole length of the farm to be used as part of a new turnpike, now Route 9.

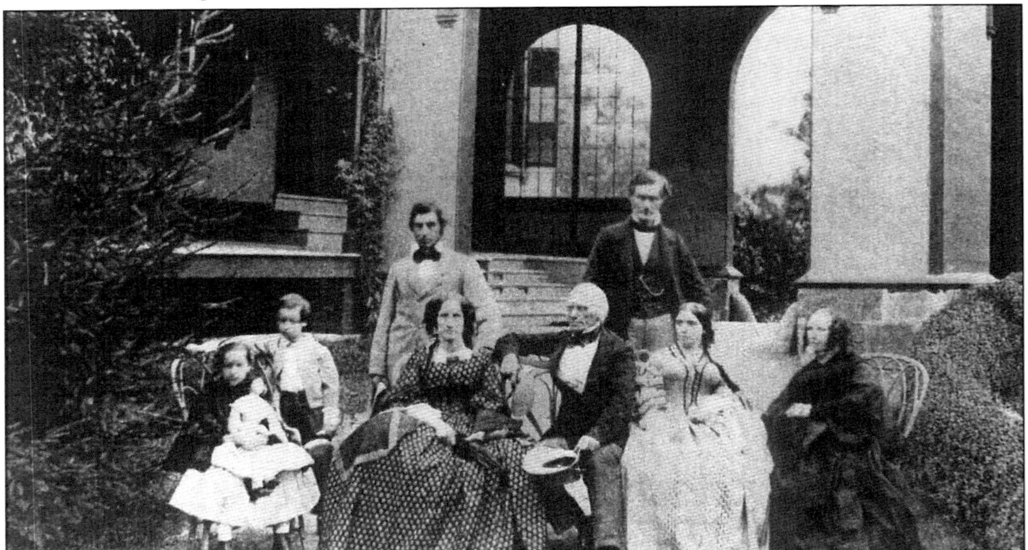

Locust Grove with S.F.B. Morse and Family, c. 1860. (Samuel F.B. Morse Historic Site [SFBMHS].) In 1847, S.F.B. Morse bought Locust Grove, the site of various Livingston houses. He noted then that the imminent coming of the railroad would "bring New York within two hours of us." In conjunction with the architect Alexander Jackson Davis, he remodeled the house in the style of a Tuscan villa. He also had the grounds and gardens developed in the style of Andrew Jackson Downing, one of the most influential landscape architects of the nineteenth century. The property was later purchased by the Young family.

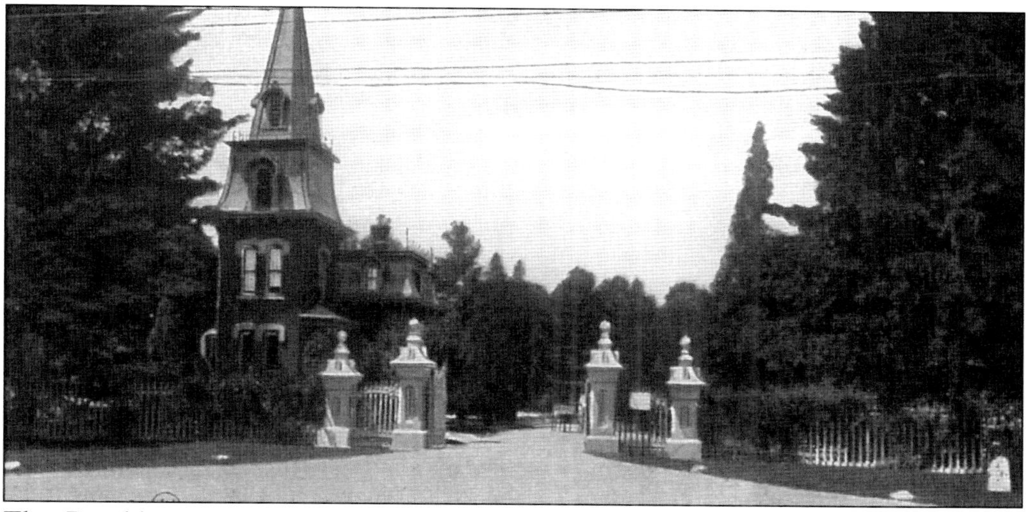

The Poughkeepsie Rural Cemetery. (DCHS.) The rural cemetery movement reached Poughkeepsie in 1851. Until then, churchyards usually served as cemeteries, but these were filling up and were being encircled by increasing development. Matthew Vassar acquired forty-four acres that had been part of the Allen Farm at Eden Hill with plans to use it as a cemetery or as an estate. In fact, the Cemetery Association founded in 1852 chose land across the highway from the Vassar property and the Poughkeepsie Rural Cemetery was dedicated in the following year.

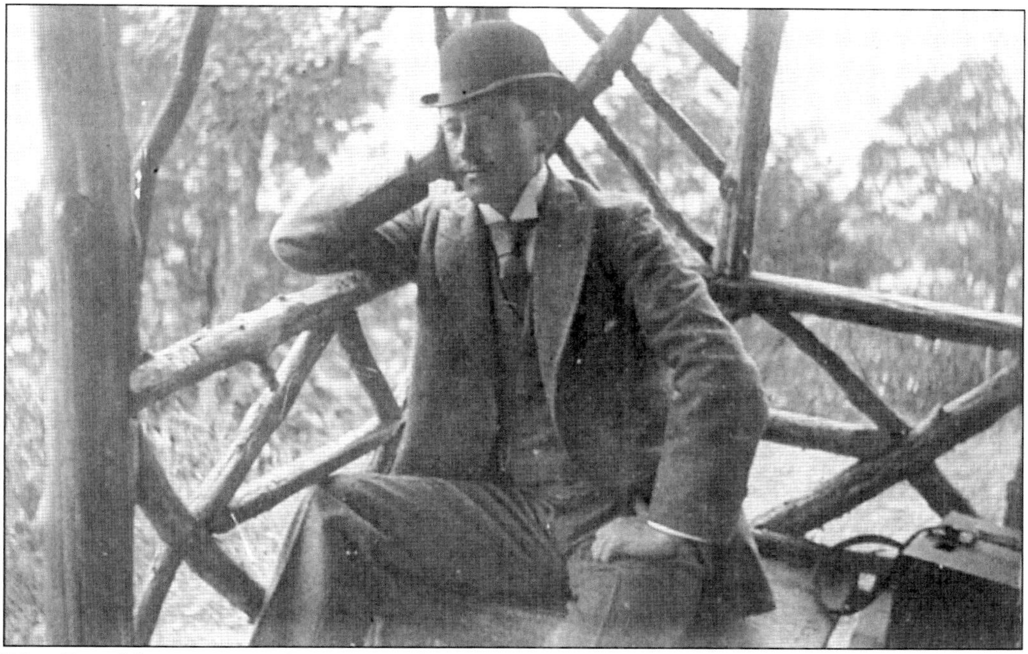

The Poughkeepsie Rural Cemetery/Lover's Leap, Late Nineteenth or Early Twentieth Century. (Norma Van Kleeck [NVK].) Barnard D. Van Kleeck is seated in the summer house at "Lover's Leap" in the cemetery. Legend has it that two Indian lovers jumped to their death there. Note the size of the camera beside Mr. Van Kleeck, who enjoyed taking photographs himself.

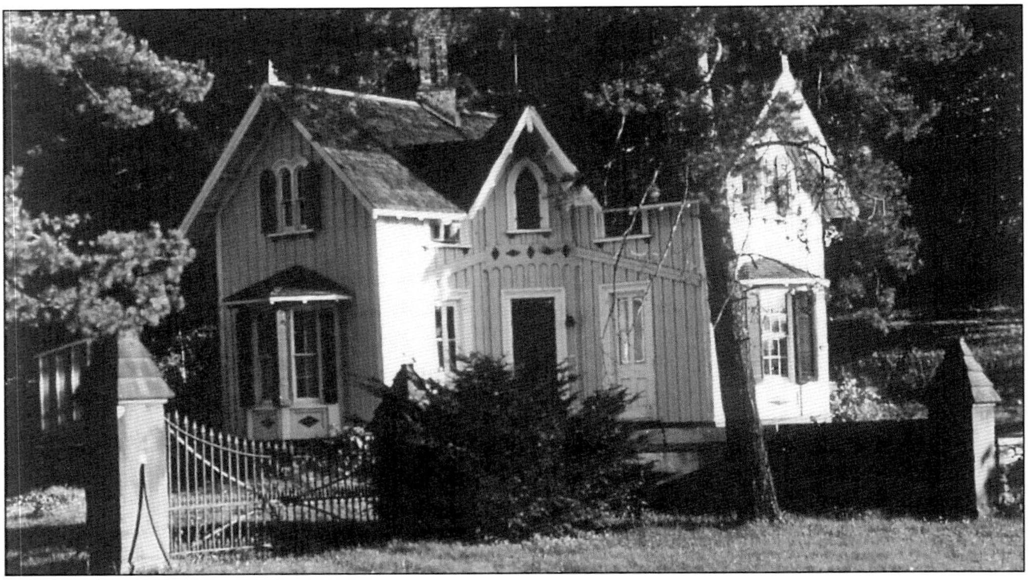

The Gatehouse at Springside. (Springside Landscape Restoration, Virginia Hancock.) Matthew Vassar hired Andrew Jackson Downing, the foremost landscape architect of the day, to design what became known as Springside. Before Downing's death in 1852, the gardener's cottage, the stable and carriage house, the porter's lodge, the roads, paths, ponds, and fountains had been built and hundreds of trees planted. Vassar opened the landscaped grounds to the public for their enjoyment, making Springside Poughkeepsie's first de facto public park.

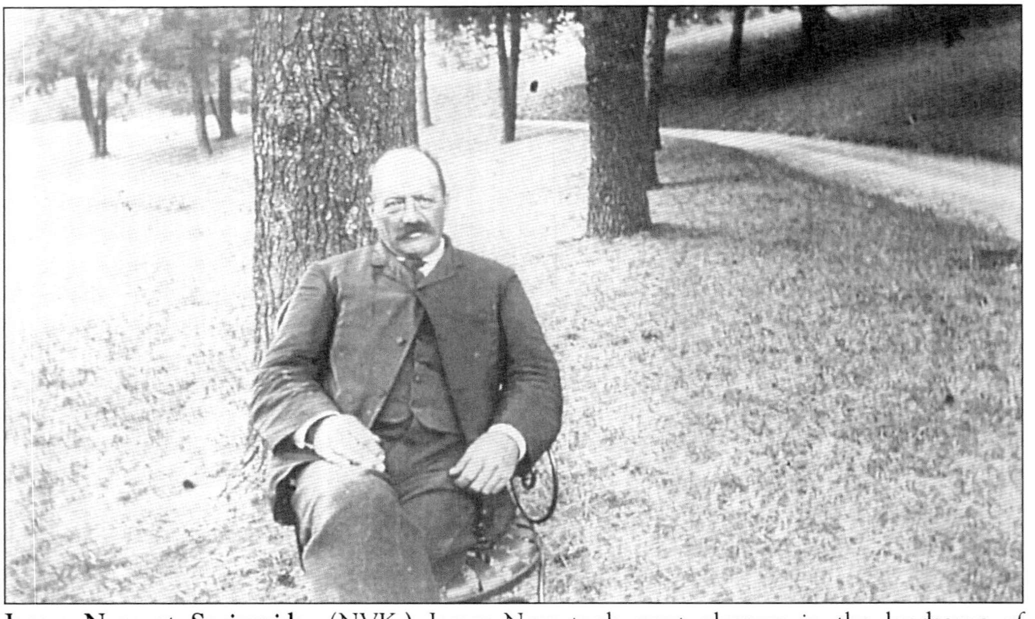

James Near at Springside. (NVK.) James Near took great pleasure in the landscape of Springside. Downing had designed the park-like grounds of the estate to illustrate his principles of the beautiful and of the picturesque. To him the beautiful consisted of flowing lines such as the gently curving path and mature trees, while picturesque qualities were to be found in rugged outcroppings and gnarled trees.

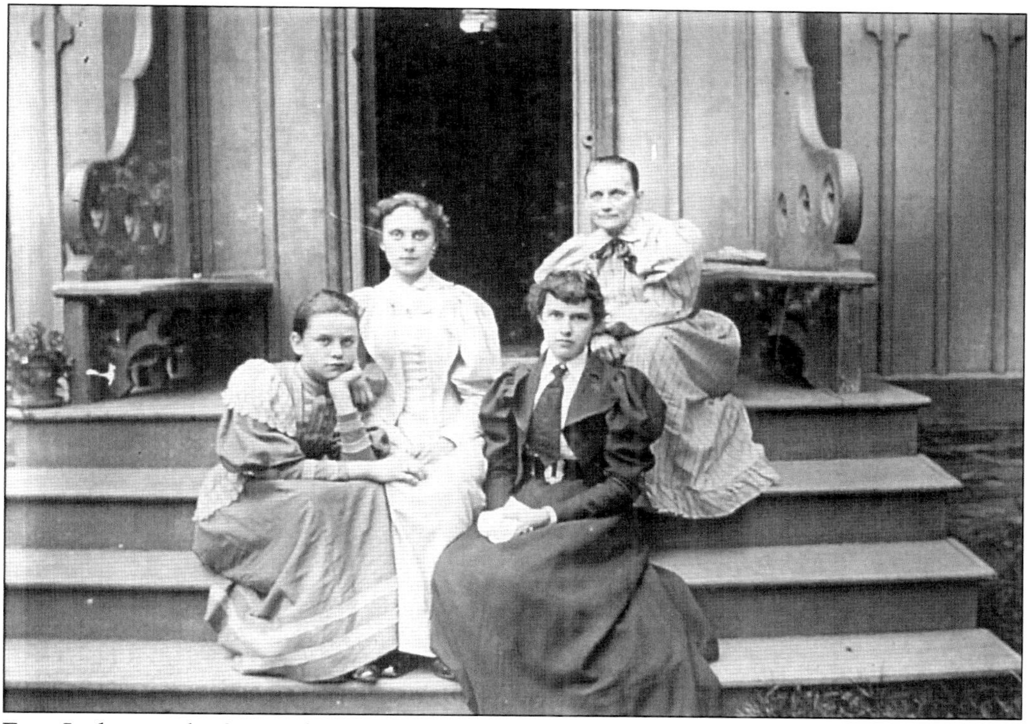

Four Ladies on the Steps of the Gardener's Cottage at Springside. (NVK.) Gathered on the front steps are Lotta R. Brown (later Mrs. Anthony), Florence C. Brown (later Mrs. Moore), Mary Near (Mrs. James Near), and Margaret Near (later Mrs. Van Kleeck). A main villa was never built, so Matthew Vassar used the gardener's cottage as his summer residence. It was among the very few examples of Downing's skill as an architect.

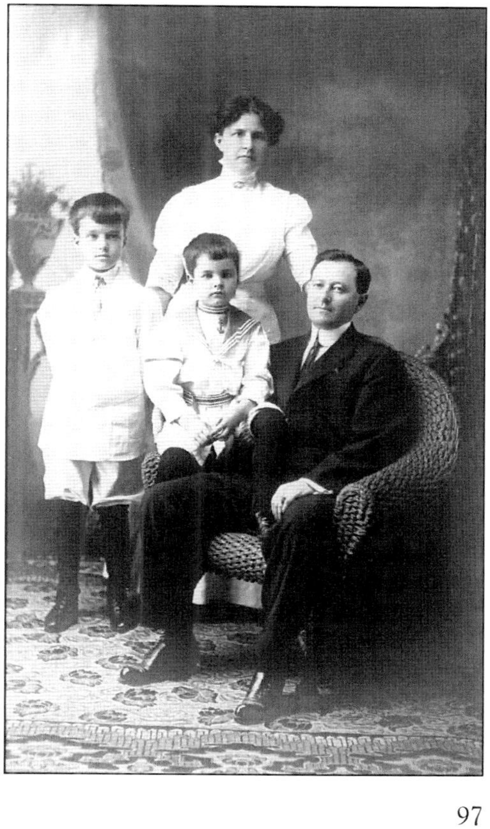

The Van Kleeck Family, c. 1910. (NVK.) This branch of the Van Kleeck family that had ties to Springside lived on the increasingly developed south side of the city at the time when lovely homes began to sprout up the length of Hooker Avenue. Shown here are Ralph, Dudley, Barnard D. (photographer at Lover's Leap), and Margaret (James Near's daughter.)

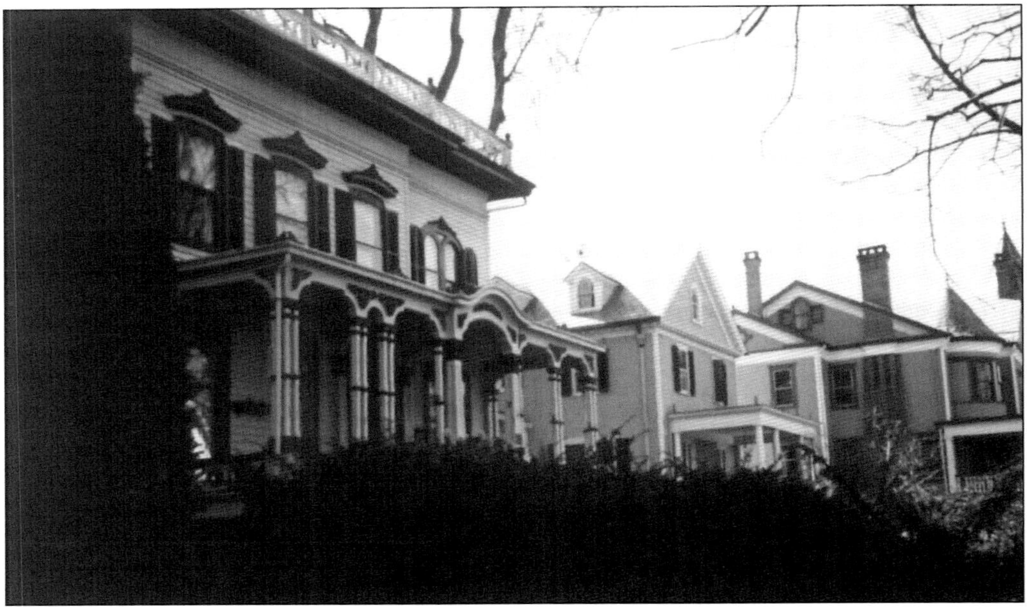

Garfield Place. (DCHS, JG.) Garfield Place illustrates the expansion of the village and later city of Poughkeepsie to the south. The first house on South Liberty Street (renamed Garfield Place in 1881 after the assassination of the president) was built in 1851 by George Corlies. Among the notable residents on the street have been Charles P. Luckey of Luckey Platt, Edward Storm, who installed the first residential water tap in 1872, and Milo Jewett, president of Vassar College.

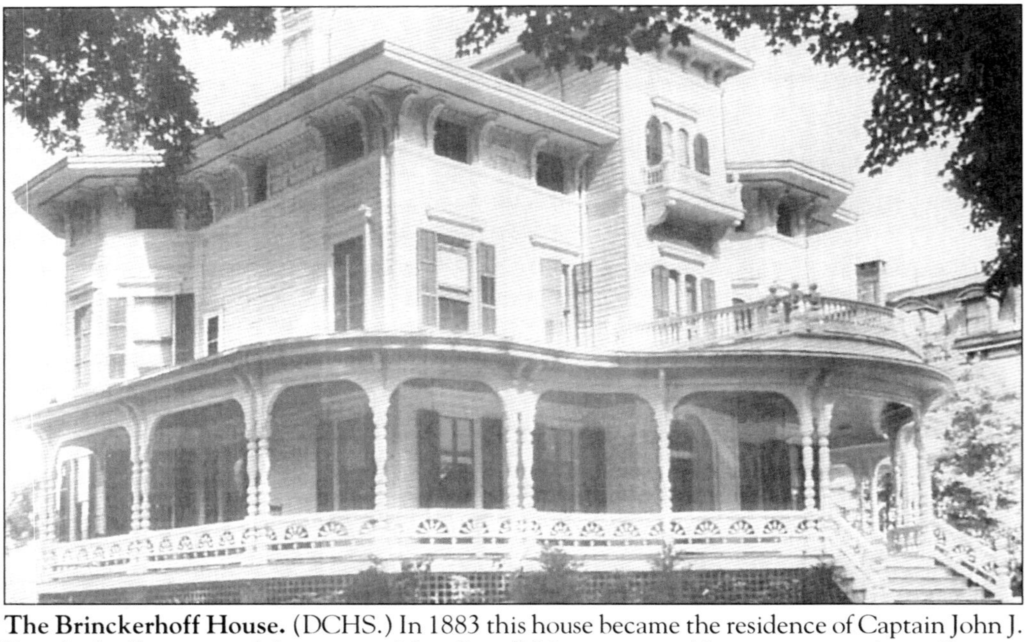

The Brinckerhoff House. (DCHS.) In 1883 this house became the residence of Captain John J. Brinckerhoff, captain of the steamer *Mary Powell*. Note its resemblance to a steamboat. Captain Brinckerhoff also had a large interest in the Poughkeepsie Transportation Company and owned dockage along the river.

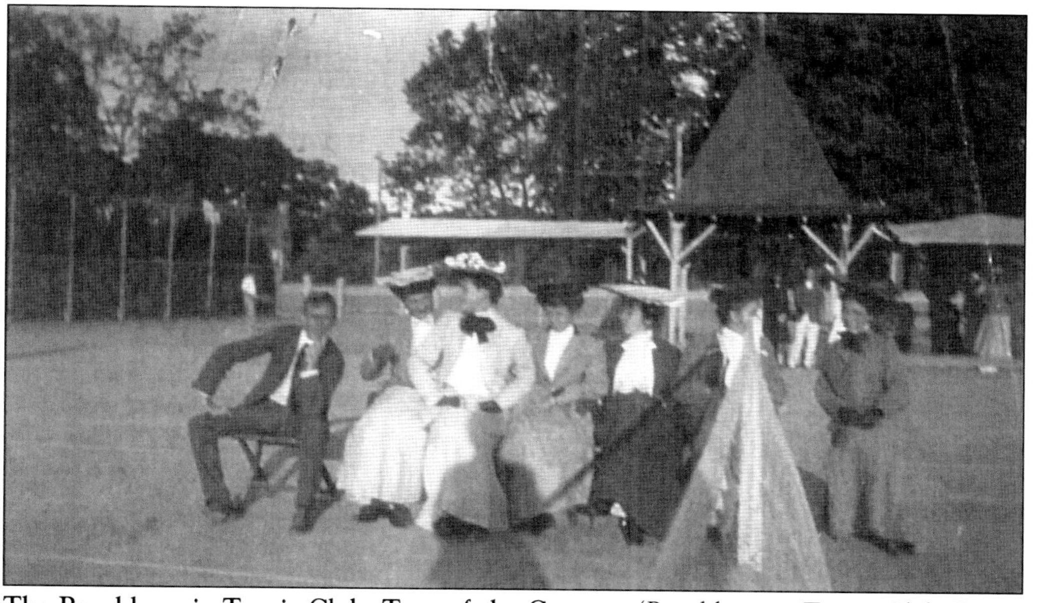

The Poughkeepsie Tennis Club, Turn of the Century. (Poughkeepsie Tennis Club, Rocco Staino.) The Poughkeepsie Tennis Club was organized in 1890, and the first club house was on a knoll on the corner of Dwight Street; however, this burned down in 1893. The club then purchased property on the corner of Hamilton Street and built its present clubhouse. Some spectators at early tennis games may have also played the gentle game of flirtation.

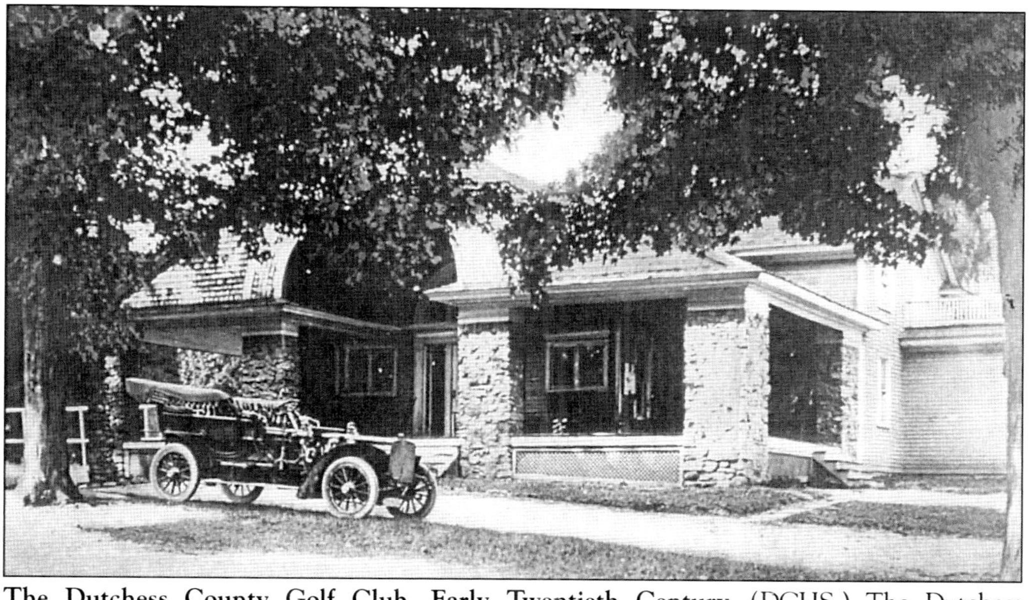

The Dutchess County Golf Club, Early Twentieth Century. (DCHS.) The Dutchess County Golf Club was organized in 1897. John E. Adriance, one of the donors of the Adriance Memorial Library, was its first president. In 1901 it was incorporated as The Dutchess County Golf and Country Club. Members enjoyed its beauty as they combined pleasure with perhaps some business (even in those days) while playing a leisurely game of golf.

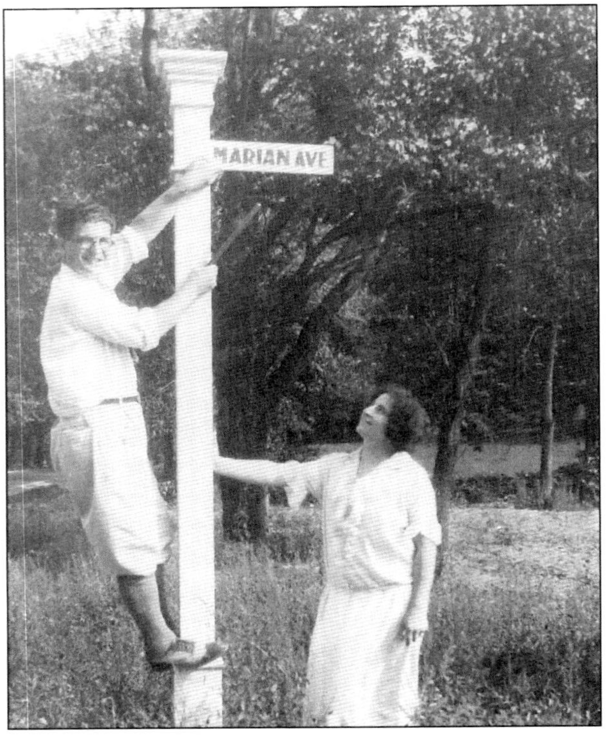

Marian Avenue, c. 1920s. (DCHS.) This photograph of John Marian and his wife is another illustration of the growth of the city to the south. Opposite Cherry Street on Hooker Avenue, Marian Avenue continued the trend exemplified by the development of the Whitehouse Farm and property on Whitehouse Avenue, Barnard Avenue (Howell Avenue), Crescent Road, Lockerman Avenue, and Adriance Avenue. A prominent real estate developer was James E. Sague, whose first wife was Clarence Kenyon's sister.

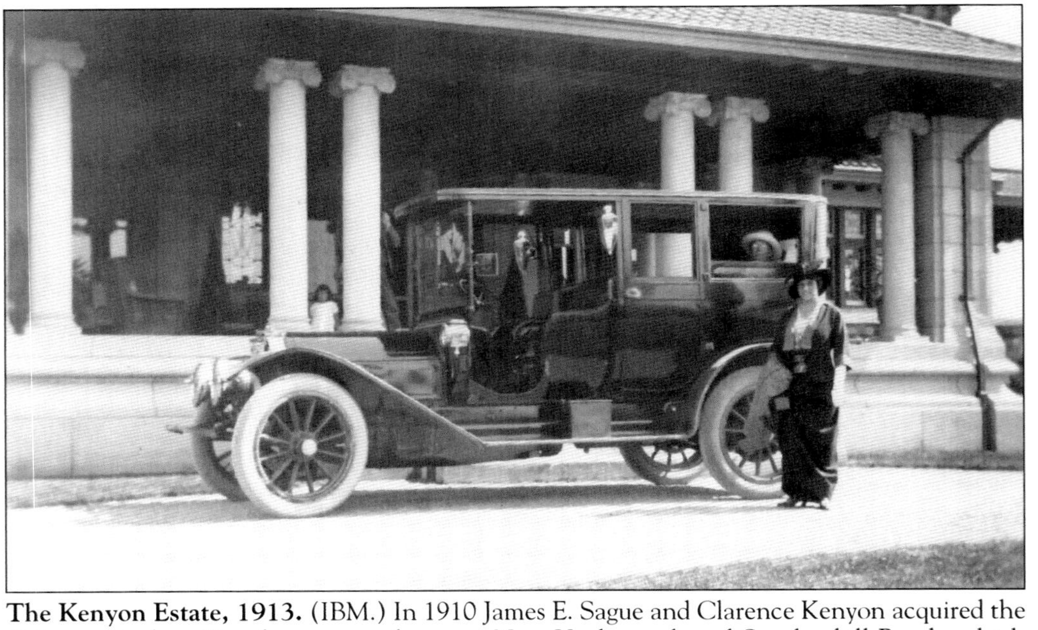

The Kenyon Estate, 1913. (IBM.) In 1910 James E. Sague and Clarence Kenyon acquired the 500-acre Andrew Boardman estate between New Hackensack and Spackenkill Roads, which they then divided. Mr. Kenyon, a successful Brooklyn businessman, came to live in Poughkeepsie in 1913 in this Mediterranean style structure designed by Percival M. Lloyd, who had also done the FIAT building. In 1944 the house was sold to IBM to use as a "modern research and engineering laboratory."

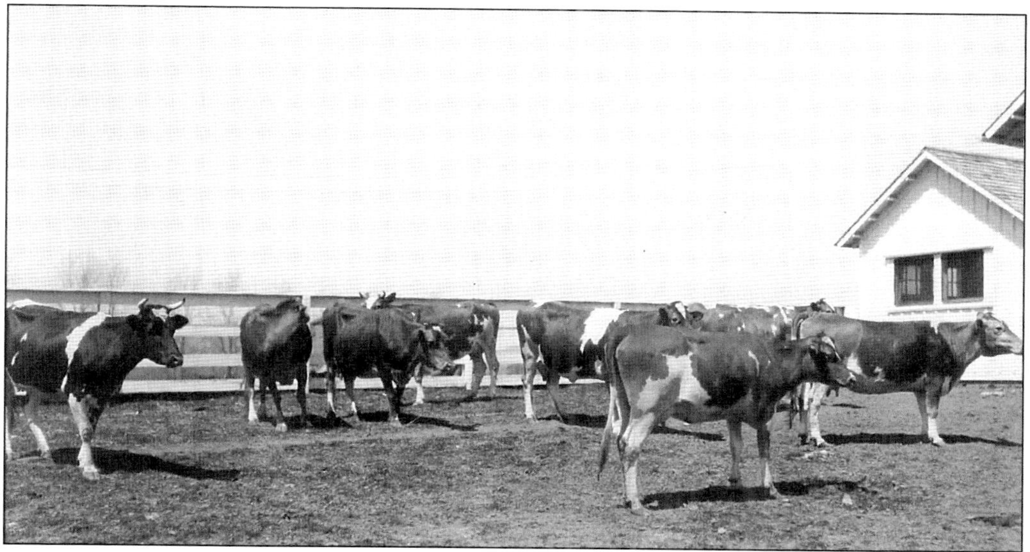

The Site of Oakwood Friends School. (Oakwood Friends School [OFS].) Cows continued to graze even after Oakwood Friends School had purchased the 75-acre Coleman farm at the junction of Route 9 and Spackenkill. Continuing its tradition as the City of Schools, Poughkeepsie had actively and successfully encouraged the school to relocate to Poughkeepsie after it suffered a fire at its Union Springs site in 1917. The school was started in Millbrook as the Nine Partners School.

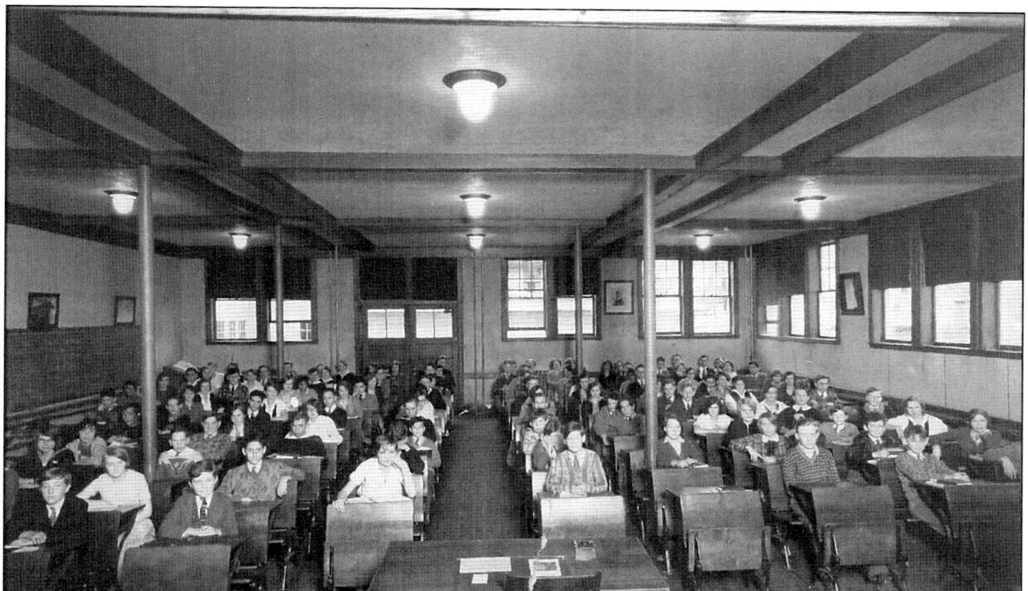

A class at Oakwood Friends School. (OFS.) Students at Oakwood Friends School are seen in the Meeting Room after the move to Poughkeepsie. The first co-educational boarding school in the country, it continued to have both boarding and day students. The educational mission of the school emphasizes the value of the individual, respect for the diversity of the group, a shared search for truth through the Friends Meeting for Worship, an opportunity for creative participation in the arts, and an emphasis on service to the larger community.

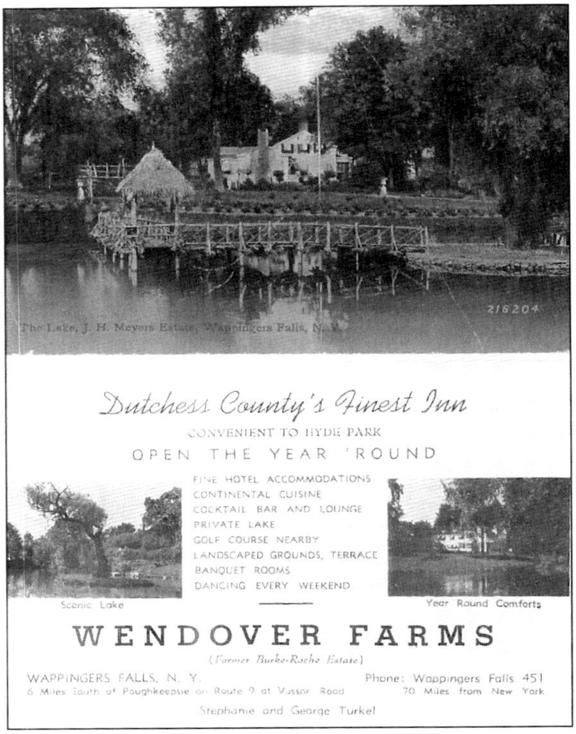

Wendover Farms. (TPH.) Farther south on Route 9 was Wendover Farms. Located on the corner of Route 9 and Vassar Road, it was a popular destination for families and couples from the 1930s to the early '50s. A beautifully landscaped farm with duck ponds and a gazebo, it was a delight to the eyes of passing motorists.

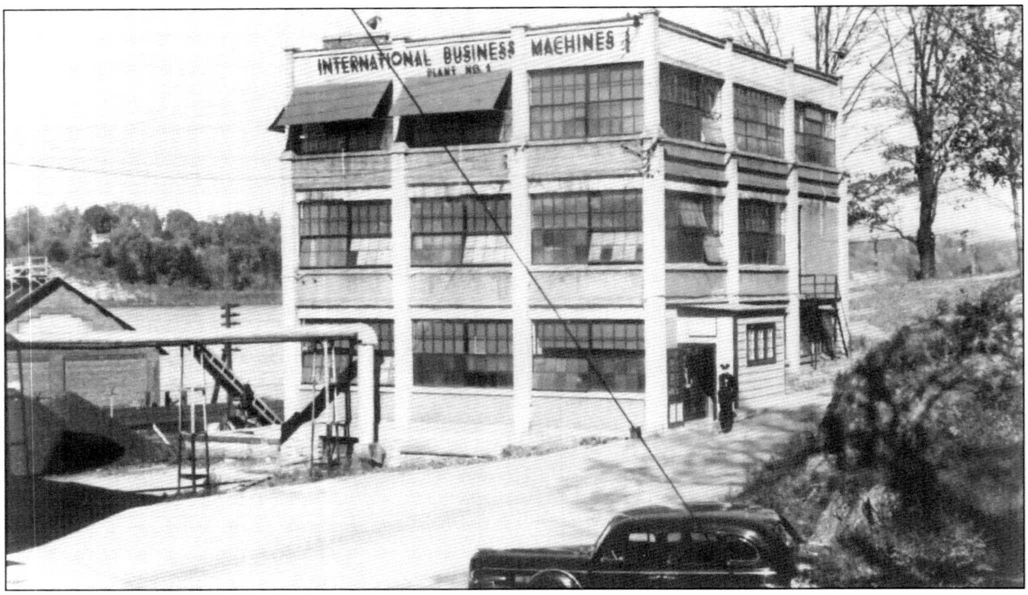

The Delapenha Factory/IBM. (IBM.) In 1941 the Munitions Manufacturing Corporation, a subsidiary of IBM, purchased approximately 215 acres of land and buildings on the Hudson River about 5 miles south of the city. It merged with IBM in 1942 and the organization became known as International Business Machines Corporation. Included in the original parcel were two factories: one devoted to preserving fruit and spices and the other to packing and storing olive oil. A gristmill was also on the site.

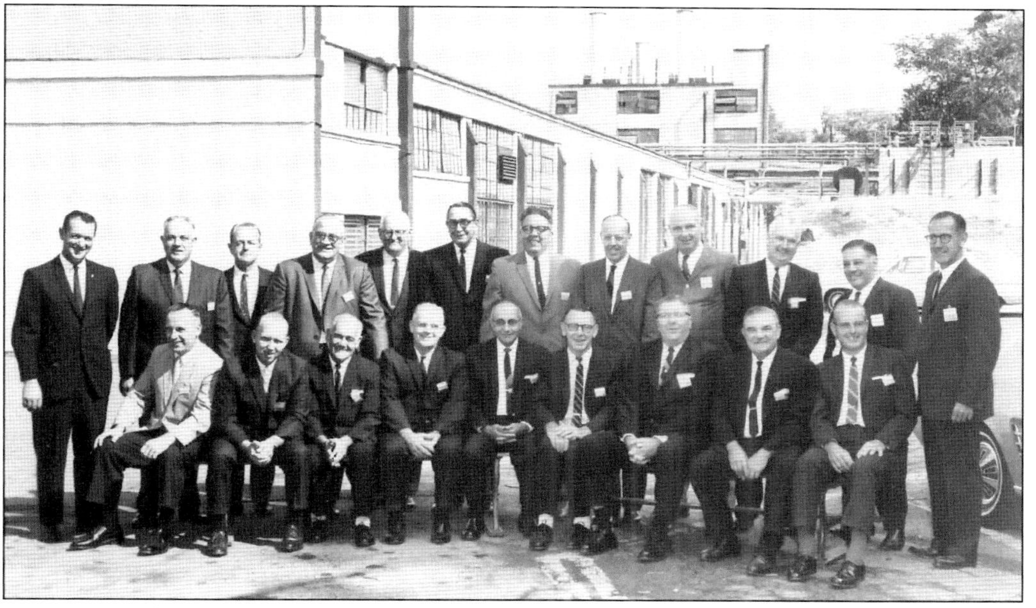

A Reunion of 1941 IBM Workers. (IBM.) When people heard that IBM was hiring in 1941 and applied and got jobs, they probably had little idea that they would spend their working lives at a company that would grow at a phenomenal rate and change the economic base of Poughkeepsie and the county for over half a century.

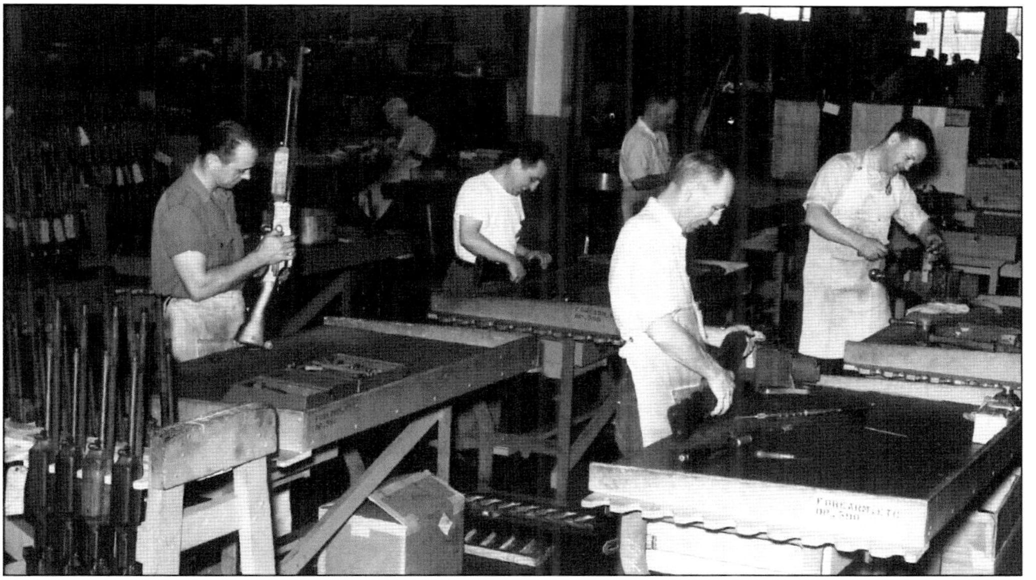

Munitions Workers at IBM, Early 1940s. (IBM.) Set up to manufacture war munitions for the U.S. government, the plant made a variety of aircraft cannons and rifles. After the war, the Poughkeepsie facility began to produce card punchers and sorters, and in 1948 IBM dedicated a 250,000-square-foot manufacturing building on South Road. The principal speaker, General Dwight D. Eisenhower, then president of Columbia University, said: "We are dedicating this magnificent building to the future of America." For Poughkeepsie as well as for the world, this future would be unimaginably different from the past.

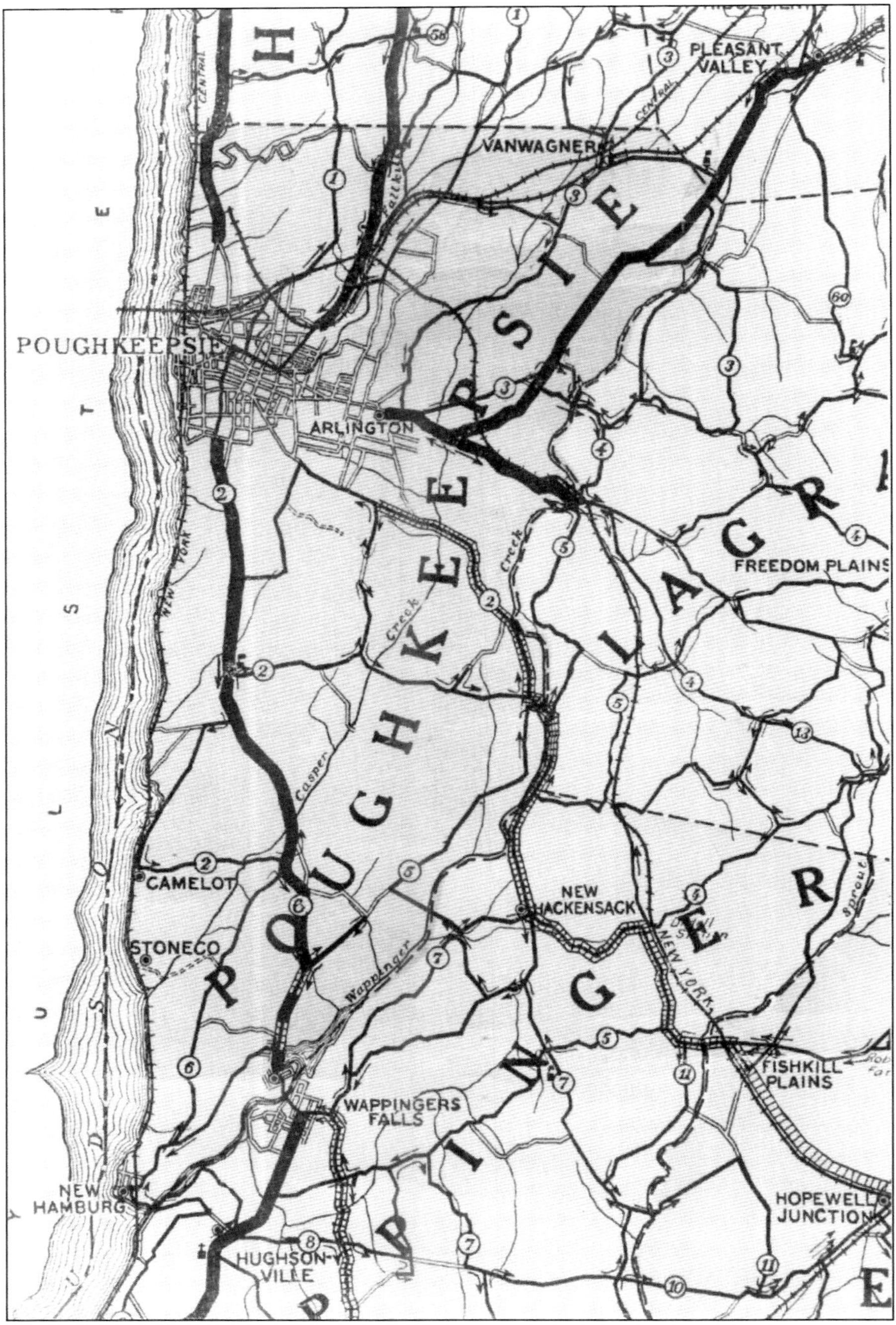

A County Postal Route Map, 1910. (Walter and Virginia Anderson [WA], PK.) An early-twentieth-century map not only shows the postal stations in the town but also illustrates the growth of transportation infrastructure. Rail lines along the Hudson and crossing it met in Poughkeepsie, where they extended northeast and southeast into New England. Eastman's and Vassar's vision of a central rail corridor was in place. New streets and roads extended from the city and major roads were being improved.

Five

Connections

In this final chapter, people are seen in a variety of activities and arenas which brought them together: government, business, celebrations, work, play, and communications. Governmental boards plan, community organizations meet, the king and queen of England visit, wars are fought, churches hold picnics, teams play football, and families celebrate together. Individuals also were a significant force in uniting people within Poughkeepsie and linking it to the wider world. Geography and demographics, intellectual and technological developments, entrepreneurship, aesthetics, culture, family, religion, and politics have all affected the development of Poughkeepsie. This chapter gives glimpses of how the community changed from the end of the seventeenth to the mid-twentieth century. When local history began to be recorded, change was slow. Communities were small and walkable. Distance and ability to communicate were defined in terms of how many miles could be walked or ridden on a horse. The railroad, horse cars, electric trolleys, buses, and, most of all, automobiles, changed the definition from how far it was to how long it took to get there.

By 1950 the city and town differed greatly from the tiny settlement that earlier defined the place named Poughkeepsie. The speed of change was accelerating. What would happen in the last half of the twentieth century was still unknown.

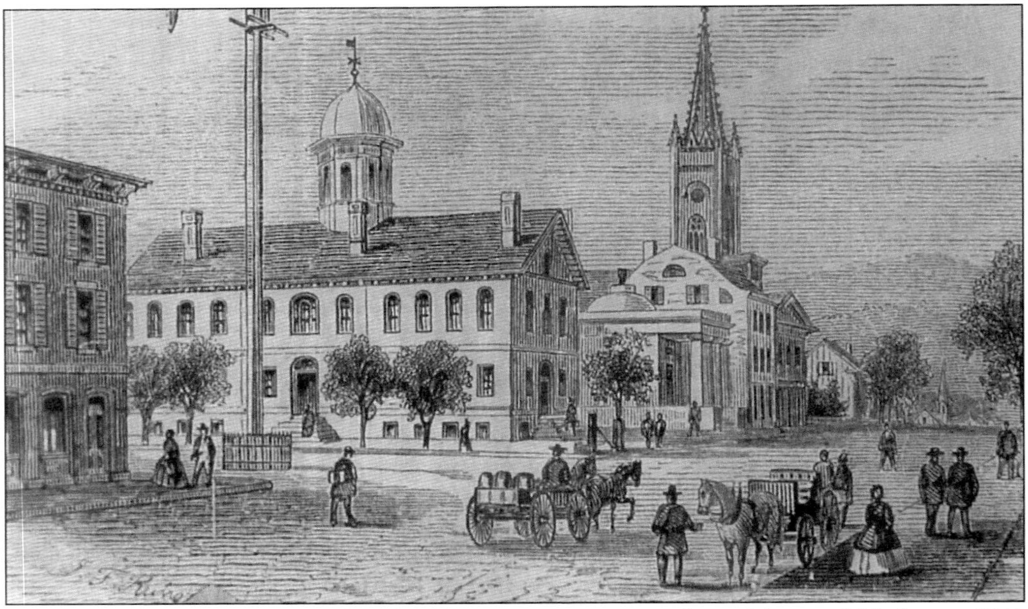

Liberty Pole at Main and Market. (PJ.) A Lossing engraving shows Main and Market in 1861 during the Civil War when patriotic spirit ran high and citizens showed their support of the Union through liberty poles and flag raisings. The center of county, town, and city government was duly marked by these symbols of unity. The county courthouse, where the supervisors met, is located in the center on the left, with its liberty pole opposite the entrance. Two doors beyond the dome and columns of the Poughkeepsie Trust Company (in the center) is the Greek Revival facade of Poughkeepsie City Hall and Market.

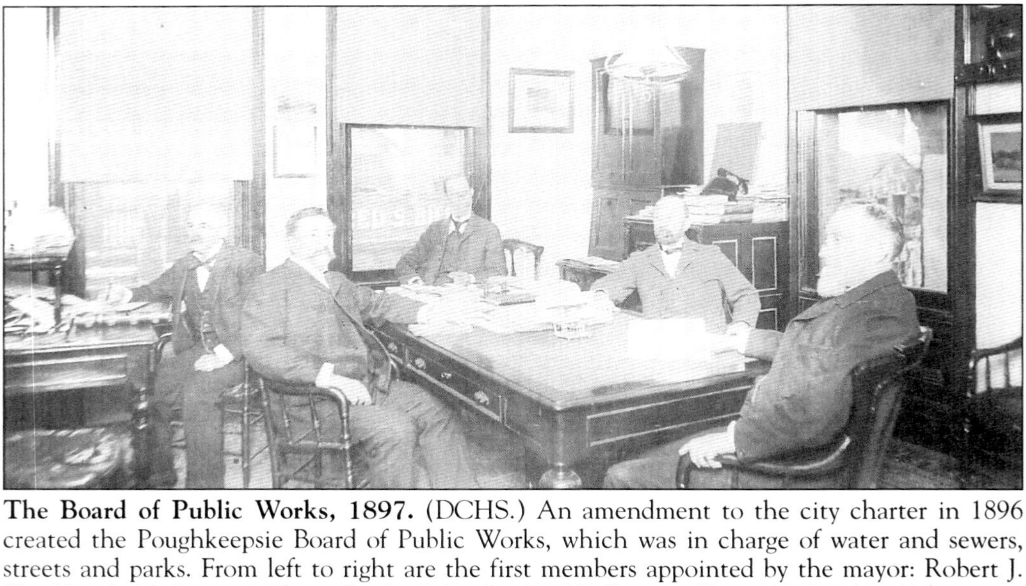

The Board of Public Works, 1897. (DCHS.) An amendment to the city charter in 1896 created the Poughkeepsie Board of Public Works, which was in charge of water and sewers, streets and parks. From left to right are the first members appointed by the mayor: Robert J. Shields (clerk), James B. Platt, Charles E. Fowler, Dr. W. Case, and James E. Dutcher. Subsequent boards were elected until 1901, when the appointment of the members of all such boards became a mayoral prerogative. The decisions of the board connected residents in the most tangible and physical sense.

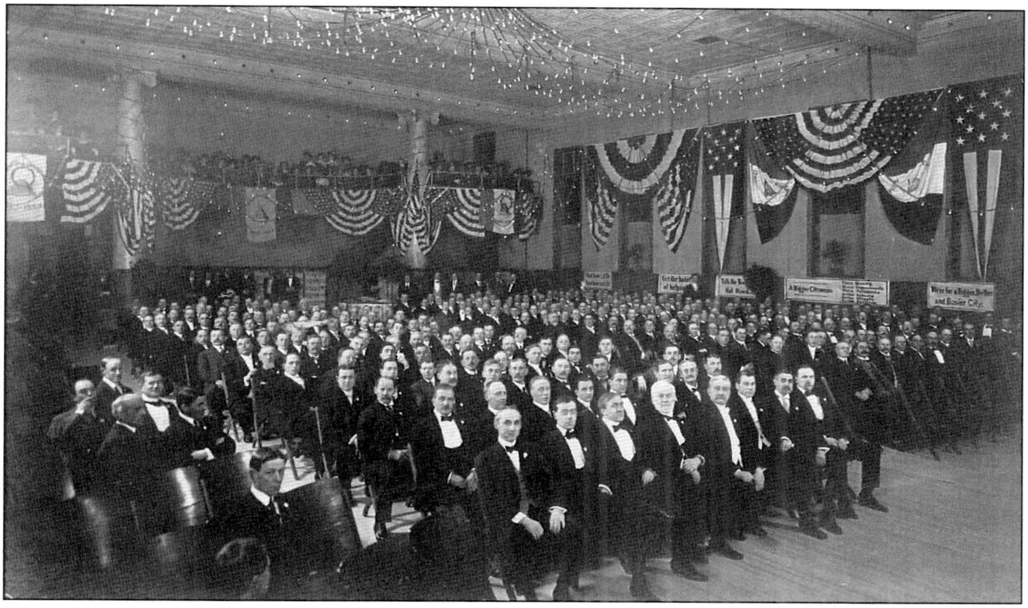

The Chamber of Commerce, 1910. (AML.) Shown here is the chamber of commerce meeting at the Columbus Institute on February 23, 1910. The board of trade, the merchants' association, and the civic league had merged because it was thought by some that there "were too many organizations in the city with the same purpose, that of uplifting the city." While continuing to work diligently for that goal, chamber members also enjoyed lighter moments, such as their 1921 annual dinner when Miss Gladys James, "direct from the Moulin Rouge," led the entertainment.

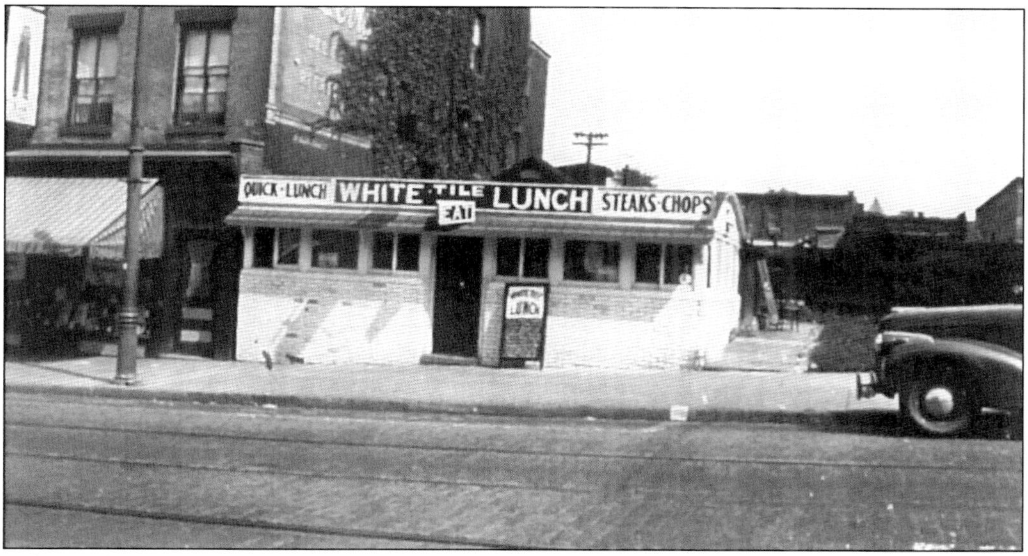

White Tile Lunch. (DCHS, WH.) The tiny White Tile Lunch at 175 Main Street was the kind of place that became a de facto neighborhood clubroom where "regulars" paid their dues with a daily cup of coffee on the way to work or a sandwich at lunch. The proprietors in the 1930s and '40s, Evangelos Krimezos and James Andreakos, represented another new population group coming at the turn of the century from Greece and the eastern Mediterranean.

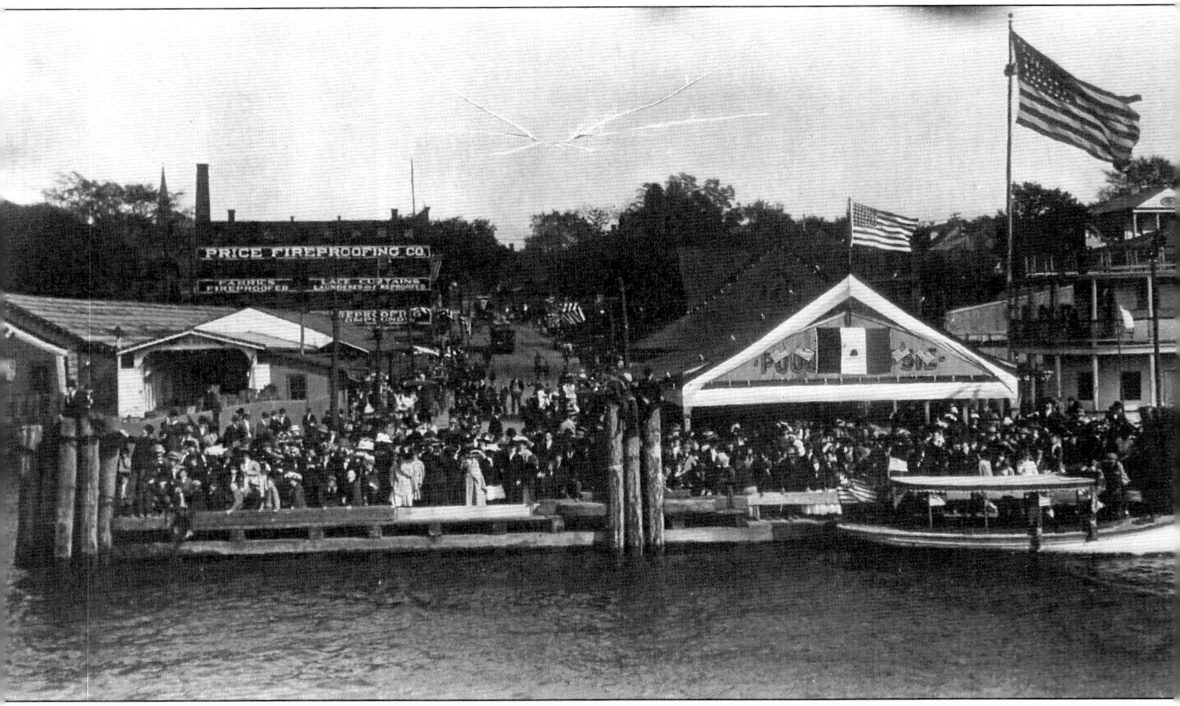

The 1909 Hudson-Fulton Celebration. (DCHS.) Crowds of participants in the Hudson-Fulton Celebration of 1909 mobbed the Main Street dock to welcome replicas of Henry Hudson's ship *The Half Moon* and Robert Fulton's steamboat *Clermont* reenacting their voyages of 1609 and 1807. The year-long celebration in communities from New York City to Albany prompted a groundswell of interest in regional history as material for festivity and consequent economic development. Festivals included land and river parades accompanied by fireworks, pageants, speeches, and special street lighting displays.

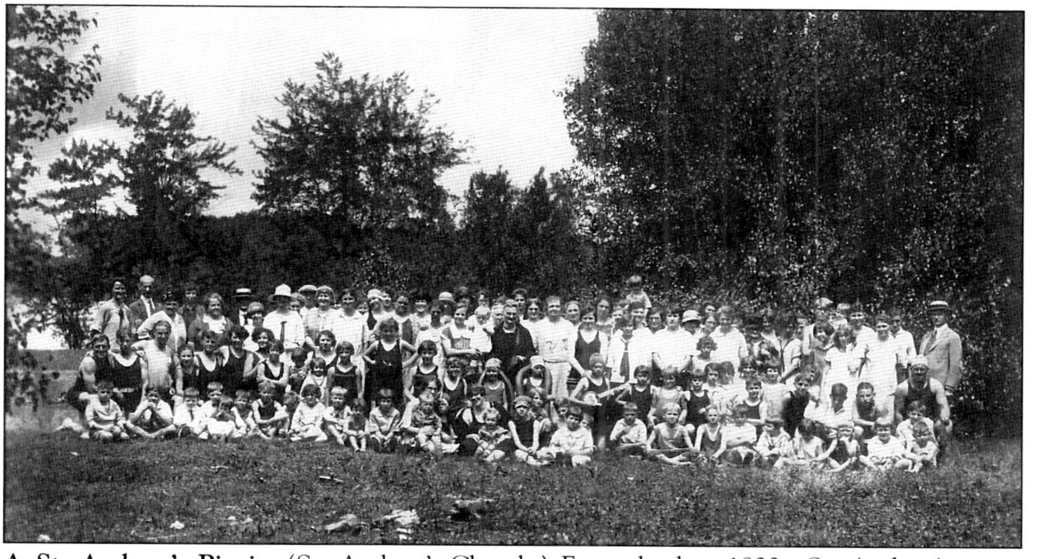

A St. Andrew's Picnic. (St. Andrew's Church.) From the late 1800s, St. Andrew's was a growing High Episcopal mission church begun by St. Paul's to meet the needs of parishioners in the Arlington hamlet. By 1933 it had a permanent rector, Father Harold Thompson, and a newly renovated sanctuary at 853 Main Street. Proud church leaders, their wives, and children looked forward to informal gatherings like the annual church picnic to relax and "connect" as a church family.

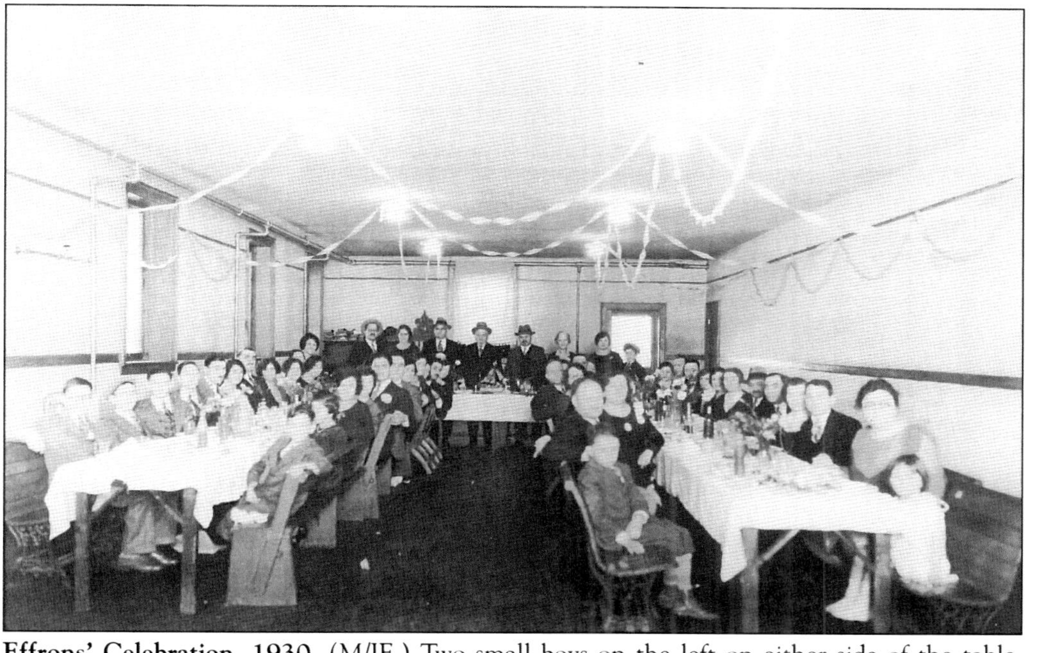

Effrons' Celebration, 1930. (M/JE.) Two small boys on the left on either side of the table, Marshall and Jesse Effron, attended a dinner before the trip of their grandfather, Benjamin Weiner, to Poland and Israel. He was not a rabbi nor officially a teacher, but his scholarship was greatly respected by the entire Jewish community. When he died, as a special tribute, his funeral cortege passed in front of the synagogue.

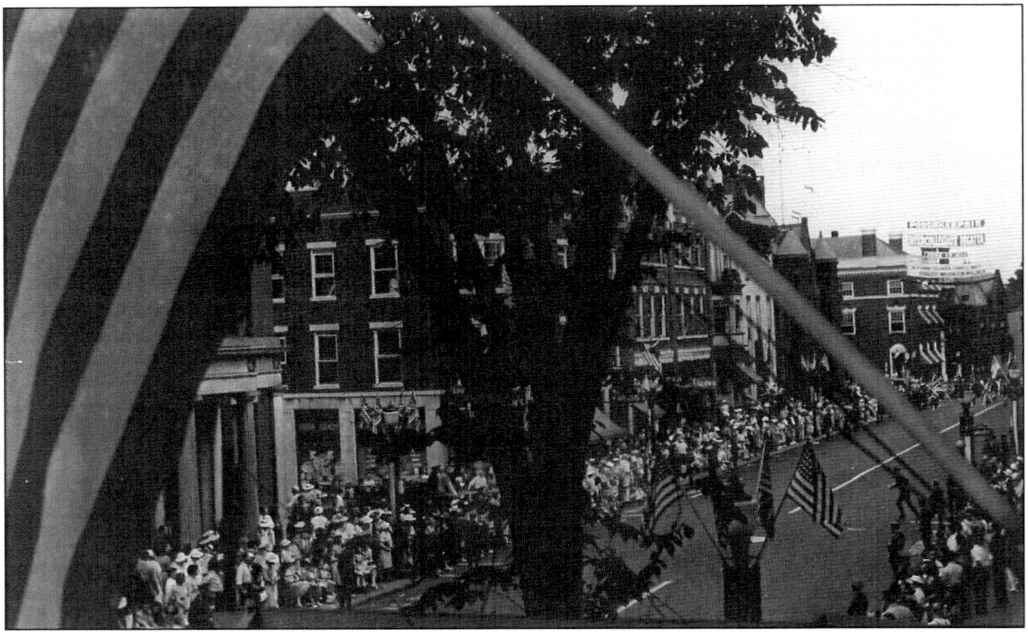

A Visit by the British Royal Family. (PJ.) The visit of King George VI and Queen Elizabeth of England in 1939, with war on the horizon, was a memorable event for Poughkeepsians looking forward to the annual regatta or a trip to the World's Fair. The motorcade route up Albany Post Road from the New York City Fairgrounds, despite uncertain weather, was lined for hours by police, troops, well-wishers, and hero-worshippers hoping for a glimpse of the royalty Americans had rejected in 1776.

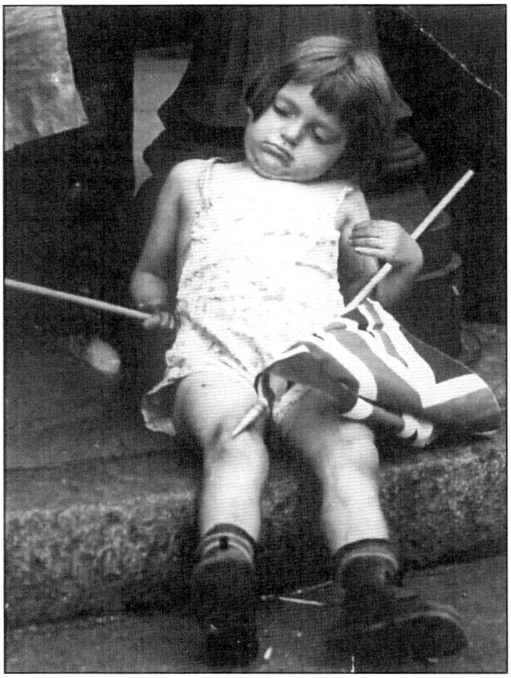

A Napping Well-Wisher. (PJ.) Flag and balloon sellers did well during the wait, but as the hours ticked by, even the most stalwart were having trouble with their aching feet and drowsy eyes. This little sleeper with the droopy flags found rest on the curb. One hopes that the frenzy of the eventual arrival of the king and queen woke her in time for her own memorable moment.

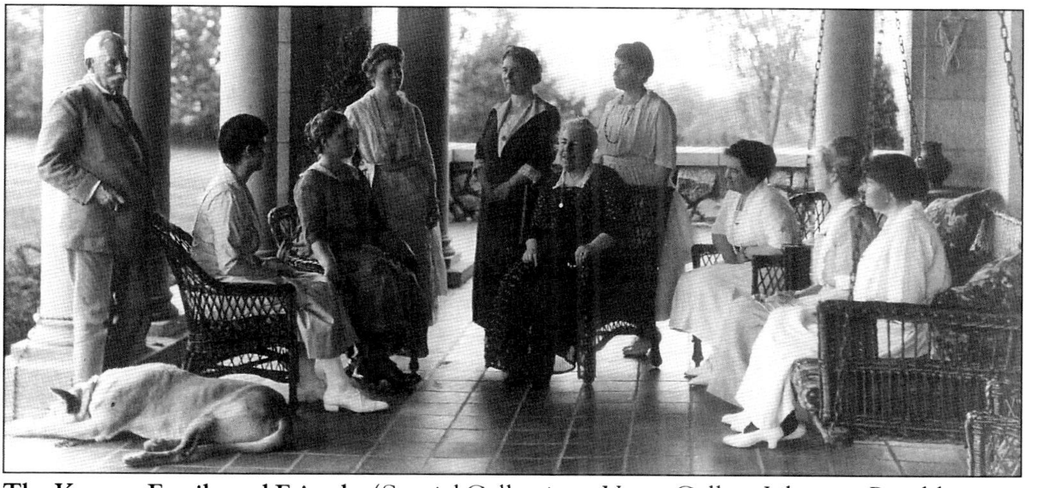

The Kenyon Family and Friends. (Special Collections, Vassar College Libraries, Poughkeepsie, NY.) Helen Kenyon (center right, standing), her family, friends, and Great Dane are shown on the porch of her home. Miss Kenyon, Vassar Class of 1905, was dedicated to the college and used her considerable talents to raise funds for it. Bridging the gap between "town and gown," she was equally active on behalf of the wider Poughkeepsie community.

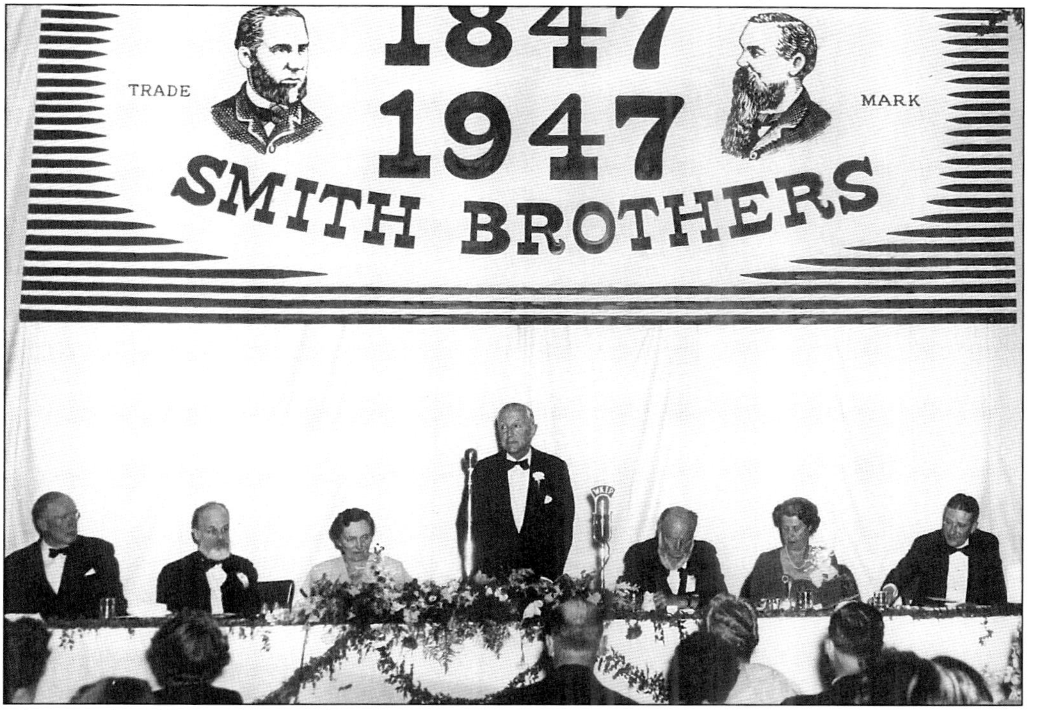

The Head Table at the Smith Brothers 100th Anniversary Celebration, 1947. (ARMcC.) Another family gathering that seemed to include most of Poughkeepsie—the celebration of the Smith Brothers cough drop business in 1947—was one of the largest ever held in the city of Poughkeepsie. Shown here is the head table. From left to right are Mayor Frank Doran, W.W. Smith II, his wife Grace, Ellison Capers, Robert J. Smith, his wife Dorothy, and Frederic A. Smith (County Clerk, no relation).

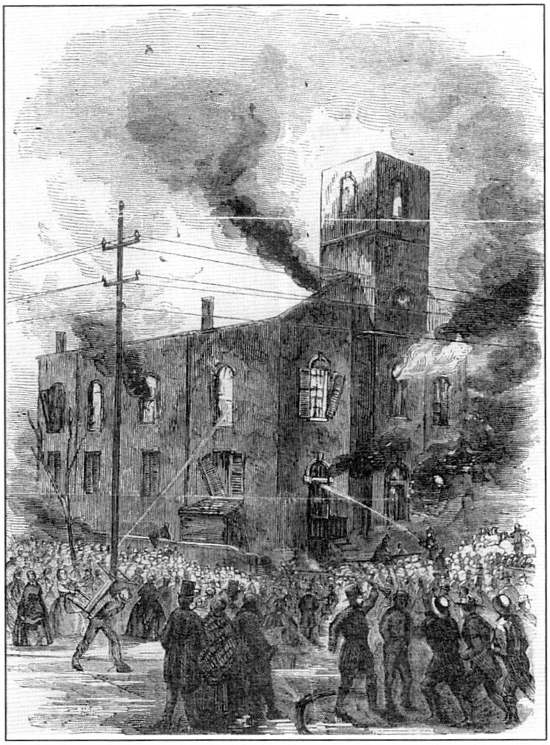

The Reformed Dutch Church Fire, 1857. (AML.) On January 18, 1857, the Reformed Dutch Church on Main Street caught fire, the burning steeple a "fearful column of fire ascending far up towards the clouds." Only one of many fires that changed the Poughkeepsie landscape, other blazes affected the courthouse (1785 and 1806), the south side of Main Street to Academy Street (1836), the block bounded by Catharine, Main, and Crannell Streets (1857), the north side of Main Street east of Garden (1870), the Whitehouse Factory (1879), the glass works (1897), Reynolds Elevator and Gas Works (1898), Morgan House (1917), and the Windsor Hotel (1944.) Fire company volunteers responded in numbers.

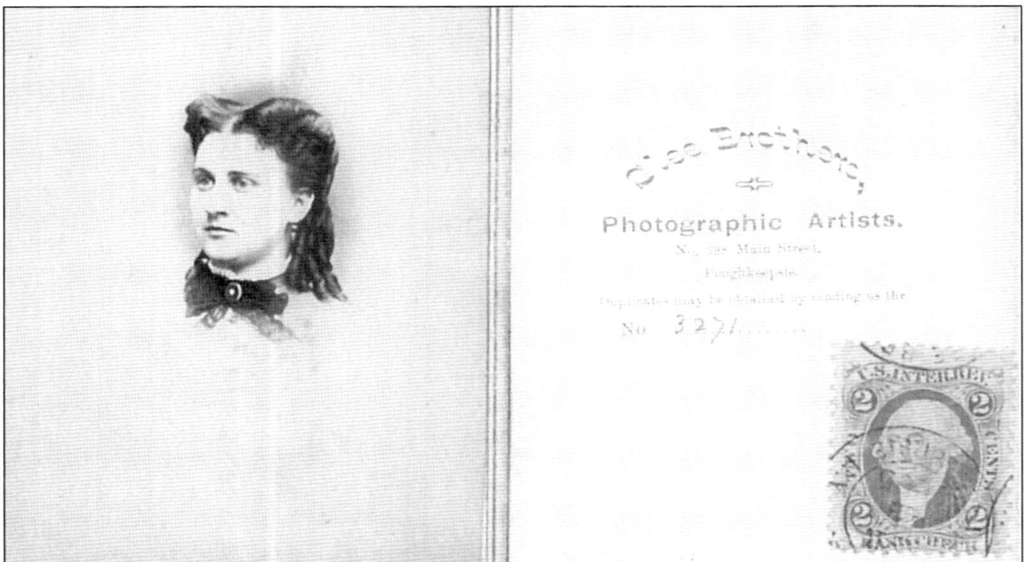

Revenue Stamps, Civil War era. (James and Anita Emrich.) While the costs of war in human terms are sometimes hard to measure, the money required to pay for war is all too concrete, as any photographer during the Civil War could attest. During that era, required revenue stamps were affixed to photographs and the proceeds were used to help fund the war. Unlike today when almost everyone has a camera, in those days it was necessary to visit the studios of professional photographers; this fact assured a constant stream of revenue to the government.

World War I Troop Transport. (MKD.) What appears to be Japanese subway stuffing is the old Main Street passenger terminal during World War I. Poughkeepsie sent troops off to war on government troop trains. The comfortable accommodations marketed by the railroad for more than half a century were forsaken in favor of getting as many people as possible from point A to B in the shortest period. Following the war, a new terminal was built a block north that really did attend to passenger comforts.

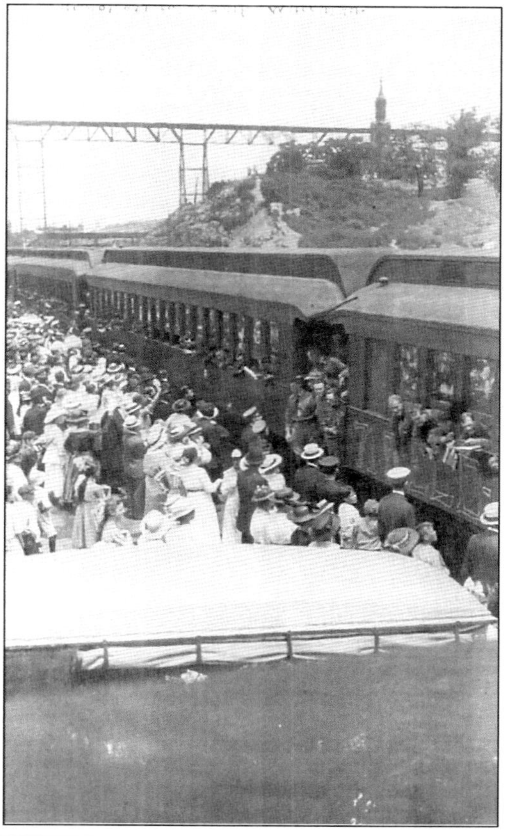

Company K at Camp Whitman. (AML.) At the start of World War I the United States armed forces had only 200,000 members. Four and a half million more volunteered or were conscripted during the course of that war. Typical among them was Isaac E. Tompkins (center right, tree trunk), posing here at Camp Whitman where members of Company K, First New York Volunteers, from Poughkeepsie's armory unit trained. He was eventually sent home, deferred as a married man with a six-year-old daughter to care for.

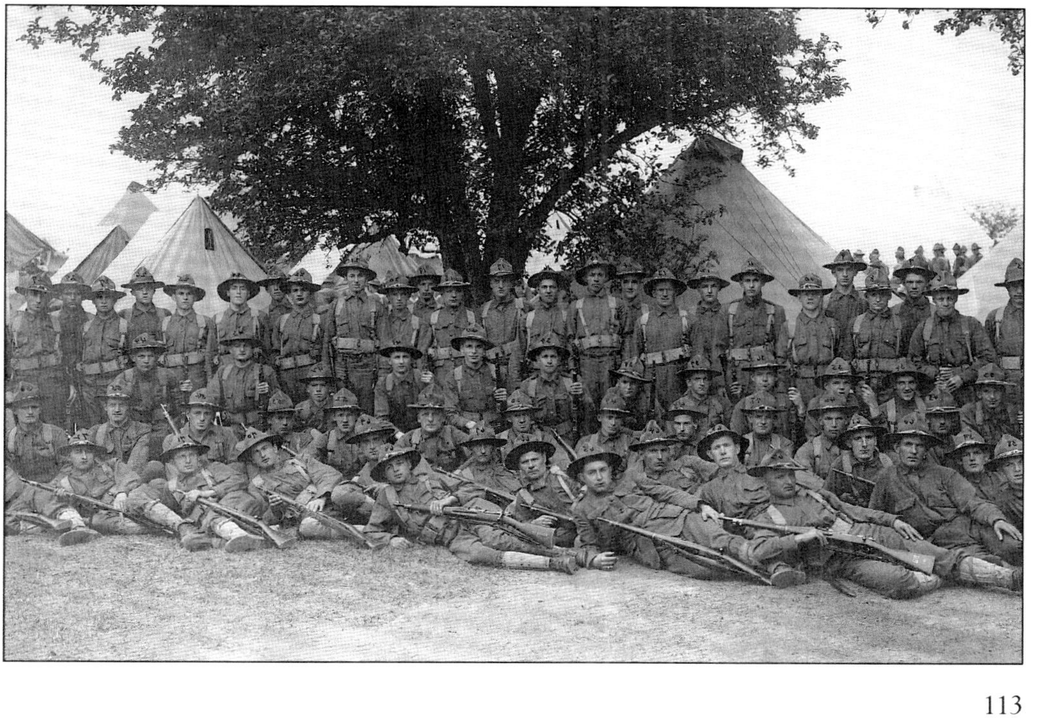

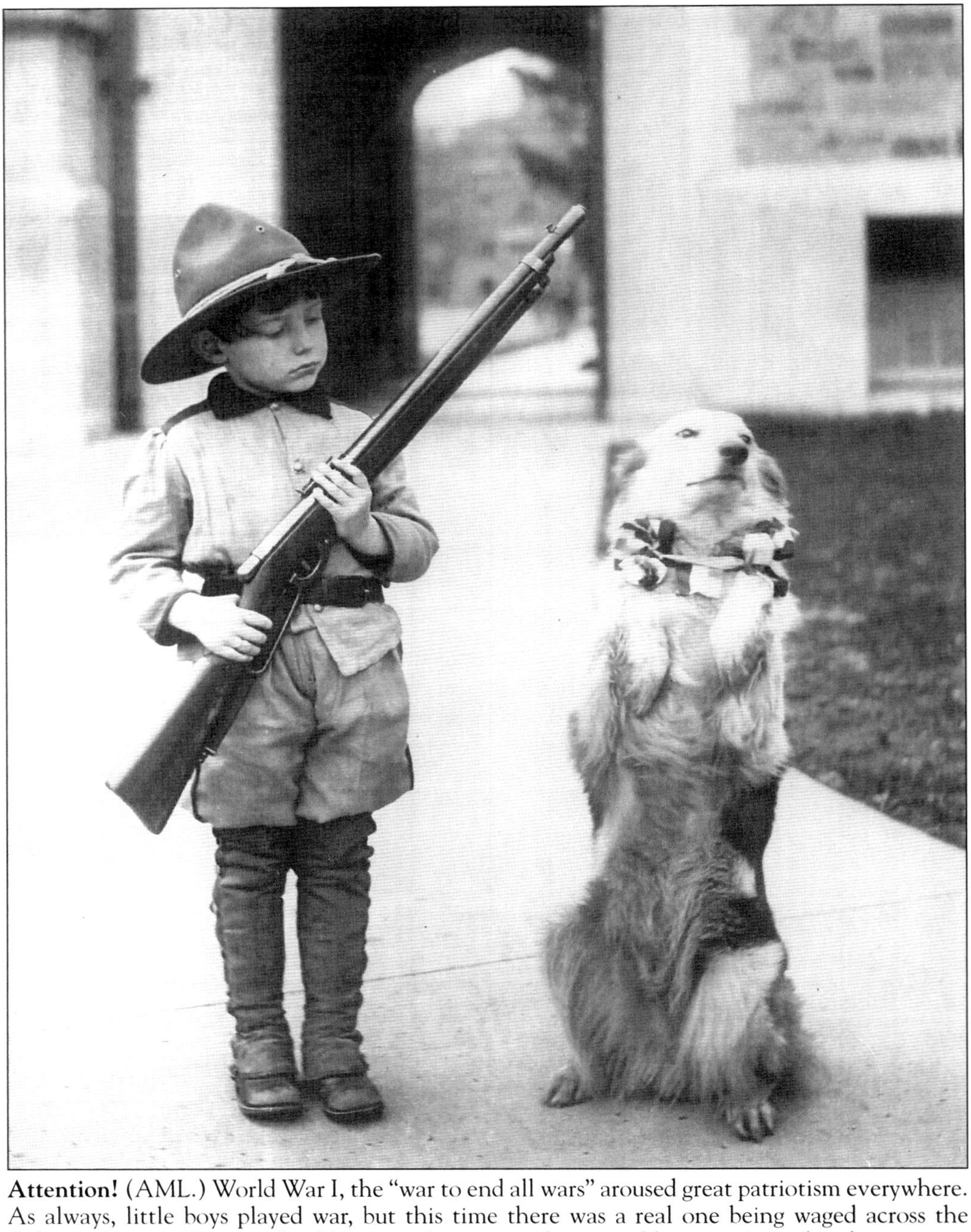

Attention! (AML.) World War I, the "war to end all wars" aroused great patriotism everywhere. As always, little boys played war, but this time there was a real one being waged across the Atlantic Ocean. This small soldier must have spent hours and hours training his dog to come to attention. He obviously succeeded, as evidenced by the photograph taken in front of Vassar College Main Gate.

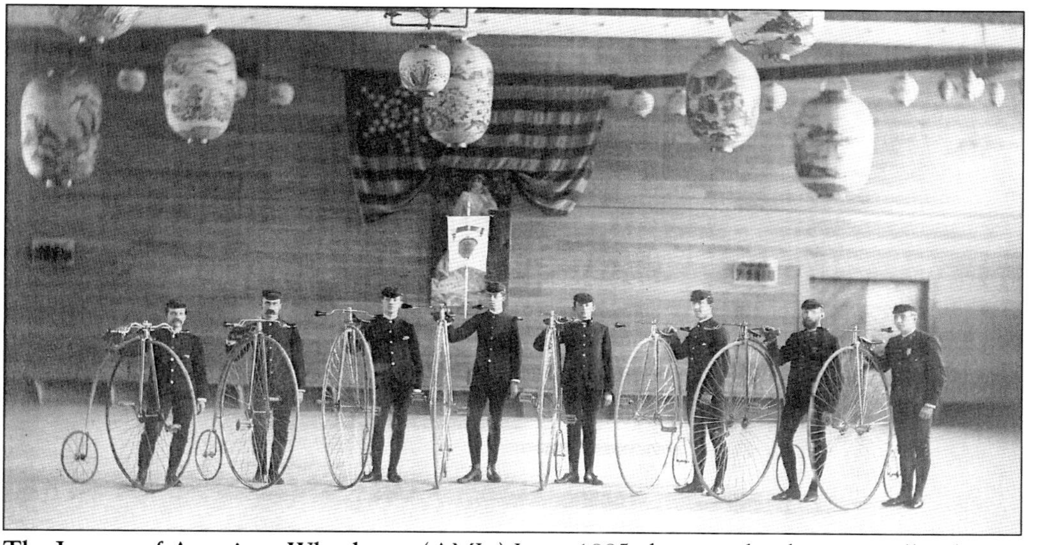

The League of American Wheelmen. (AML.) In an 1885 photograph taken in a roller skating rink on Market Street, members of an early bicycle club, "The League of American Wheelmen," show off their "wheels," as bicycles were then called with good reason. Technical improvements rapidly increased the popularity of the bicycle as a recreational vehicle, prompting the establishment and growth of other clubs: the Ariel Wheel Club, the Poughkeepsie Bicycle Club, and the Century Cycle Club, whose members, meeting in their clubhouses, sponsored social outings and races.

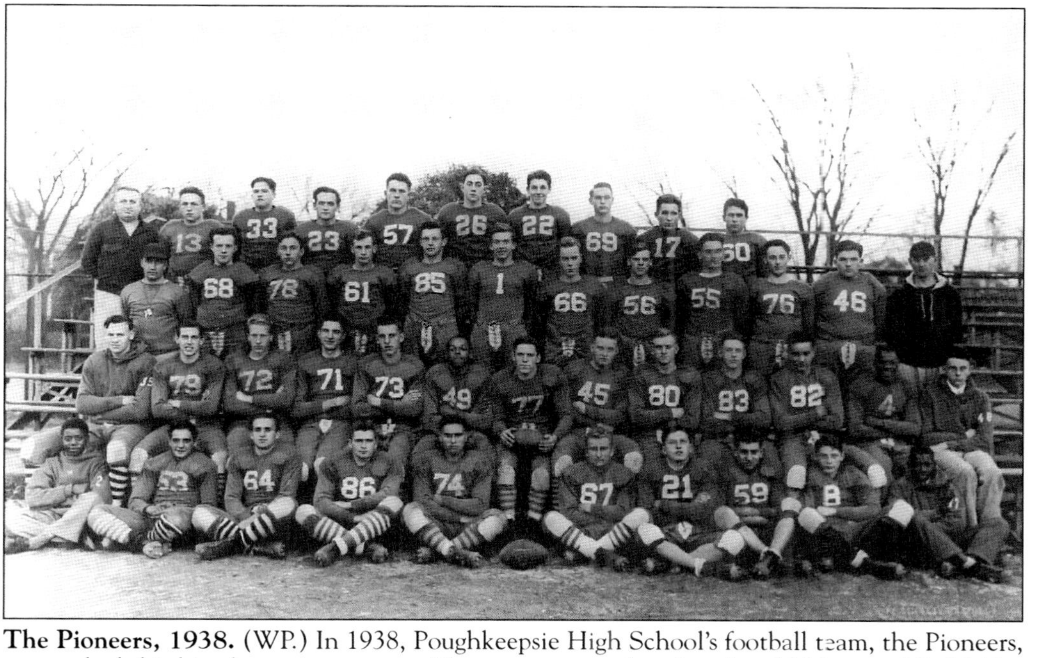

The Pioneers, 1938. (WP.) In 1938, Poughkeepsie High School's football team, the Pioneers, was ranked third in the entire country. The games were played at the old Memorial Field (the present-day site of Poughkeepsie High School) and sometimes drew as many as four thousand people. For forty years Sam Kalloch was the coach, always emphasizing teamwork. As one player recalled, "We just loved to play the game!"

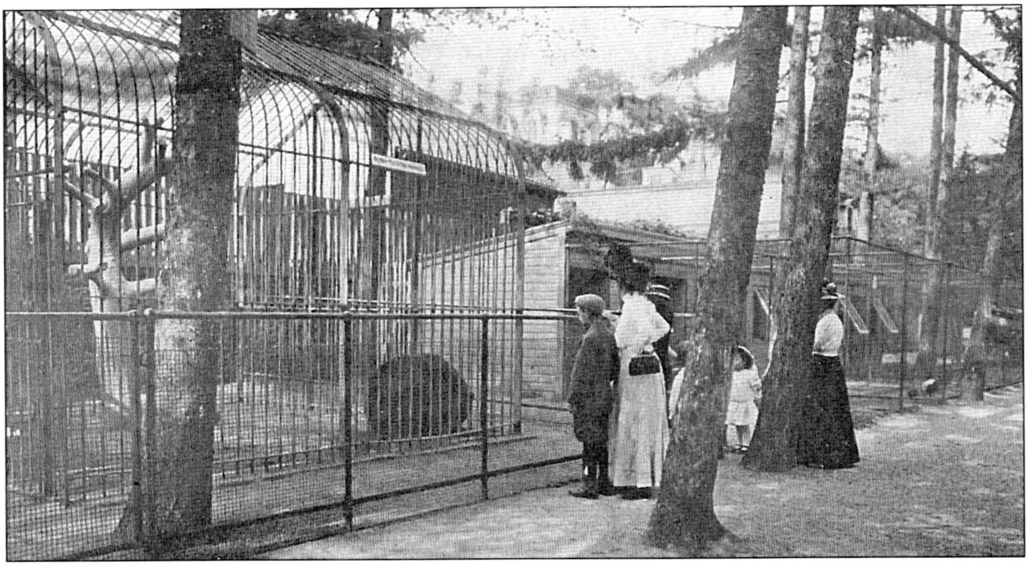

Eastman Park Zoo. (MT.) In 1865 Harvey Eastman bought property on the corner of Montgomery and Market Streets and laid out his estate that came to be known as Eastman Park. Trees and shrubbery abounded amidst gently curving drives. Skating, band concerts, and baseball games all contributed to the enjoyment of the public to whom Eastman had opened the grounds about 1867. In 1909 the city acquired the property. The zoo continued to operate until the 1930s, but its denizens included only two bears and a few birds.

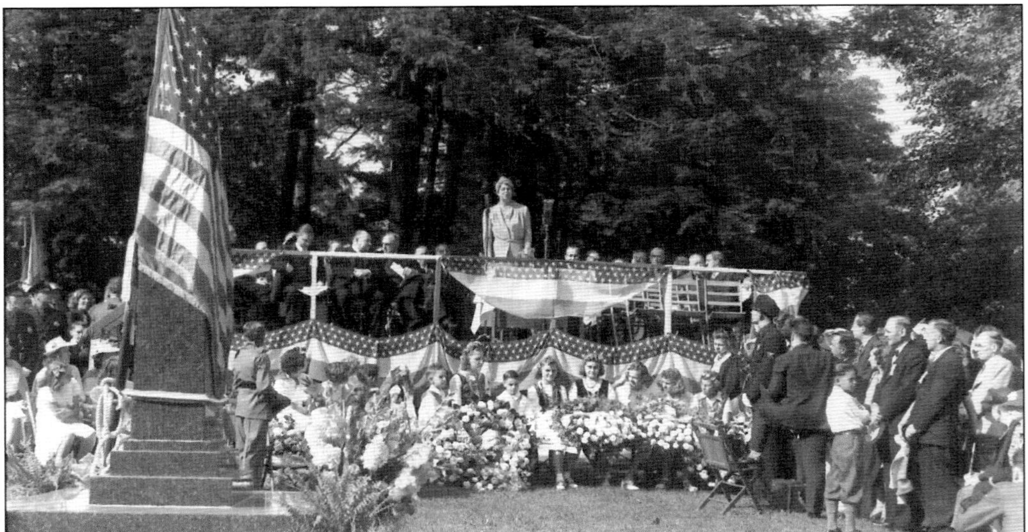

The Pulaski Park Monument Honoring General Casimir Pulaski, 1940. (PJ.) In Pulaski Park on North Road a monument to General Casimir Pulaski was unveiled in 1940 amid crowds of admirers of the Polish general who had been so helpful to the American people during the Revolution. Among those present were Eleanor Roosevelt, Father Kaminski, William Ciolko, Mayor Schrauth, Judge Morschauser, Monsignor Connelly, and Lucille Zajkowski, themselves representative of several of the various nationalities that contributed to the diversity and progress of Poughkeepsie.

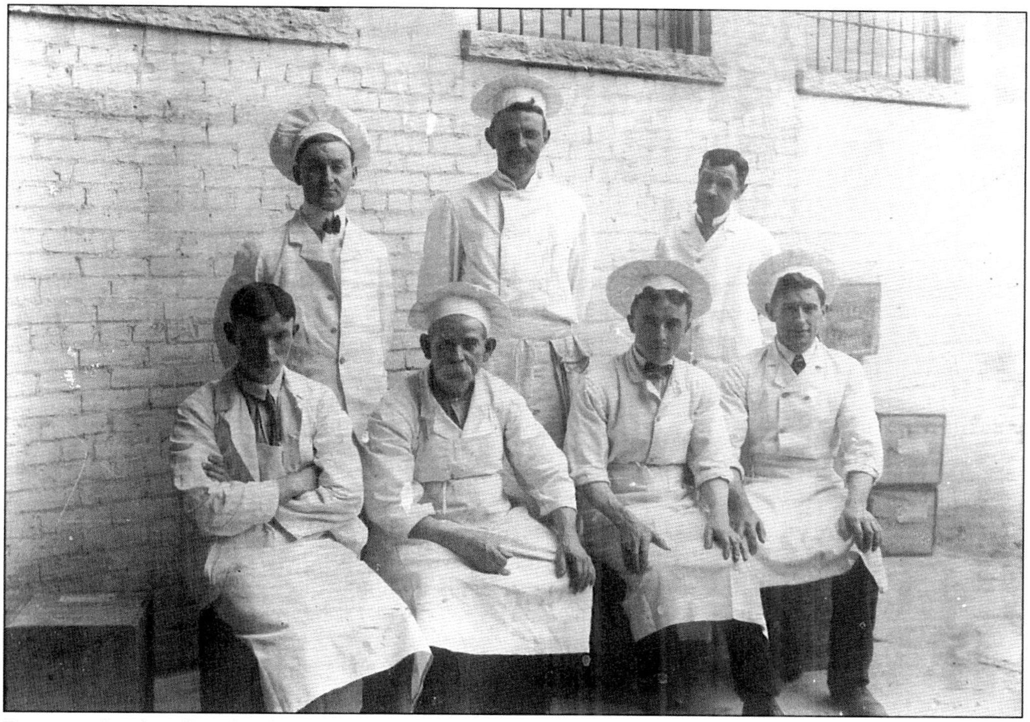

Resting Cooks. (BA/LE.) Among those wonderful glass negatives turned up by Lucy Edgcomb and Catherine Bala was this one of a group of cooks believed by Bardavon historian Annon Adams to be Smith Brothers staff on a "time-out" after preparing a meal for an Opera House function. Other photographic evidence indicates that Mr. Slater, the carpenter and fireman, also did some of the photography.

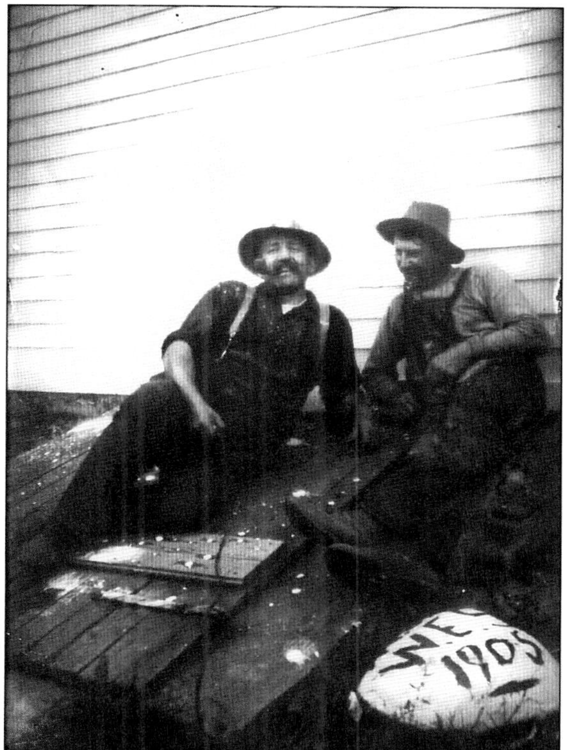

Resting Painters. (CB.) One pleasant day in 1905, William Slater and a friendly neighbor or family member painted a house and had the memorable event recorded for posterity by the other person who created some of those glass negatives. The smiles on their faces indicate satisfaction with a painting job done well enough to merit a signature as a work of art and a well-deserved restful pipe. The cellar door would have pleased Jackson Pollack.

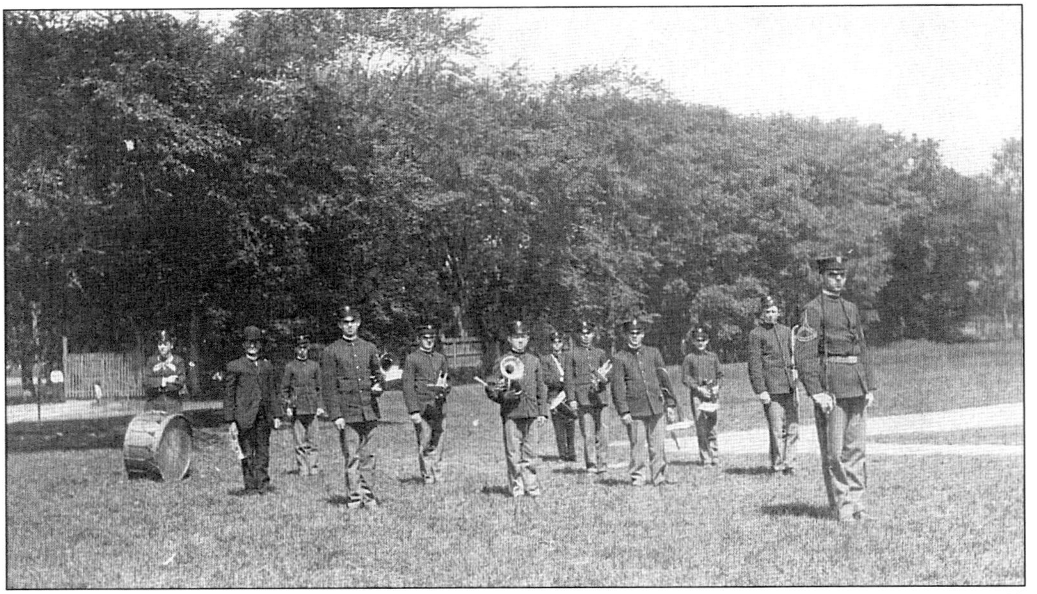

Riverview Academy Band Members. (MMB.) Young Aylmer Musselman (fifth from left) made "playing" his work. As a student at Riverview Academy at the turn of the century, he was proudly chosen first cornetist in the academy band. As an adult this man of many talents became a professional musician and teacher, as well as the director of the Franklin D. Roosevelt High School Band, which consistently won awards in competitions.

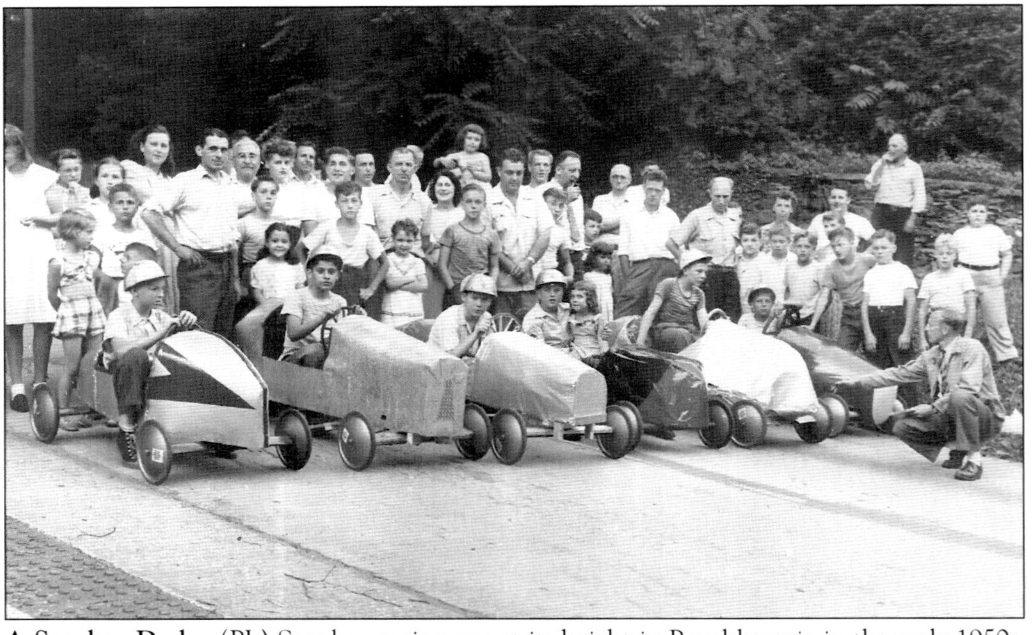

A Soapbox Derby. (PJ.) Soapbox racing was at its height in Poughkeepsie in the early 1950s. Everyone turned out for races first run from Brickyard Hill on the Dutchess Turnpike, and later on safer Academy Street. In a series of national run-offs, young contestants had to find sponsors who would receive advertising on the cars. Proud parents, not permitted by the rules to assist in racer design or construction, were happy to be included in news photographs.

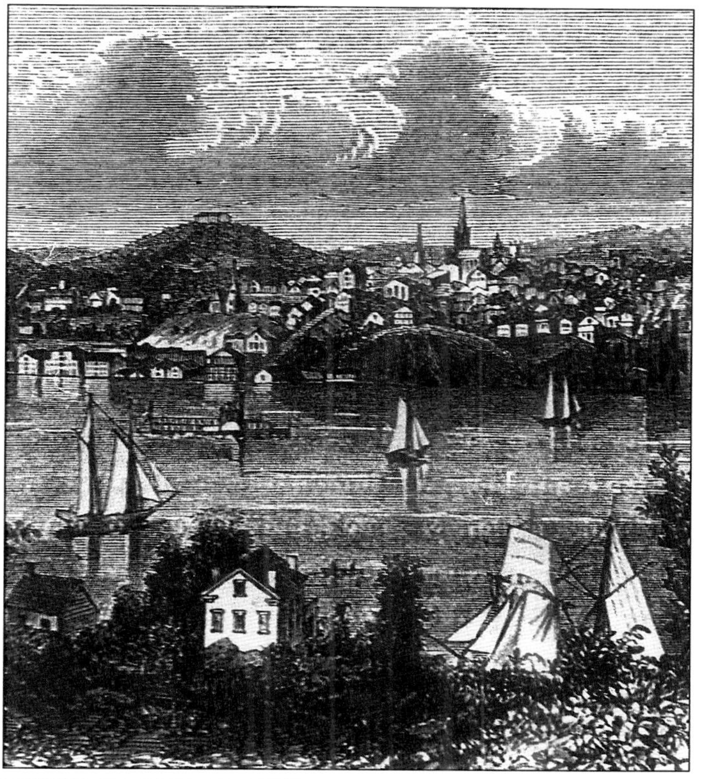

Poughkeepsie, Seen from Lewisburg c. 1840. (DCHS.) For centuries the river was the main road in the Hudson Valley, filled with everything that floated, from three-masted schooners and paddlewheelers to ferries and sloops. Shipbuilding in Poughkeepsie was a healthy industry that during the Revolution built warships and when this engraving was made was producing and sending out whaling ships. This engraving of the view from Lewisburg (Highland) shows just how busy it could get.

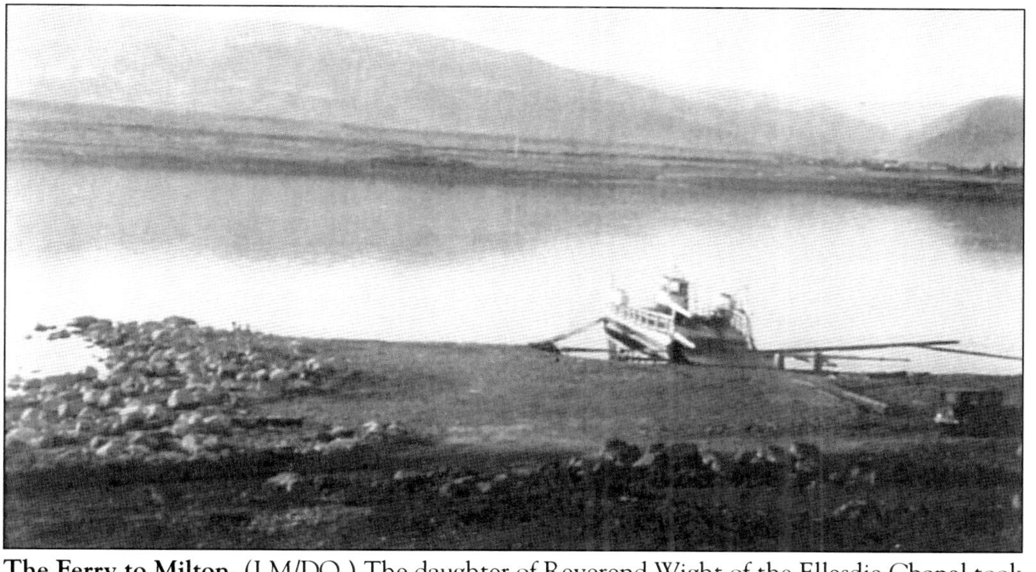

The Ferry to Milton. (LM/DO.) The daughter of Reverend Wight of the Ellesdie Chapel took this photograph of the ferry between New Hamburgh and Milton at the turn of the century. The ferry that had operated since the eighteenth century appears to have changed very little. The lack of customers may be attributed to competition from Poughkeepsie and Beacon (where there were larger ferries driven by powerful steam engines) or it may simply represent the smaller market in New Hamburgh.

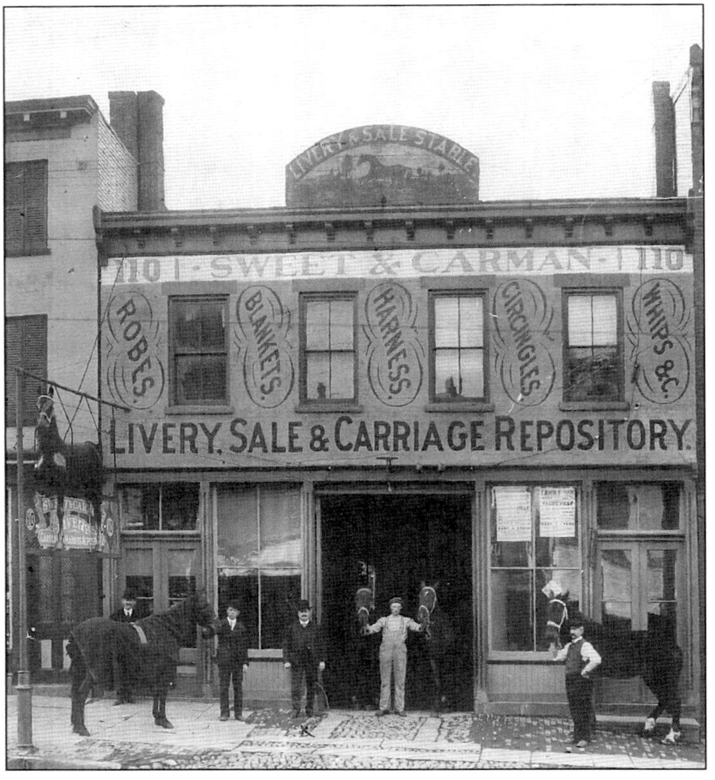

The Sweet and Carman Livery Stable. (AML.) The problem of where to park your horse while shopping or doing business in the city in the days before motorized vehicles was similar to that faced by today's motorists. It was solved in the same way it is handled today, with horse "garages" called livery stables. The old city directories show quite a number which, like Sweet and Carman, also sold livery supplies. When autos came along, many of the stables became garages.

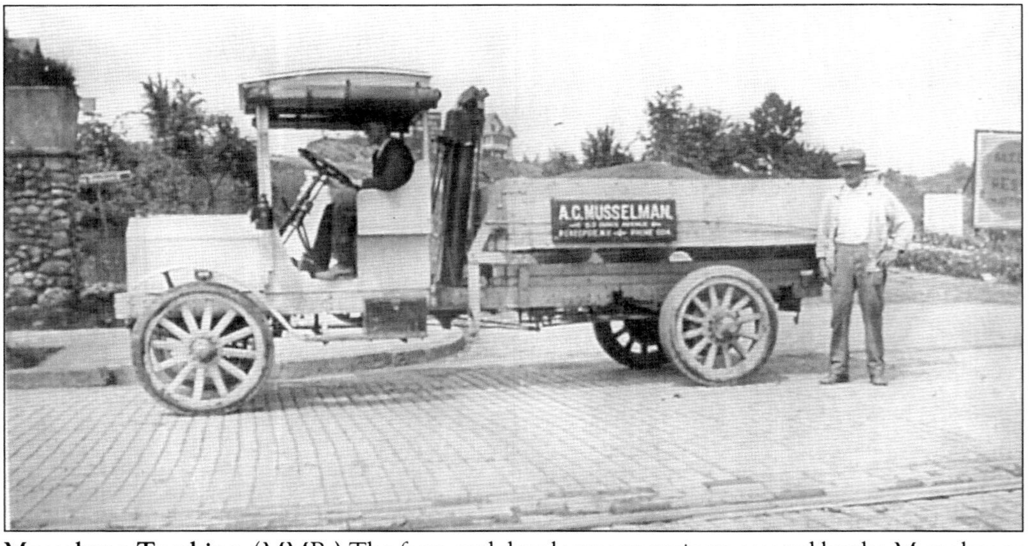

Musselman Trucking. (MMB.) The farm and development projects created by the Musselmans were not the family's only entrepreneurial adventures. At the turn of the century, they started a trucking business with two teams of horses, who apparently were thought of as business partners, named and cherished. When engines replaced horsepower, Musselman Trucking retired Dan, Bob, Dick, and Prince and purchased their first trucks.

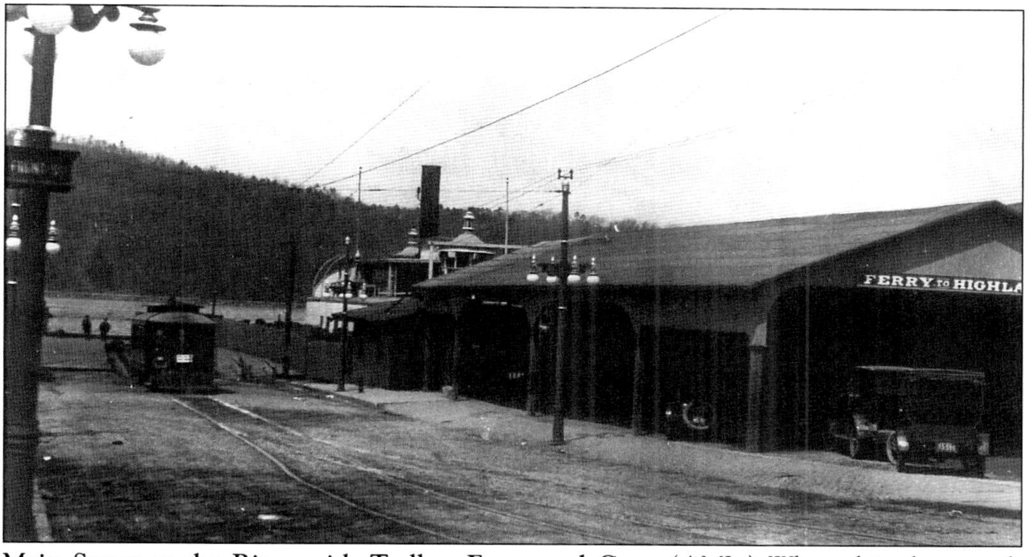

Main Street at the River with Trolley, Ferry, and Cars. (AML.) When this photograph was taken, who would have guessed that only one mode of transportation pictured would last far beyond the mid-twentieth century? Perhaps one could have supposed that trolleys would be replaced by buses, and ferries by a bridge, but who could have known the impact of the automobile on the land use patterns of the city and town? With the automobile came unimaginable freedom of movement, and, eventually, the almost complete discontinuation of public transportation.

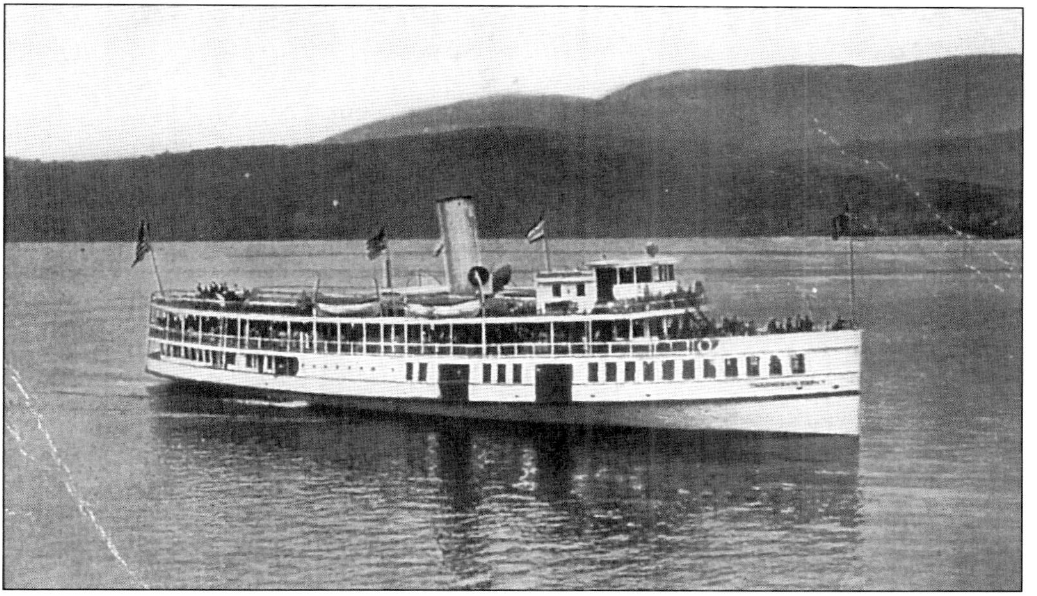

The Chauncey M. Depew Dayliner. (WA.) Robert Fulton's successful steamboats started a whole new river industry. Night boats and day boats sped up and down the river breaking records for half a century until the coming of the railroad. The Hudson River Dayline kept going successfully by slowing down a bit, allowing passengers to take in the scenery. Dayliners from New York City to Poughkeepsie were popular until the mid-twentieth century.

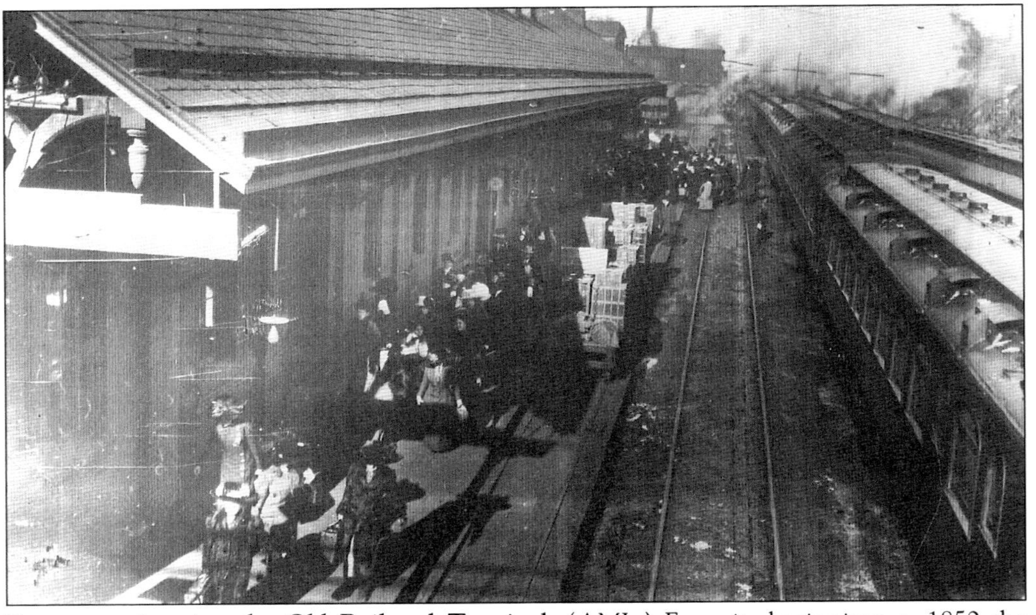

Passengers Leaving the Old Railroad Terminal. (AML.) From its beginnings *c.* 1850 the Hudson River Railroad Line included both passenger and freight services and marketed the speed and comfort that it could provide travelers. The passenger terminal was adjacent to Main Street, accessible by stairs to other transportation. Poughkeepsie, where travelers changed trains, was often the end of the line for immigrants, who got off and stayed here.

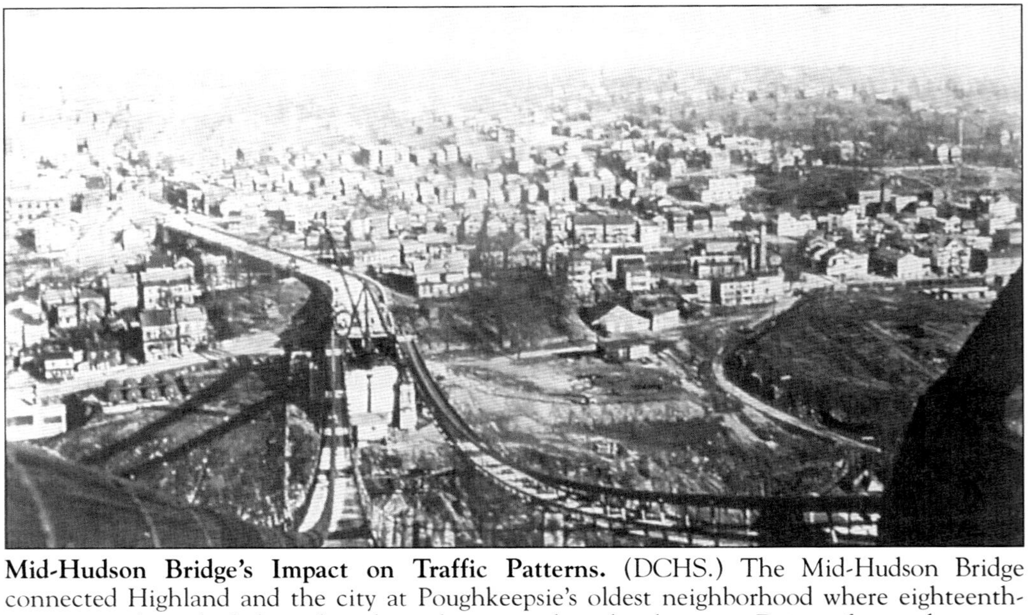

Mid-Hudson Bridge's Impact on Traffic Patterns. (DCHS.) The Mid-Hudson Bridge connected Highland and the city at Poughkeepsie's oldest neighborhood where eighteenth-century roads snaked through industrial areas and worker housing. Drivers from other parts descended into a maze of narrow streets only to face Church Street hill, with a slope like Mt. Everest and a stoplight at the crest. Once on Market Street, traffic came to a screeching halt in the crowded center of town.

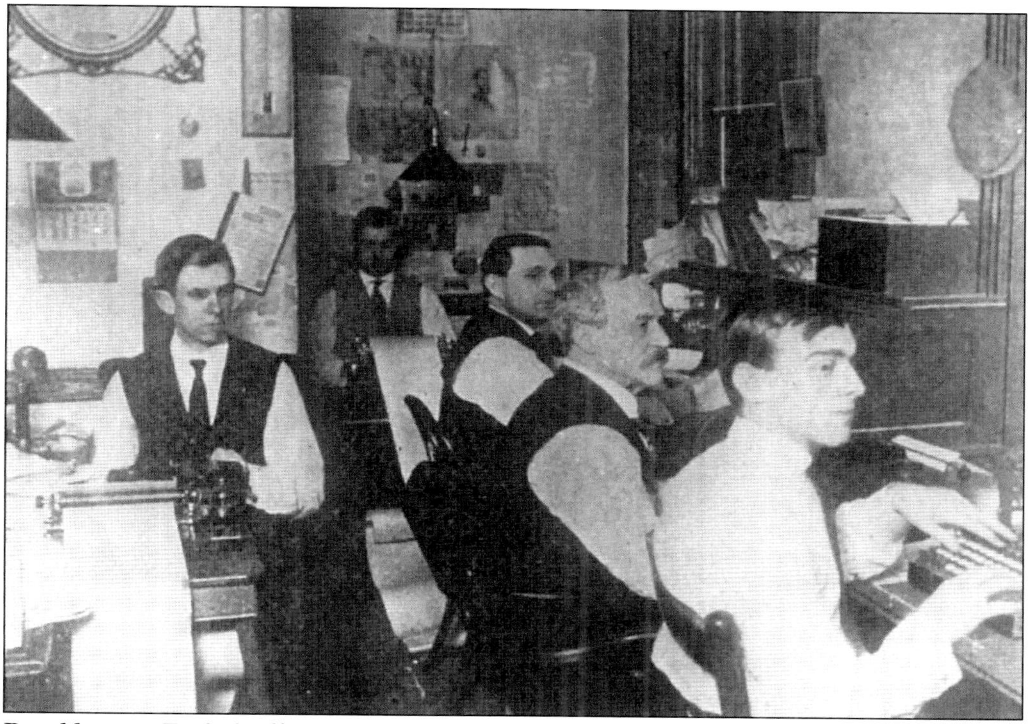

***Poughkeepsie Eagle* Staff, 1911.** (PJ.) Some people cook. Some people paint. And some people write for a living. The staff of the *Poughkeepsie Eagle* on Liberty Street earned their living as news hawks for a predecessor of the *Poughkeepsie Journal.* Seen from left to right are Reporter Edwin Overocker, Telegraph Operator Lyle E. Wigg, City Editor George W. Davids Jr., Reporter Theodore W. Davis, and Budding Attorney Philip Mylod (then a college student), hard at work getting out a special edition observing "50 years of achievement."

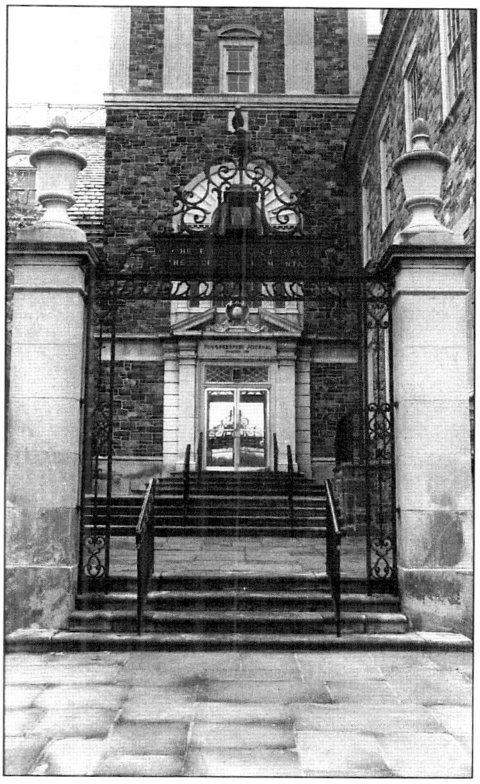

The Poughkeepsie Journal Building. (PJ.) "Here Shall the Press the People's Right Maintain" is the timeless motto over the entrance to New York State's oldest newspaper, the *Poughkeepsie Journal.* It was established in 1785 by Nicholas Power, a one-man communications center with a few hundred customers, who also was postmaster, set his own type, and ran a reading room. This impressive building was constructed in 1941. It houses the management, reporters, pressmen, marketing, and distribution staff, and the huge modern presses needed for a current daily circulation of 44,000.

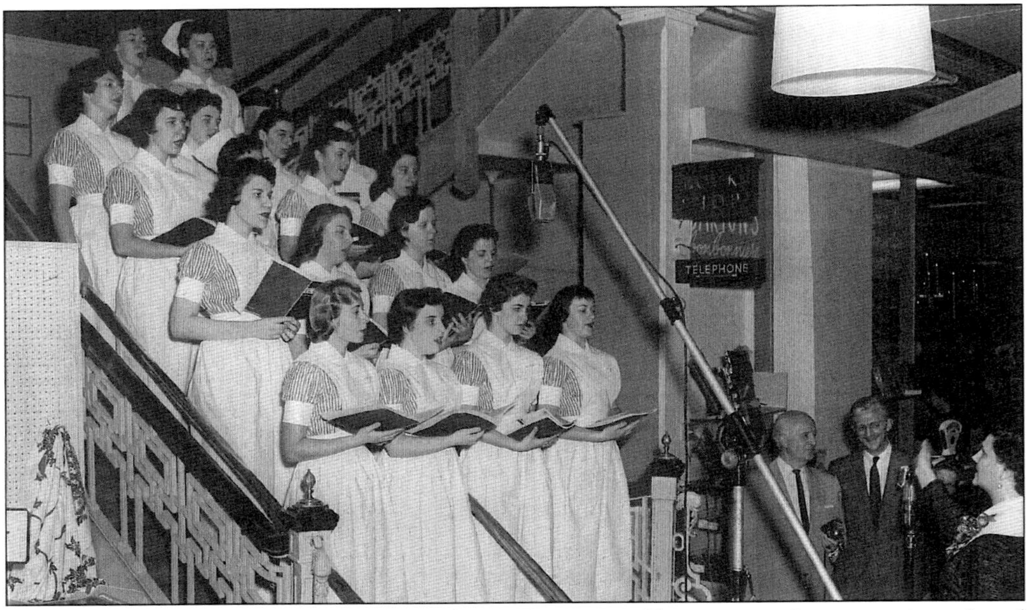

Broadcasting From Luckey's. (JS.) In the 1940s a new Christmas tradition was introduced by Luckey's and Wallace's, which was to remain open late into the night for "Men's Night." Fashion shows, bargains, and entertainment—including nursing school carolers on the steps beneath Luckey's stained glass window of Hudson's Half Moon—lured male shoppers. Popular broadcaster John Kuhn and William Geckle from management were on hand to interview customers for WKIP, Poughkeepsie's earliest radio station (licensed c. 1941). The new communications medium captured everyone's attention.

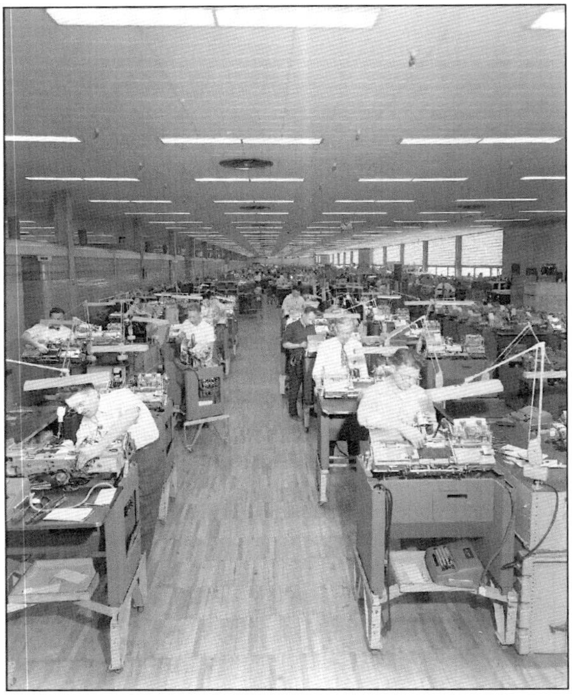

IBM Card Punch Assembly, 1950. (IBM.) Shown here in the main plant that was completed in 1948 is the assembly room for the card punchers, which produced the punch cards necessary for data processing. They were in some ways the precursors of computers, the vehicles for communication in the future. In fact, in fewer than ten years, employees would be assembling computers in the same room.

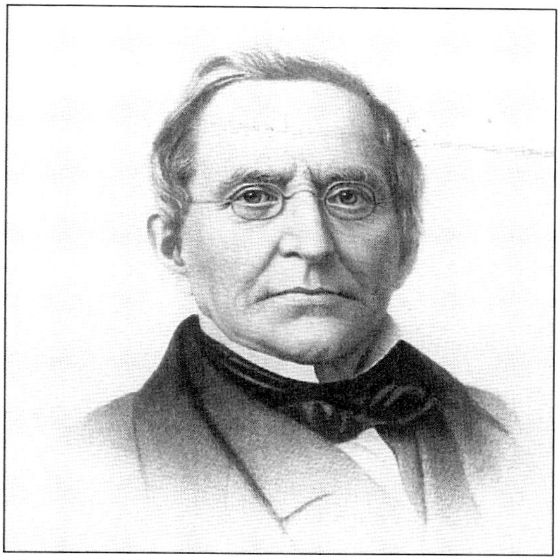

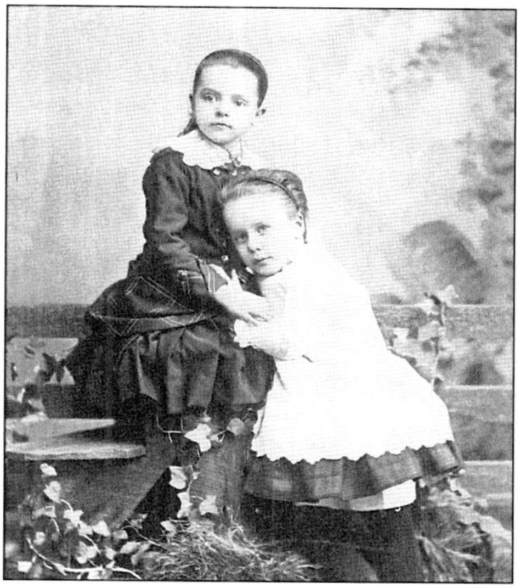

Matthew Vassar (1792–1868). (AML.) A successful businessman, one of the organizers of two Poughkeepsie banks, a leader in the formation of the Poughkeepsie Whaling Company, a member of the Improvement Party and president of the village board, an early and energetic supporter of the Hudson River Railroad, Matthew Vassar would be remembered for his lasting impact on Poughkeepsie . . . even if he had not also founded Vassar College. He said: "If we only follow on in the old beaten paths we will make no progress. We can do no more than others have done before us. . . . My motto is progress."

Helen Wilkinson Reynolds (1875–1943). (AML.) The serious little blonde girl (right) matured into the source of much of our most reliable historical scholarship. Helen Reynolds, from an old Poughkeepsie family, used her good connections and detective instincts to train herself in documentary research and interpretation. A fine writer and careful editor, she produced the *Dutchess County Historical Society Yearbook* for over twenty years. As city and county historian, she worked with FDR and the New York State Archives to make local historical resources accessible and appreciated.

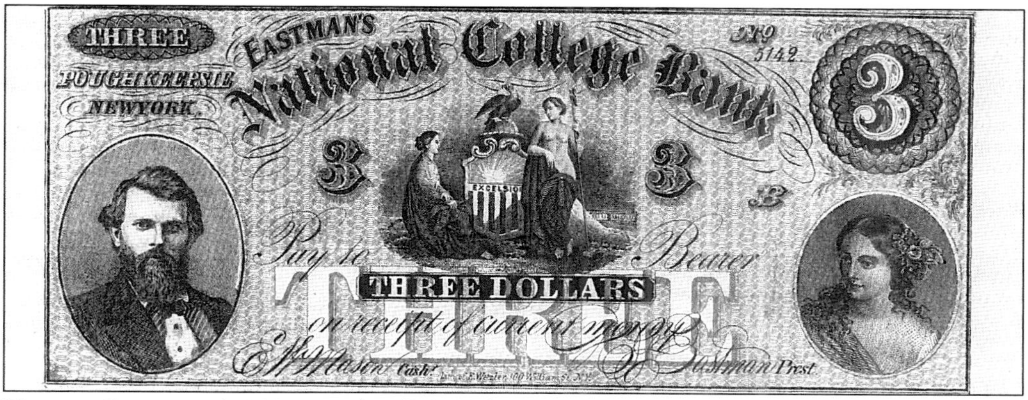

Harvey Eastman (1832–1878). (DCHS.) Entrepreneur extraordinaire and enthusiastic community leader, Harvey Eastman established Eastman College, a business college that used a "hands-on" method of learning, creating its own money and establishing its own stock market to teach business practices. Always an energetic visionary, he actively supported the construction of the Poughkeepsie and Eastern Railroad and the railroad bridge. He was elected mayor in 1871 and reelected in 1878. He died in office.

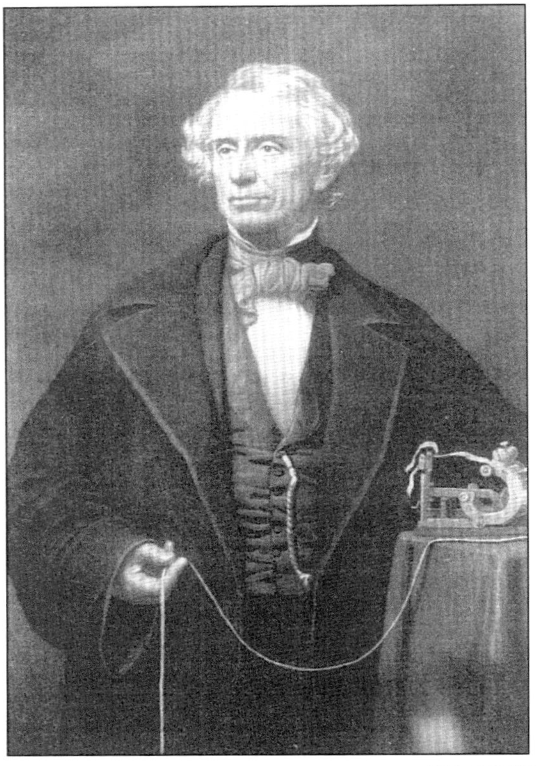

S.F.B. Morse (1791–1872). (SFBMHS.) An accomplished artist himself, S.F.B. Morse not only enhanced the beauty of his estate Locust Grove, but he also contributed to many institutions in his adopted home of Poughkeepsie, including the Children's Home, the Presbyterian church, and Vassar College. It is, however, through his invention of the telegraph, the first non-physical means of transferring information, that he achieved international fame. Through the telegraph, in effect the first Internet, Poughkeepsie became directly connected to the wider world.

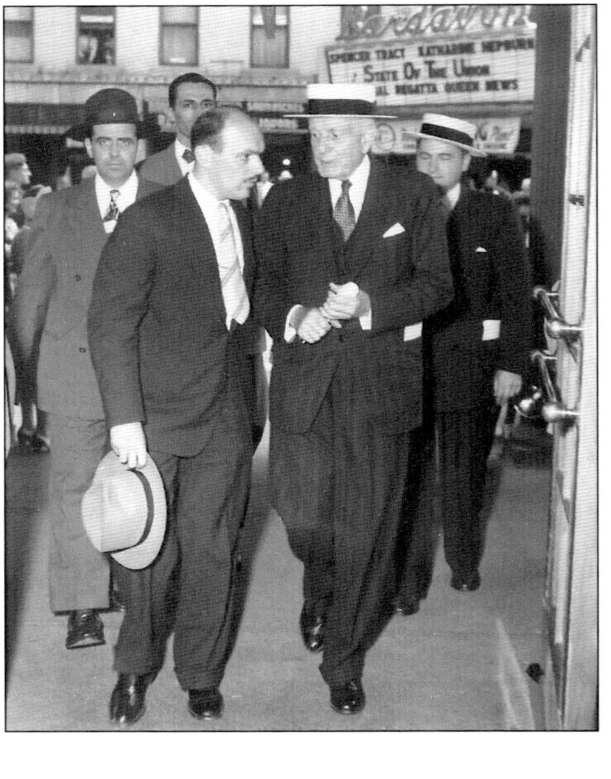

Thomas J. Watson Sr. (1874–1956). (IBM.) On June 26, 1948, IBM dedicated Building 002 on South Road. Seen here stopping at the Nelson House that day are Thomas J. Watson Sr., Major Schultz (of the state police), Detective Martin, C. Love, and Walter Averill. Unlike the other individuals who have helped to shape Poughkeepsie, Thomas J. Watson Sr. never lived in Poughkeepsie. However, the impact of his decision to locate IBM there was profound and prophetic of the time when more and more decisions that significantly affect communities are made far, far away.

Acknowledgments

A work like this is not the result of the authors' efforts only. It is the product of the generous sharing of information and resources by an entire community. The authors are grateful to the following organizations and individuals who provided encouragement in our research and access to information used in the preparation of this book:

- Adams Fairacre Farms: Mark Adams
- Adriance Memorial Library: Myra Morales, Lyn Lucas, Dora Schisler
- Bardavon 1869 Opera House: Annon Adams, Lucy Edgcomb, Elizabeth Oakley, James Storrow
- Bowdoin Park Archeological and Historical Association: B. Buchanan
- The Children's Home of Poughkeepsie: Frank Dwyer
- City of Poughkeepsie: Colette Lafuente
- Cunneen-Hackett Cultural Center: Virginia Hancock
- Dutchess County Clerk's Office: Bill Paroli Jr. and the staff of the records room
- Dutchess County Department of Planning and Development: John Clarke
- Dutchess County Historical Society: Erica Blumenfeld, Eileen Hayden, Lorraine Roberts, Jon Hayden
- Dutchess County Landmarks Association: Stephanie Mauri
- Fitzgerald Tile Company: the Fitzgerald family
- Franklin Delano Roosevelt Museum and Library: Raymond Teichman
- Greater Poughkeepsie Area Chamber of Commerce: Jack Tarleton
- Hatfield Metal Fabrication: Ann Hatfield
- Hudson River Psychiatric Center: Sharon Backus, Leonard Peluso, James Regan
- IBM Corporation: Stephen Cole
- Maplewood Apartments: Frances A. Knapp
- Marist College: Timmian Massie
- The McCann Foundation: John J. Gartland
- Oakwood School: Tracy Gartelmann
- Poughkeepsie Day School: Pat Prunty
- *Poughkeepsie Journal*: Richard Wager, Meg Downey, Larry Hughes, Mary Ann Gardinier
- Poughkeepsie Post Office: Tom Nucifore, Ellen Mooney, Al Thomas
- Poughkeepsie Tennis Club: Rocco Staino
- Pronto Printer
- Smith Metropolitan AME Zion Church: Walter Patrice
- Springside Landscape Restoration: Virginia Hancock
- Town of Poughkeepsie: Jean Murphy
- Vassar College Libraries, Special Collections: Nancy S. MacKechnie
- Vassar-Warner Home: Marjorie Thompson
- Vassar Temple: Marjorie Katz
- Samuel F.B. Morse Historic Site: Raymond Armater

Thanks also go to the following:

Walter and Virginia Anderson, Leonard Babiarz, Catherine Bala, Mrs. Manley Behrens, Judith A. Bleakley-O'Neill, Ada Booth, Donald and Elizabeth Budd, Patsy Newman Costello, Jean and Ed Cote, Mary Kaye Dolan, Joseph J. Dosio, the Jesse and Marshall Effron families, James and Anita Emrich, Edwin and Bernice Fitchett, William D. Ghee, Lori Gilmore-Morris, Esq., Donald Goddard, Frank Hanlon, Elinore Frank Haverkamp, Eileen Mylod Hayden, Gilbert Hilderbrand, Janice A. Hilderbrand, David R. and Valerie A. Hinkley, Timothy P. Holls, Norma and William Hubbard, Katherine Hull, Christine Jacoby, Raymond Kearney, Mrs. James W. Key, Peter Klose, Catherine Kondor, Dave Krzeminski, Lawrence J. Majewski, Margaret and Antonio Marquez, Arthur B. McComb, Jeanne Opdyke, Dewey Owens, Walter Patrice, Mr. and Mrs. Herbert Saltford, Leonard Peluso, Lorraine Roberts, Todd Scheff, Mae Schneeweiss, Jonah and Joan Sherman, Mary Lou Sotanski, Margaret Spingler, Mark Tallardy, Marjorie Thompson, Mona Vaeth, Norma Van Kleeck, and Barbara Corliss Velletri.

Special thanks is due to the board of the Dutchess County Historical Society, whose faith in the authors made the book possible. We are extraordinarily grateful to Eileen Hayden and Erica Blumenfeld for their generosity in sharing information, for locating needed historical materials, and for overlooking the intrusions on staff time and Clinton House space dictated by our study. We thank Myra Morales, too, for her patience with our research at Adriance Memorial Library. A final word of recognition is due our long suffering and endlessly good-natured spouses, Tom Spence and Bill Ghee. Without their patient endurance of the myriad impacts on home, family, and business schedules, and without the frequent gifts of time and thought, we could not have completed our work.

Joan Spence and Joyce C. Ghee

Reading List

Dutchess County Historical Society, ed. *Dutchess County Historical Society Yearbooks*. 1914–1995. An index of articles is available at the society's headquarters at the Clinton House, 549 Main Street, Poughkeepsie, NY 12601.

Hasbrouck, Frank. ed. *The History of Dutchess County, New York*. Poughkeepsie, NY: S.A. Matthieu, 1909. Especially Chapter XV, "Town and City of Poughkeepsie," by Edmund Platt, pp. 199–257.

Jeanneney, John and Mary L. *Dutchess County A Pictorial History*. Norfolk, VA: The Donning Company, Publishers, 1983.

Platt, Edmund. *The Eagle's History of Poughkeepsie From the Earliest Settlements 1683 to 1905*. Poughkeepsie, NY: Dutchess County Historical Society, 1987.

Smith, James H. assisted by Hume H. Cale and Wm. R. Roscoe. *History of Duchess County, NY with Illustrations and Biographical Sketches of Some of its Prominent Men and Pioneers*. Syracuse, NY: D. Mason & Co., 1882. Reprinted by the Dutchess County Historical Society, 1980. Especially chapters xxix–xxxix, pp. 357–439.

Smith, Philip H. *General History of Dutchess County from 1609–1876*. Pawling, NY: Published by the author, 1877. Especially "Poughkeepsie," pp. 332–371.